TABLE OF CONTENTS

Other titles in the Finding Your Ancestors series:

Finding Your Irish Ancestors
Your Swedish Roots
Finding Your African American Ancestors
Finding Your German Ancestors
Finding Your Mexican Ancestors

FINDING YOUR
CANADIAN
ANCESTORS

A BEGINNER'S GUIDE

SHERRY IRVINE AND DAVE OBEE

Library of Congress Cataloging-in-Publication Data

Irvine, Sherry.
  Finding your Canadian ancestors : a beginner's guide / Sherry Irvine, Dave Obee.
    p. cm. — (Finding your ancestors series)
  Includes bibliographical references and index.
  ISBN 978-1-59331-316-6
  1. Canada—Genealogy—Handbooks, manuals, etc. I. Obee, Dave, 1953– II. Title.
  CS82.I78 2007
  929'.10720971--dc22

                              2007025824

Published by Ancestry Publishing, a division of
The Generations Network, Inc.
360 West 4800 North
Provo, Utah 84604
www.ancestry.com

First Printing 2007

10 9 8 7 6 5 4 3 2 1

Printed in the United States of America.

Original map data provided by The Atlas of Canada http://atlas.gc.ca/ © 2007.
Produced under license from Her Majesty the Queen in Right of Canada,
with permission of Natural Resources Canada.

CG—Certified Genealogist is a service mark of the Board for Certification
of Genealogists and is used under license by associates who meet prescribed
genealogical competency standards.

PREFACE

Canada is a large and diverse country. It has a long history in which many nations played a part. These factors make Canadian history interesting and will make your genealogical research equally absorbing.

Canada's size and diversity also influence its records, which are similarly varied and at times complex. For example, responsibility for administrative matters, and thus government record keeping, is split between a federal government in Ottawa and the governments of ten provinces and three territories. The organization of this book has been influenced by these factors.

We begin with remarks on a few subjects that need some explanation up front, such as frequently used Web resources, changes to websites, and the use of library services. In the chapters we guide you through Canadian genealogical records, first by record type and then according to province. There are separate chapters on finding geographical information and information about special groups, such as Aboriginals, Acadians, and Loyalists.

The book ends with four appendixes covering research techniques, pitfalls, using the Internet, and timelines for Canadian history.

We would like to thank the many genealogists, archivists, and librarians who answered our questions, in particular the staff at the Canadian Genealogy Centre.

A book like this could not be written without the encouragement and interest of colleagues, friends, and family. Many helped out, and we appreciate their support. We would like to single out for special thanks Laura Hanowski, Ann Leeson, Sarah Obee, and Russell Irvine.

If you find errors, we take full responsibility and ask that you let us know.

Sherry Irvine, Courtenay, British Columbia

Dave Obee, Victoria, British Columbia

BEFORE YOU START

Most of us with Canadian ancestors find connections in more than one province or territory, but it is unlikely we will be researching in all of them. With this in mind, we recommend you read chapters one through twelve first and then select from the others those directly connected to your research, whether that be a special group, province, or territory. Changes in boundaries, described in the text, will tell you whether or not you should read about the records of an adjacent region.

We mention some search tools, resources, and data websites frequently throughout the book. These deserve a separate introduction and some summary notes.

THE WEB IS ALWAYS CHANGING

As we were busy with final checks to this manuscript, the Library and Archives Canada website completely changed its look and many of its functions. That is an excellent reminder that websites large and small are evolving all the time. Addresses change, and long, printed lists of URLs quickly become dated. For this reason, lists at the end of each chapter concentrate on the most important websites for data, background information, and other links. We also provide full website names, which will help you find any relocated websites using a search engine.

You can save yourself time and frustration by keeping track of important sites. This may be easy if you visit them frequently, but you may want to find a favorite information website that you can rely on to maintain up-to-date listings. You can read more about gateway sites in Appendix C.

You also need to be aware of additions and changes within sites. Look for the site map of a favorite website and for any tools it has to help you get around, such as an internal search engine or a catalog.

LIBRARY AND ARCHIVES CANADA

Library and Archives Canada (LAC) is a single entity combining the former National Library and National Archives as well as the Canadian Genealogy Centre. Chapter 1 tells you about LAC in more detail. These are the three search tools available on the LAC website referred to most often in the book.

- AVITUS—Directory of Canadian Genealogical Resources; it has links to hundreds of other websites and it is often mentioned in the guides to resources found at the Canadian Genealogy Centre website.
- AMICUS WEB—Canadian national catalog of published sources held in Canadian libraries; the LAC collection can be searched alone, or all can be searched together. Available from the main website search facility and from some pages in the Canadian Genealogy Centre site.
- Index of Topics—An index to topics at the Canadian Genealogy Centre website and an important reference source for information on Canadian

genealogy; to facilitate browsing, all topics are grouped by letters of the alphabet. The descriptions of each topic vary in length and take you to other areas of the LAC website, to external sites, or to search tools such as AVITUS and AMICUS.

The Index of Topics at the Canadian Genealogy Centre Website
<http://www.collectionscanada.ca/genealogy/022-904-e.html>

Note the menu bar item, Sources by Topic, is in white, indicating it has been selected; and the last item in the list on the left, Index of Topics, was clicked.

FAMILYSEARCH

FamilySearch is the name of the genealogy website of The Church of Jesus Christ of Latter-day Saints (LDS). *FamilySearch* is also an umbrella term for all genealogy activities. LDS resources are available to the public at the Family History Library (FHL) in Salt Lake City, through a network of Family History Centers around the world, and online at FamilySearch.

The FamilySearch website is extensive. It includes many databases and good research advice. These are described in more detail in Appendix C.

The FHL, Family History Centers, and the Family History Library Catalog (FHLC) are mentioned in nearly every chapter of this book. We recommend you check the library's resources as a standard step in any search for available records. If you check the FHLC on a regular basis, you will become familiar with its resources and avoid the possibility of overlooking helpful genealogical sources.

We suggest you take time to practice searching the catalog by place-name and by keyword. When doing a place search it is a good idea to check listings under local place-names, the name of the province, and under Canada.

ANCESTRY

Ancestry's Canadian website includes a large collection of census data, vital records, immigration lists, and fully searchable books. The largest and most frequently used resources can be accessed from the home page, and you can use the Search tab on the menu bar to locate detailed lists of databases arranged by province; clicking the tab takes you to a page with an interactive map of the provinces.

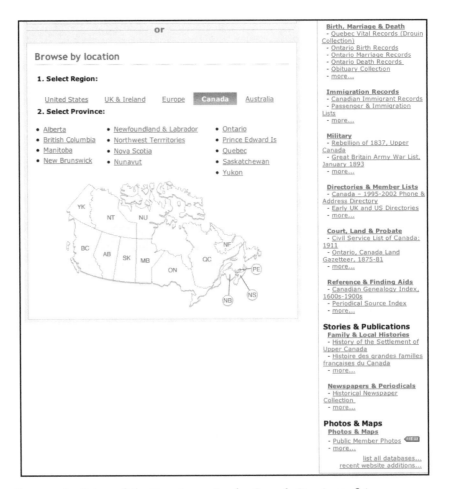

Interactive Map of the Provinces in the Search Portion of Ancestry.ca

LIBRARY AND ARCHIVES CANADA

The most comprehensive single resource for Canadian genealogists is found a few blocks west of Parliament Hill in Ottawa and, thanks to the Internet, it is as close as your home. Library and Archives Canada (LAC) is putting many of its most valuable resources online and creating a central access point on its Canadian Genealogy Centre website.

The roots of LAC can be traced back to 1872, when the federal government created the Public Archives of Canada. The organization's role was simple: to collect and preserve the unpublished documentary heritage of the Dominion.

In 1953 the government established the National Library of Canada as a repository for the nation's printed works. In 1967, the archives and the library were brought together in one building in Ottawa, and in 1987 the name of the archives was changed to National Archives of Canada.

In 2003 the National Library and the National Archives introduced their joint website, the Canadian Genealogy Centre, but that was just a hint of what was to come. In 2004 the two organizations were merged to become Library and Archives Canada.

Library and Archives Canada collections include the following:

- More than 2.5 million architectural drawings, plans, and maps from the sixteenth to the twenty-first centuries
- More than 21 million photographic images dating back to the 1850s
- Portraits of more than 1 million Canadians
- More than 270,000 hours of video and sound recordings
- Textual records and publications for federal, provincial, territorial, and foreign governments
- Textual records from individuals and groups such as church organizations

- Newspapers from across Canada, including everything from dailies to ethnic publications
- More than 3 million megabytes of information in electronic format, including more than 9,500 Canadian periodicals and books
- More than 71,000 hours of films
- Millions of books. Under Canadian law, two copies of every book published in Canada must be deposited with Library and Archives Canada.

The resources of LAC are essential to Canadian family history research. The commitment of LAC to the Internet means that no matter where they are, genealogists have relatively easy access to millions of pages of documents.

EXPLORE THE LIBRARY AND ARCHIVES CANADA WEBSITE

The LAC website, in its Web address, goes by the name Collections Canada, which appropriately indicates the breadth and variety of material available. The home page presents several ways to help you get around.

Figure 1-1. The Library and Archives Canada Website
<http://www.collectionscanada.ca/index-e.html>

The black area, center top, is a title format common to every Government of Canada Web page; only the background varies. Five of the six menu bar links near the top of the page relate only to Library and Archives Canada: Français (or English)

Home, Contact Us, Help, and Search. The sixth link (canada.gc.ca) takes you to the main Government of Canada page.

The rest of page helps you navigate within LAC's online resources. You are likely to use four links more than the rest.

- Search All
- In the Spotlight
- What We Have
- Canadian Genealogy Centre

Search All

The *All* in Search All indicates that the search spans the entire LAC website, its catalog of published holdings, a selection of descriptions of the archival holdings of LAC, and the catalogs of 1,300 other libraries. The results of this comprehensive search are presented by category in the following order: library, archives, website. You see the first five results in each category, and you can choose to see more.

If you look closely on the home page search area you see, in plain text, Search only, which allows you to search one category at a time. If you select one of these options, you are taken to another search box on a different Web page. There are additional options to choose from when you elect to explore only library or archives content.

Library and Archives Canada Search Tool
This view shows the Library Search option. You can see the Advanced Search and Search Tips links and the buttons to toggle on and off to set the extent of your search.
<http://search-recherche.collectionscanada.ca/amicus/search.jsp?Language=eng>

The Search Tips link is not available at the home page but appears when you access the search from among the options on the black menu bar. An Advanced Search option appears whenever you are in a search of a single category.

In the Spotlight

The center of the home page puts four items in plain view, highlighting exhibits, sections of the website, and news. These change regularly.

What We Have

You find What We Have in the red column on the left. Within it On Our Website is an extremely useful tool, listing resources in three different ways: alphabetical, topic, and product. Try each of the arrangements, browse through the titles, and try a few links.

Half-forgotten databases or research guides can usually be found when you have three ways to look for them. In addition, you can use the What We Have listings if you are having difficulty finding something within the Canadian Genealogy Centre site.

Also within What We Have is the section Our Popular Resources. Presently it has very few entries, but that will change. It is intended to be a quick route to the most visited subpages, such as the Canadian Genealogy Centre, and to popular individual records and resources.

THE CANADIAN GENEALOGY CENTRE

You may be tempted to dive right into the databases, but there is a better way. At the Centre's home page, select the Sources by Topic tab, and then pick from the choices on the left side of the screen. There are eleven:

- Aboriginals and Ethno-Cultural Groups
- Births, Marriages and Deaths
- Government
- Immigration
- Military
- Publications
- Census
- Land
- Employment
- Other Topics
- Index of Topics

Each of the first ten topics has subsections that appear as soon as a topic is selected. For example, click on the Land item, and it opens up three more: Land Petitions, Provincial Land Records, and Land Grants to Veterans. You will also find valuable background information and directions for finding indexes and databases. The Index of Topics takes you to short articles on dozens of resources, not all of them included in the other ten sections.

There are innumerable resources online at the LAC website, from huge collections such as the census enumerations to smaller ones such as Divorce in Canada, 1841–1968. Some are based within the Canadian Genealogy Centre subsite, but not all. We will list a few here. Your tours around the site using search tools described here or URLs listed at the end of each chapter will turn up many more.

Census

- Images from 1851, 1901, 1906 (Prairie Provinces only), and 1911. There is also a head-of-household index to Ontario's returns from 1871. Eventually the site will include scanned images of all available censuses since 1851.

Immigration

- Images of passenger lists, 1865–1922
- Index to immigration records, 1925–1935
- Arrivals of Home Children, 1869–1930
- Montreal Emigrant Society Passage Book, 1832
- Port of New Westminster Register of Chinese Immigration, 1887–1908
- Upper Canada and Canada West Naturalization Records, 1828–1850

Military

- Soldiers of the South African War, 1899–1902
- Soldiers of the First World War, 1914–1918
- War Diaries of the First World War

Land

- Western Land Grants, 1870–1930
- Lower Canada Land Petitions, 1764–1841

First Nations / Métis

- Maps of Indian Reserves of Western Canada
- Métis Scrip (certificates that could be redeemed for cash or land)
- Red and Black Series

Other Sources

- Canadian Directories—Who Was Where
- Canadian Patents, 1869–1894
- Ward Chipman Papers on Loyalists, 1777–1785
- Electoral Maps of Canada

BEYOND COLLECTIONS CANADA

From the LAC Website

The LAC website looks outward as well. AVITUS and AMICUS take you to databases, information, and library catalogs elsewhere on the Web.

The Links tab on the Canadian Genealogy Centre site has subsections of its own:

- Genealogical Societies
- Provincial and Territorial Archives

- University Research Centres
- Libraries
- Reference Sites
- Religious Archives
- Family History Library
- Other Archives in Canada
- International
- Provinces and Territories

The section headings are mostly self-explanatory. The last item is a miscellaneous collection of links not listed in any other part and arranged by province and territory. This is a good place to quickly find links to other repositories, societies, and research centers.

Other Federal or Canada-wide Sources

There are several other federal or Canada-wide resources that you may find useful that are not under the LAC umbrella.

Canadiana.org—Formerly the Canadian Institute for Historical Microreproductions, this organization is dedicated to preserving library materials and making them accessible to a wider audience. It has placed scans of thousands of documents on its website and has many others available at major libraries on microfiche. The collection includes Canadian pamphlets, monographs, serials, annuals, and periodicals up to 1994 on microfiche. It can be searched online, although not all documents are available for viewing on the Internet. The others are available for purchase or can be viewed at major libraries.

Our Roots—This site offers a tremendous collection of local histories, with a comprehensive index pointing to scanned images of the pages. These local histories were usually written by people living in the communities featured. Our Roots has been created through the collaboration of libraries, universities, colleges, archives, historical associations, businesses, and individuals across Canada.

Peel's Prairie Provinces—This website, at the University of Alberta, features a comprehensive collection of material related to the Prairies up to 1953, originally produced on microfiche by the National Library of Canada. The search engine allows you to search for individual names within thousands of documents and then search within the results on a geographic basis. The searches will take you directly to original document images.

Geographical Names of Canada—It's possible to search current or historic place-names.

Histori.ca—This website has been created to foster the teaching of Canadian history and to encourage students to take an interest in Canada's past; a widely used reference work, the *Canadian Encyclopedia*, is available free at this website.

Canadian Patents Database—A searchable index leads you to images of the patent documents. The site will also lead you to the Canadian Trade-Marks Database, which covers from 1865 to the present day, as well as databases of copyrights and industrial designs.

Canadian Civil Aircraft Register—Did your ancestor own an airplane?

WEBSITES

Canadiana.org: <www.canadiana.org>
Canadian Civil Aircraft Register: <www.tc.gc.ca>
Canadian Genealogy Centre:
    <www.collectionscanada.ca/genealogy/index-e.html>
Canadian Patents Database: <patents1.ic.gc.ca>
Geographical Names of Canada: <geonames.nrcan.gc.ca>
Histori.ca: <www.histori.ca>
Library and Archives Canada: <www.collectionscanada.ca>
Our Roots: <www.ourroots.ca>
Peel's Prairie Provinces: <peel.library.ualberta.ca>

BIBLIOGRAPHY

Gilchrist, J. Brian, and Clifford Duxbury Collier, comps. *Genealogy and Local History to 1900: A Bibliography Selected from the Catalogue of the Canadian Institute for Historical Microreproductions (CIHM) [Genealogie et histoire locale d'avant 1900: une bibliographie tiree du catalogue de l'institut canadien de microreproductions historiques (ICMH)]*. Ottawa: Canadian Institute for Historical Microreproductions, 1995.

Treasures of the National Archives of Canada. Toronto: University of Toronto Press, 1992.

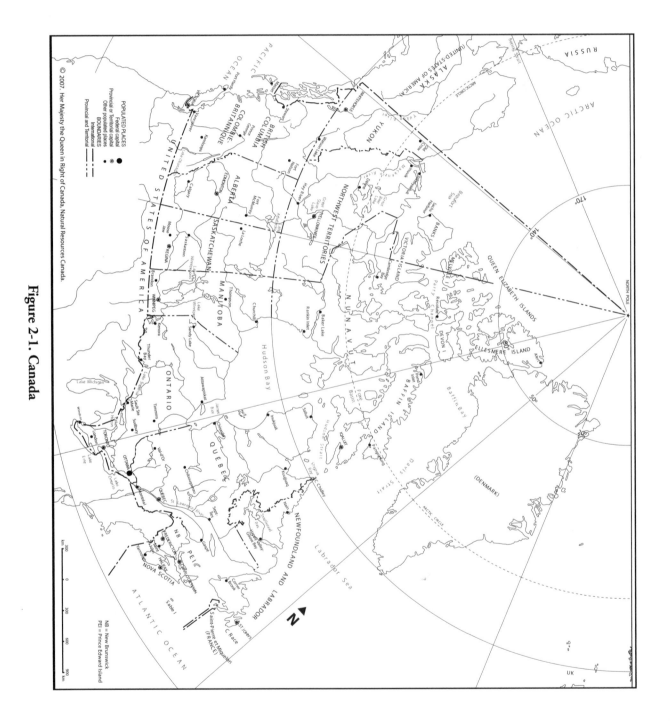

Figure 2-1. Canada

CANADIAN GEOGRAPHY AND FINDING LOCALITIES

Geography and genealogy go hand in hand. It is impossible to do quality research into your family's history without understanding the geography of your ancestors' lives.

The first step is to determine where they lived. That will usually be easy, but often you will need to do some digging. Canada has more than 300,000 official geographic names, along with many more unofficial ones, and thousands of names have been changed over the years. Maps, atlases, and gazetteers can help you find locations and see how one spot related to the region around it. By making it easier to understand an area, these works can help direct researchers to where records will be found.

Canadian places have acquired their names for many different reasons. Some were named for early settlers, others for the locations where the settlers originated. Some were named for royalty, others for businesspeople, and one—Flin Flon, Manitoba— drew its name from a science fiction character, Flintabbattey Flonatin.

Many place-names are based on words the Indians used. *Canada*, for example, is drawn from the Huron word *Kanata*, meaning "settlement" or "village." *Winnipeg*, the name of the capital city of Manitoba, as well as a lake and a river, is derived from the Cree word *Winnipi*, which is translated as "dirty water" or "murky water."

Other notable place-names inspired by Indian words include Ottawa ("traders"), Toronto ("trees standing in water"), Kamloops ("meeting of the waters"), and Chicoutimi ("end of deep water"). Some names are simply translations of Indian names. These include Medicine Hat, Yellowknife, Thunder Bay, and Grand-Mère.

The most remarkable string of names in Canada is on the Canadian National Railway line in Manitoba and Saskatchewan. As you head west, towns are in alphabetical order, starting with Arona and Bloom in Manitoba and ending with Zeneta in Saskatchewan. After that, the cycle begins again.

When searching for a place-name, the first step is to check for clues that might point you to a location. Look for references in other records, such as obituaries, local histories, genealogies, and official records. If possible, gather information on other members of the family who may have some information that will help get you started. Your ancestors did not live their lives in isolation, so look for common migration patterns.

Finding a community is just the start. You need to determine the community's jurisdiction—the province, county, or district, for example, that would hold the relevant records. Jurisdictions have changed many times as boundaries have been redrawn. Make a note of all of the jurisdictions that apply, with special emphasis on ways they have changed and when changes took place.

Along with looking outside the community or district, you should look into it as well. Try to determine the precise location of your ancestor's house or farm, and find out what else was in the neighborhood.

SOURCES FOR NAMES

Along with the names that have been changed or lost over the years, you might need to find a location that is still around but is simply so small that it's not included on road maps. With luck you will have other evidence, such as the name of the nearest large community, the name of the province, or the location of the local courthouse or registry, that will help you narrow your search.

It should be possible to find the location for just about every Canadian community, no matter how small. Try using these resources:

- **Gazetteers.** These are basically geographical indexes or dictionaries, and they have been published in Canada for more than two hundred years. They list communities and other locations, such as mountains and lakes, and provide key information to help you find them.

    The 1873 edition of *Lovell's Gazetteer of British North America*, available as a reprint, contains references to 6,000 places. The 1908 edition of the same book had references to almost 15,000, reflecting the increase in the number of settled areas. Several other early gazetteers have also been republished in recent years.

    Many of the early gazetteers were privately compiled and published. The federal government is still publishing comprehensive ones on a province-by-province basis. The federal government also has a website, Geographical Names of Canada, that has databases of both current and historic place-names. Provincial governments also have published gazetteers.

- **Directories.** These are primarily designed to list the names of businesses and civic officials, but the ones that cover provinces or regions also have identifying information that will help you find communities. Many old directories are available on microfilm or microfiche at archives or large public and university libraries.

- ***Canadian Almanac and Directory.*** The name has changed several times since this annual publication was launched in 1848; it was known for several years as *The Canadian Almanac and Directory and Repository of Useful Knowledge.* Until 1980 the almanac included a list of post offices and railway stations in Canada. Most large libraries have back issues, a transcript of the 1861 list is on the CanGenealogy.com website, and several editions from the 1800s are on the Internet Archive website. An extensive list of almanacs is on the Library and Archives Canada (LAC) website.
- **Maps and atlases.** Beyond the basics—such as highway maps and atlases—you should look for maps and atlases that cover small areas such as counties. They will often show the smallest settlements and even community halls that are in the middle of nowhere but still carry a name of some sort. Check local sources, such as municipal offices, to see what is available for your area.

  An excellent source of detailed local information would be a topographic map printed by Natural Resources Canada. These maps come in two scales—1:50,000, or 1 centimeter for every .5 kilometer, and 1:250,000, or 1 centimeter for every 2.5 kilometers.

  These maps are the most comprehensive maps available for Canada. They include roads, buildings, urban development, boundaries, railways, lakes, rivers, streams, mountains, valleys, slopes, wooded and cleared areas, place-names, water feature names, and highway names. They are available through government-authorized resellers across Canada.

  Many old maps and atlases have been reprinted. The county atlases of Ontario, for example, were first published in the 1870s and were made available again a century later. More recently, they have been made available on the Internet.
- **List of post offices.** The LAC website has a database of old post offices and postmasters. Some of these post offices disappeared years ago, but the database includes enough information to help you determine where they were.

230 OTTAWA CITY DIRECTORY.

PRESCOTT.

A town on the River St. Lawrence, at the junction of the Grand Trunk and St. Lawrence and Ottawa Railways, in the Township of Augusta, County of Grenville, 12 miles from Brockville, 45 from Ottawa, 113 from Montreal and 220 from Toronto. Population, 3000.

Adams, Mrs., boarding house, King.
Anderson, D., fruits, &c.
Armstrong, Capt. W., landing waiter, Customs.
Bacon, Ebenezer, tanner and leather dealer, Water.
Baines, J., chemist and druggist, King.
Beaufort, E., & Son, dining saloon, Junction.
Belgard, Henry, foreman, *Telegraph*.
Benson, W. T.
BIRKS, GEORGE, chemist and druggist, King.
Blacklock, Mrs., milliner, King.
Blair, Rev. George, principal Union Grammar and Common schools.
Bleakley, Mrs. R., milliner.
Bleakley, Robert, saddler.
Brackenbury, Miss, teacher.
Bradley, John, grocer, King.
Brady, James, mariner, King.
Brouse, H. A., exchange broker, fruits and confectionery.
BROUSE, W. H., M.D., P.M.
Brown, Geo. W., exciseman.
Buchanan, Colin, teller, Merchants Bank.
Buckley, James, forwarder, general merchant.
Buckley, John, forwarder, general merchant.
Burke, Rev. J., Church of England.
Burton, Rev., Presbyterian.
BYRNE, PETER, editor and prop *Telegraph*, bookseller, &c., King.
Cairns, James, builder.
CAMP, WM., accountant, R. P. LaBatt.
Canadian Inland Navigation Co., L. H. Daniels, agent.
Chartier, A., boarding house.
Clarke, Macneil, M.P.P., barrister.
Coates, Jas., insurance agent.
Coates, Thomas, stoves and tinware, King.
Coons, S. M., cabinet-maker, King.

Figure 2-2. A Page from *Hunter, Rose & Co.'s City of Ottawa Directory for 1870–71*
<http://www.collectionscanada.ca/canadiandirectories>

PITFALLS

Genealogists sorting out geography need to understand several possible pitfalls, including changed names, lost names, duplicate names, and changing jurisdictions.

Changed Names

Place-names change for different reasons. Many changes were made in the eighteenth century after the British assumed control of what had been French territory, and more

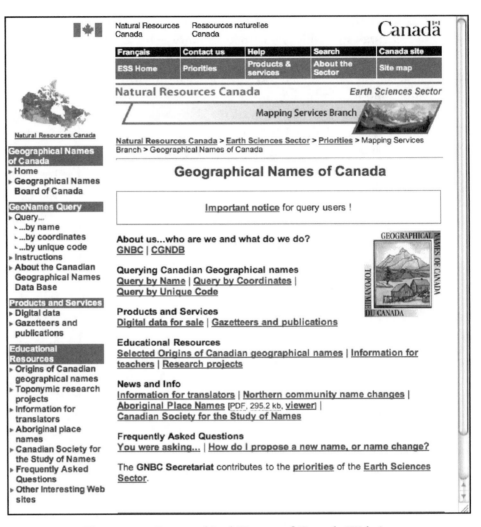

Figure 2-3. Geographical Names of Canada Website
<http://geonames.nrcan.gc.ca/index_e.php>

changes have taken place every year since then. If you simply cannot find the place you are looking for, check a reference book, such as a gazetteer or directory, printed during the time your family lived there. That might provide a clue to the community's location that will help you find the modern name.

Some communities, such as Kitchener, Ontario, have had several names. When Kitchener was founded in 1799, it was known as Sand Hills because of the sand dunes in the area. Then it became Mount Pleasant, then Ebytown, after Mennonite leader Benjamin Eby. In 1841 it became Berlin, named for the German capital. That name lasted until 1916, when the town name was changed because of anti-German sentiment. The name *Kitchener* came from Lord Kitchener, a British field marshal who drowned in the early days of World War I.

Other names have simply evolved. Fredericton, New Brunswick, was originally Fredericktown, but two letters were dropped soon after the name was assigned in 1785. Skaha Lake, in British Columbia's Okanagan Valley, has had three names. It was also known as Lac de Chien and as Dog Lake. All three names mean the same thing—"dog," in English, French, and native Okanagan.

Sometimes it's hard to argue with the decision to change names. Regina, Saskatchewan, was formerly known as Pile of Bones.

French-language names for Quebec's towns, cities, and counties are widely known across Canada. It has not always been that way. At one time, English speakers would use *Seven Islands* instead of *Sept-Îles* or *Three Rivers* instead of *Trois-Rivières*. You may still find the English names in old documents.

In recent decades, Indian names have been given to northern communities that had previously carried English names. Those changed include Frobisher Bay (now Iqaluit), Port Brabant (now Tuktoyaktuk), and Notre-Dame-de-Koartec (now Koartec). Some of these communities have seen more than one change; for example, Great Whale River became Poste-de-la-Baleine, then Kuujjuaraapik in 1992.

Virtually every community in Canada has changed street names and street numbering systems. Within large cities, ward boundaries change as well—Toronto had at least a dozen variations in its ward system in the nineteenth century alone, which is important to remember when dealing with the census. Check local sources such as libraries for guides to these changes.

Lost Names

Many small settlements have disappeared over the years, with the only remaining trace being a faded sign or a line on a map—and, of course, references in genealogical records. For example, the town of Phoenix, British Columbia, was once considered the largest community north of San Francisco and west of Chicago. There's nothing left anymore; it's just one of many Canadian communities to rise and fall in a matter of months.

To find communities that have disappeared, check old gazetteers and, if you know the rough area, maps. Old directories also might lead to a location.

Town names can disappear because communities amalgamate. For example, Galt, Hespeler, and Preston in Ontario came together as Cambridge. Fort William and Port Arthur were amalgamated to form Thunder Bay. In Quebec, Hull was one of four community names that disappeared with the amalgamation that created Gatineau, and Beau Repaire became part of Pointe Claire. Additional major amalgamations took place in Quebec in 2001.

Small towns can disappear as a larger neighbor expands. Dufferin, British Columbia, was swallowed up by Kamloops. Calgary took over Montgomery and Bowness. And so on. The former names sometimes—but not always—survive as the names of neighborhoods in the larger communities.

Sometimes the name has not changed, it's just that the residents do not use it. That often happens with small communities next to large ones. It's easier to mention a city as well known as Vancouver, after all, than to specify a village such as Anmore.

Duplicate Names

Do not assume that you will have an easy time just because you have found a reference to a well-known community. There might be more than one with the same name. For example, a reference to Victoria could refer to British Columbia's capital—or to any one of the eight other places with that name.

And Victoria is not the worst offender. Canada has sixteen Mount Pleasants, fifteen Centrevilles and Lakeviews, fourteen places named Pleasant Valley, and thirteen named Fairview.

Even a name such as Red Deer, which might seem odd enough to be unique, has been used more than once. Alberta has the city of that name, but you will find Red Deer Creek, Red Deer Forks, Red Deer Hill, and Red Deer River in Saskatchewan.

Changing Jurisdictions

The tendency to change names isn't confined to local communities; it affects provinces and territories as well.

Ontario used to be known as Upper Canada but became Canada West in 1841 and Ontario in 1867. Quebec was Lower Canada until 1841, then Canada East, and became Quebec in 1867. Prince Edward Island was Île St. Jean at first, then St. John Island, then Prince Edward Island.

Many boundaries have changed as well. The Northwest Territories, for example, used to be much larger, taking in all of Alberta, Saskatchewan, the Yukon, and Nunavut, as well as the northern regions of Manitoba, Ontario, and Quebec. Always consider the date of the document you're dealing with. If you have one that refers to "Medicine Hat, N.W.T.," for example, it's the city we know today as Medicine Hat, Alberta. Before 1905 the city was in the territorial district of Assiniboia, or Ass. for short.

Within each province you might also find changing names and changing boundaries for districts. Many genealogical records are filed with counties, districts, municipalities, or other local governments, and if you know where to look you will be able to save time and frustration.

In Ontario, for example, the county of Brant was formed in 1852 from parts of three other counties: Wentworth, Oxford, and Halton. Before they were created, Ontario had districts rather than counties, which can be confusing. If you are interested in the county of Brant, for example, you might find yourself dealing, depending on location and time frame, with the Western, Niagara, London, Home, Gore, or Brock districts.

Beyond that, jurisdictions are not consistent from region to region. A township in Ontario is different from a township on the Prairies. A lot in Prince Edward Island refers to a large block that includes many parcels of land, while a lot elsewhere is usually the smallest legal unit of property.

WEBSITES

Atlas of Canada: <atlas.gc.ca>

Geographical Names of Canada: <geonames.nrcan.gc.ca>

Internet Archive: <www.archive.org>

Post office database (on the Library and Archives Canada website): <http://www. collectionscanada.ca/archivianet/post-offices/index-e.html>

BIBLIOGRAPHY

Government of Canada. *Gazetteer of Canada.* (Series; one for each province, plus one for Northwest Territories—including Nunavut—and one for the Yukon. Publication dates vary.)

Hamilton, William B. *The Macmillan Book of Canadian Place Names.* Toronto: Macmillan of Canada, 1978.

Hayes, Derek. *Historical Atlas of Canada.* Vancouver: Douglas and McIntyre, 2002.

Kerr, D. G. G. *A Historical Atlas of Canada.* 3rd ed. Don Mills, ON: Thomas Nelson, 1975.

Murray, Jeffrey S. *Terra Nostra, 1550–1950: The Stories behind Canada's Maps.* Sillery, QC: Septentrion, 2006.

Rayburn, Alan. *Dictionary of Canadian Place Names.* Toronto: Oxford University Press, Toronto, 1997.

GLOSSARY OF PLACES

Acadia: Original name of Nova Scotia, first used in 1603. Acadia included all territory between the St. Lawrence River and Gulf and the Atlantic Ocean. New Brunswick and eastern Maine were part of Acadia. In 1784, New Brunswick was separated from Acadia, and the remainder was renamed Nova Scotia.

Canada East: The name of Quebec from 1841 to 1867.

Canada West: The name of Ontario from 1841 to 1867.

Cape Breton Island: Part of Nova Scotia, but a separate jurisdiction from 1784 to 1820.

Île Royale: Now Cape Breton Island, Nova Scotia.

Île Saint-Jean (or Island of St. John in English): The name was changed in 1799 to Prince Edward Island. Part of Nova Scotia until 1769.

Klondike: Region in the Yukon made famous by a gold rush that started in 1896.

Lower Canada: The name of Quebec from 1791 to 1841.

New Caledonia: Name given to an area in British Columbia west of the Rocky Mountains between the fifty-second and fifty-fifth parallels.

New France: The name given to France's possessions in North America from 1534 to 1763. New France included the Great Lakes and the Mississippi Valley, although modern-day Quebec was the most important part of it.

North Western Territory: From 1821 to 1869, including much of western and northern Canada.

Northwest Territories: One of the three territories now north of the sixtieth parallel. From 1869 to the early 1900s it was known as the North-West Territories and included much of western and northern Canada, including much of Ontario and Quebec. Land was lost to Manitoba in 1870, 1881, and 1912; Alberta and Saskatchewan in 1905; the Yukon in 1898; Ontario in 1889 and 1912; and Quebec in 1898 and 1912.

Nova Scotia: Now a province, but formerly a colony that, until the late 1700s, included modern-day Prince Edward Island and New Brunswick.

Quebec: The name refers to a modern province. From 1763 to 1791, Quebec included all of Upper Canada, which eventually became Ontario.

Rupert's Land: Drainage basin of the Hudson Bay, granted to the Hudson's Bay Company in 1670 and sold to the government of Canada in 1869. Also known as Prince Rupert's Land.

Selkirk Grant: Land in southern Manitoba that was opened for settlement in 1812.

Upper Canada: The name of Ontario from 1791 to 1841.

Vancouver Island: A colony from 1849 to 1866, when it was united with the colony of British Columbia to form what in 1871 became the province of British Columbia.

IMMIGRATION

Most Canadians descend from immigrants who arrived in the last four hundred years. The first arrivals came from Europe, though early settlements were vulnerable and not always supported by governments back home. Permanent communities were costly and reduced the profits to be made from fishing, hunting, and trading with the native population.

Attitudes toward colonization were influenced by strong personalities, such as Samuel de Champlain, who persuaded the French courts and investors to back his efforts to explore and settle the territory across the Atlantic. Economics were another factor. In Newfoundland it became necessary to protect shore facilities like jetties and sheds year round, and, in defiance of government policy, people began to overwinter. A military expediency to counter the fortress of Louisbourg led the British to establish the garrison town of Halifax.

As settlements grew, they would reach a point where they could defend themselves and provide for their own sustenance, which became reasons to encourage growth, both by migration and natural increase of the local population.

The Loyalists changed everything. Tens of thousands fled the American colonies during and after the rebellion there. Large numbers went to Nova Scotia, prompting the separation of New Brunswick, Cape Breton, and the Island of St. John (now Prince Edward Island). Thousands of others went to Quebec, and the influx led to the splitting of the colony into Upper and Lower Canada. The surveying of land and granting of lots helped encourage settlement. Loyalists could petition for land according to their rank; free land encouraged both further immigration and land speculation.

The flow of arrivals to Canada slowed to a trickle in the early 1800s during Britain's wars with France and the United States, although Lord Selkirk brought

FAMINE IMMIGRANTS

Some famine immigrants appear in the Grosse-Île database at Library and Archives Canada and in the Irish Immigrant database online at the Public Archives of New Brunswick. However, many of the immigrants who arrived at Canadian ports were never recorded because passenger arrival lists started years later. While you might not be able to find a specific reference to your ancestor's arrival, you can get a sense of the immigration experience. Check the books written about the famine and the voyages. This will give you an idea of what your ancestors went through.

settlers to Prince Edward Island and Red River at that time. When peace returned, the British government started to encourage immigration so the colony would have enough people to defend itself.

Most British immigrants to Canada went to Upper Canada, which is now Ontario. Irish immigration increased steadily in the first half of the nineteenth century and became a flood during the famine of 1847–1852. They came to Saint John and Quebec, where a quarantine station was established at Grosse Île in the St. Lawrence River.

In 1885 the Canadian Pacific Railway was completed, linking Ontario to the west coast by rail. The West had been opened to settlement in 1872, but the rush of settlers came with the railway, bringing people primarily from Ontario, as well as new arrivals from Scotland and Europe.

In the late nineteenth and early twentieth centuries, Canada was still seeking immigrants who wanted to settle the land, and the government looked to eastern Europe for people. Between 1896 and 1911 more than 170,000 Ukrainians settled on the Prairies. The search for farmers coincided with a period when laborers from Europe and the British Isles were looking for work in North American cities and towns, and many of the immigrants found work in industry.

A substantial number of American farmers moved to Western Canada between 1900 and 1910 after the best of the free land south of the border had been taken up. As this inflow occurred, there was a substantial outflow from Eastern Canada, particularly from Quebec to New England. Estimates of how many left depend on census figures and reports from the United States because Canada did not keep exit registers. One estimate is that 1.1 million moved south between 1911 and 1921.

Immigration to Canada peaked in 1913 and 1914, with more than 400,000 people arriving in the twelve-month period ending March 31, 1914. The boom ended with the start of the First World War four months later.

Immigration rose sharply in the mid-1920s, but the start of the Great Depression effectively shut off the flow. During the Depression, some Canadians who had moved to the United States returned.

The 1950s saw another surge in immigration, although the influx did not reach the numbers recorded in 1913 and 1914. Most newcomers headed for Ontario, Quebec, and British Columbia, in that order.

For decades, entry to Canada depended on the applicant's race. There was a strong preference for people from the British Isles or the United States and western Europe. There was prejudice of varying degrees against the rest, in particular blacks, Chinese, Japanese, those from eastern and

Figure 3-1. Passenger Manifest, Port of St. John, June 1920
Available at Ancestry.ca

southern Europe, and the Middle East. Restrictions based on race were eliminated in 1967.

Today, about 200,000 people immigrate to Canada each year.

Immigration has had a tremendous impact on Canada. The country's population increased faster than that of any other industrialized country in the twentieth century, with most of the increase coming before the First World War and after the Second World War. The number of immigrants was higher, relative to the size of the population, than it was in the United States.

IMMIGRATION RECORDS

In Canada, the earliest comprehensive passenger-arrival lists date from 1865. If your ancestors arrived before that, you will need to rely on other sources.

If they came through the United States, you might be in luck because records of American ports are available online from 1820. Records of individual ships have survived for some ports in Canada, and some other records, such as church registers, sometimes contain information on origins. So while the lack of records poses a challenge, you should not give up hope.

Your ancestor's country of origin is a factor in what records to search. Immigrants from the United Kingdom were recorded in the passenger lists but have no naturalization records up to 1947.

Before 1865

Thousands of immigration records survive, despite no organized effort having been made to keep track of new arrivals. Information on the Internet includes

- Names of 1,945 people who received aid from the Montreal Emigrant Society in 1832, on the Library and Archives Canada (LAC) website;
- Names of 3,344 people who applied for naturalization in Upper Canada or Canada West (now Ontario) between 1828 and 1850, on the LAC website;
- Names of 33,026 immigrants, taken from records of the Grosse Île Quarantine Station between 1832 and 1937, on the LAC website;
- Names of about 15,000 immigrants who arrived between 1801 and 1849 and are identified in LAC files. The searchable database is on the Ingeneas.com website;
- The Olive Tree Genealogy website includes links to many passenger lists from the nineteenth century;
- A database of 193,000 immigration records between 1780 and 1906, on Ancestry.

Some newspapers in port cities published partial lists of new arrivals, although these lists generally included prominent businesspeople, not settlers. Other possible sources for early arrivals could be church records, census records, and directories. Information on immigrants' backgrounds may appear in local histories or on tombstones. If they were still alive in 1901, their year of arrival will be shown in the census, but remember, this will have to be verified.

CHINESE ARRIVALS

If you're dealing with immigration from China, nominal registers covering the years 1885 through 1949 are available on microfilm from Library and Archives Canada. Information includes age, place of birth, occupation, date and port of arrival, as well as the amount of head tax paid. Vancouver Public Library has a website for Chinese-Canadian genealogy.

BY THE NUMBERS

Statistics from the two major ports, Halifax and Quebec, reveal a strong correlation between an immigrant's nationality and the port of entry. In 1928–1929, for example, Germans made up 16.9 percent of the arrivals in Halifax but only 6 percent of the arrivals in Quebec. Immigrants from the British Isles, on the other hand, made up 52.3 percent of the people coming through Quebec but only 24.1 percent of those using Halifax.

Arrivals from Denmark, Norway, Sweden, and Finland were also more likely to go through Halifax, while arrivals from Yugoslavia were more likely to go through Quebec. This would all have been based, of course, on the travel agents and the representatives of the steamship companies who were working in the home countries.

Passenger Lists, 1865–1935

The most common record consulted for immigration information is the passenger arrival list. Surviving records collected at major ports are held by LAC. Lists were first kept at the port of Quebec in 1865. Records up to 1935 are open for research.

Library and Archives Canada has placed images of the passenger lists on its website. The scanned images are copied from the microfilms, and the quality of the images varies widely. They can be searched by name of the ship, port of departure, port of arrival, and dates of departure and arrival. The images available are

> City of Québec, Quebec (includes Montréal), from 1 May 1865 to 13 July, 1921;
> Halifax, Nova Scotia, from January 1881 to 2 October 1922;
> Saint John, New Brunswick, from 4 January 1900 to 30 September 1922;
> North Sydney, Nova Scotia, from 22 November 1906 to 31 August 1922;
> Vancouver, British Columbia, from 4 January 1905 to 28 September 1922;
> Victoria, British Columbia, from 18 April 1905 to 30 September 1922.

Ancestry is adding indexes to all the passenger lists images available at LAC to its Canadian databases as well as indexes to the individual passenger arrival forms that were used from 1922 to 1925. Library and Archives Canada has a nominal index to more than 500,000 names for the period 1925–1935. Use the wildcard feature to ensure that a search brings up all the variations of a name, and remember that your person might not have been indexed. Another online index to the LAC passenger lists is at the website of the Nanaimo Family History Society. It contains 320,000 arrivals from 1907 through 1910.

The lists can be consulted on microfilm, and you can obtain them using interlibrary loan. Microfilms of lists up to 1908 are also available through the Family

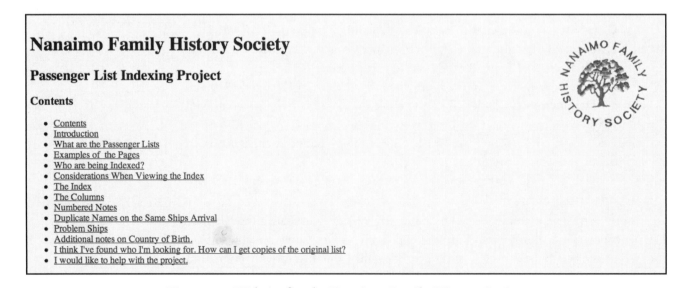

Figure 3-2. Website for the Nanaimo Family History Society
< http://members.shaw.ca/nanaimo.fhs/>

History Library (FHL). Microfilms up to 1935 are available in several large libraries in Canada, although coverage varies with each collection.

The information in passenger lists has changed over the years. The later ones offer more information, and the quality is more consistent. At the start of the twentieth century, for example, a typical passenger list provided date of departure; names of passengers; ages and gender; whether there was a head of a household on board; number of persons in the family; profession, calling, or occupation; nation or country of birth; births at sea; deaths at sea; and places of ultimate destination.

Passenger lists were arranged by port and date of arrival until 1922 and after 1925. For the three years in between, the government required individual forms (Form 30A) for each person. The forms were filed, and later microfilmed, in rough alphabetical order. The forms included the same basic information found on passenger lists.

Remember to look at records from outside of Canada. The findmypast.com website has a database of outbound passengers from the British Isles starting in 1890. This database includes passengers bound for Canada from England, Ireland, Scotland, and Wales, as well as from other countries if they passed through the British Isles on their way to North America.

Many Canadian immigrants came through American ports. Even if your ancestors came directly to Canada, it is still worth looking for distant relatives who settled in the United States because the information they provided to the authorities might provide key clues to the origins of your own family.

Ancestry has comprehensive immigration indexes for New York (the busiest port) from 1820 to 1957, as well as indexes for Boston, Philadelphia, Baltimore, and about one hundred other points of entry. More than 100 million names are included in the Ancestry collection.

Other online sources include databases of passenger arrivals at Ellis Island and its predecessor, Castle Garden, in New York.

Border Entry Records, 1908–1935

While most immigrants came through ocean ports, others entered via land ports along the American border. Some of these people had arrived at an American ocean port a few days earlier. Others had been born in the United States or had spent several years there before opting to search for yet another new home.

Until 1894 there were no limitations or restrictions placed on those crossing the border in either direction. In 1895 the United States started keeping records of people who entered the country. Canada started keeping its own records in April 1908.

Library and Archives Canada has on microfilm lists of immigrants crossing the border from 1908 to the end of 1935. These records contain information such as age, country of birth, occupation, last place of residence in the United States, and destination in Canada.

Not everyone who crossed the border was registered. Some crossed when the ports were closed or where no port existed. Many families were not registered because one

HEADING SOUTH

Along with records of arrivals in Canada, there are records for some of the people who left. The United States kept track of new arrivals on its northern border starting in 1895, and a database of more than 2.5 million names is on the Ancestry website.

A Soundex index covering lists from 1895 through 1954 is available through the U.S. National Archives as well as the Family History Library. The index to this resource, known as the St. Albans lists (named after the Vermont city where the Immigration and Naturalization Service had its main office), is complete from 1895 through 1917. From 1917 to 1927 it included only those people who entered the United States east of the North Dakota/ Montana state line. After 1927 it included only arrivals from east of Lake Ontario.

The St. Albans lists will tell you when your ancestor entered the United States and will usually also indicate when and where he or she entered Canada.

or both parents had been born in Canada or previously resided here, and they were considered returning Canadians rather than immigrants.

Border entries from 1908 through 1918 are arranged by border port and date of entry. Unindexed lists of these arrivals are available on microfilm, organized alphabetically by port, then by year and month.

From January 1919 to the end of 1924, individual forms (Form 30) were used. These records were microfilmed in a quasi-alphabetical format. In 1925, border entry lists were reinstated and were microfilmed by month. Nominal indexes cover the 1925–1935 arrivals. They are not open to the public, but LAC will search them on your behalf.

Arrivals Since 1935

Immigration records after 1935 are held in the custody of Citizenship and Immigration Canada. Send requests for copies of landing records to Citizenship and Immigration Canada in Ottawa. More information and links to the application forms are on the Canadian Genealogy Centre website.

Home Children

Between 1869 and the early 1930s, more than 100,000 children were sent to Canada from Great Britain by religious homes run by people such as Thomas Barnardo, Annie Macpherson, and John Middlemore. These children appear on passenger lists, and members of the British Isles Family History Society of Greater Ottawa have been indexing their names. The resulting database is on the LAC website.

The database includes name, age, sex, microfilm reel number, ship name, port and date of departure, port and date of arrival, name of the organization or home that sent the child, and destination. Some information in the database has been drawn from sources other than passenger lists.

Several websites and books have been devoted to the home children, so it is relatively easy to find out more about the organizations involved in your young immigrant's life.

LI-RA-MA Collection

The Likacheff-Ragosine-Mathers (LI-RA-MA) collection consists of documents created by the Imperial Russian Consular offices in Canada from 1898 to 1922. The passport/identity papers series consists of about 11,400 files on Russian immigrants to Canada, including Jews, Ukrainians, and Finns.

The files include documents such as passport applications and background questionnaires. Many of the records are written in Russian Cyrillic. An online database, including digital images of the files, is on the LAC website.

Naturalization and Citizenship Records

Naturalization and citizenship indexes from 1917 to 1951 were printed on a monthly or annual basis by the federal government. The LAC website has copies of the indexes from 1915 to 1932. These indexes include only people who were not British subjects; Canadian citizenship did not exist before 1947. So there might not be a record because nothing required that a person become naturalized.

This index might help you determine where an immigrant settled. Many new arrivals in the 1920s, for instance, listed Winnipeg as their destination, but they spent only a few days there before moving on. The naturalization index lists their place of residence after they had been in Canada for at least five years, which can guide you to other resources.

Naturalization documents are available from the federal government, but you might find references in local courts. People had to attest to their information in front of a judge, and some of those records ended up in provincial archives.

Most naturalization documents from before 1917 have been destroyed, but indexes survive.

Library and Archives Canada has a naturalization register for Ontario (at the time called Upper Canada or Canada West) from the years 1828 to 1850. A database with 3,344 references is on their website.

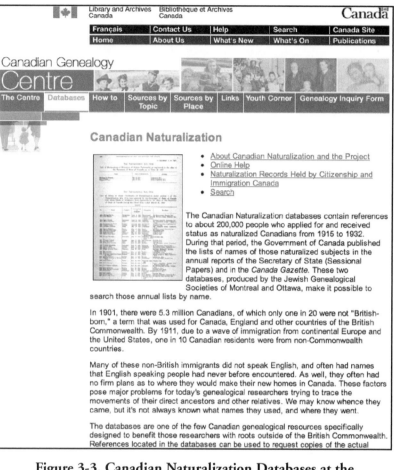

Figure 3-3. Canadian Naturalization Databases at the Canadian Genealogy Centre

<http://www.collectionscanada.ca/genealogy/022-505-e.html>

Immigration Branch Microfilms

If your ancestors arrived after 1935, passenger lists have not yet been released. There is still a chance, however, that you will be able to find information. LAC has Immigration Branch records, known as RG 76, that include information on arrivals all the way into the 1950s.

There are even a few passenger lists, but coverage is inconsistent. If you are dealing with immigrants from Holland between 1947 and 1951, you might be in luck. There are also files on people who came to Canada from Germany, Lithuania, Poland, and other countries on the European continent after World War II.

Other files deal with immigration from before 1935. The Immigration Branch microfilms could provide key details not found in the passenger lists. There are extensive files on British orphans sent to Canada early in the twentieth century, the Barr Colonists in Saskatchewan, refugees, and many others.

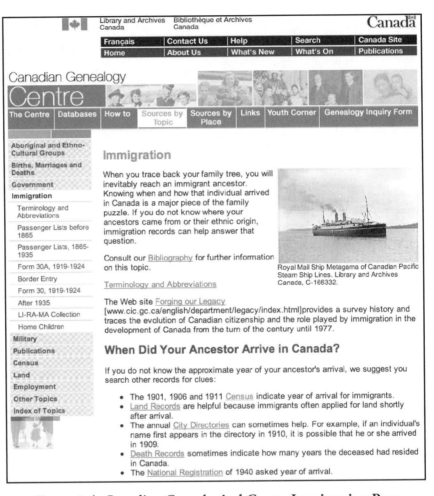

Figure 3-4. Canadian Genealogical Centre Immigration Page
<http://www.collectionscanada.ca/genealogy/022-908-e.html>

The most comprehensive index to the lists included in this microfilm series is found in the book *Destination Canada: A Guide to 20th Century Immigration Records* (Obee, 2004).

The RG 76 films are available from LAC and can be found in a variety of other locations, such as provincial archives.

WEBSITES

Ancestry.ca: <www.ancestry.ca>

Ancestry.com: <www.ancestry.com>

Canadian Genealogy Centre/Immigration: <http://www.collectionscanada.ca/ genealogy/022-908-e.html>

Castle Garden, New York: <www.castlegarden.org>

Ellis Island, New York: <www.ellisisland.org>

Findmypast: <www.findmypast.com>

Immigrants to Canada (passenger lists and background information): <ist.uwaterloo.ca/~marj/genealogy/thevoyage.html>
Immigrants at Grosse Île: <www.collectionscanada.ca/genealogy/ 022-504-e.html>
Immigration Database: <www.ingeneas.com>
Library and Archives Canada: <www.collectionscanada.ca>
Nanaimo Family History Society: <www.island.net/~nfhs/>
Olive Tree Genealogy: <www.olivetreegenealogy.com>
Pier 21: <www.pier21.ca>
Public Archives of New Brunswick/Irish Immigration: <http://archives.gnb.ca/Archives/>
Vancouver Public Library/Chinese-Canadian Genealogy: <www.vpl.vancouver.bc.ca/ccg/home.html>

BIBLIOGRAPHY

Bagnell, Kenneth. *The Little Immigrants: The Orphans Who Came to Canada.* Toronto: Dundurn Press, 2001.

Copping, Arthur E. *The Golden Land: The True Story and Experiences of British Settlers in Canada.* Toronto: Musson, 1911.

Corbett, Gail H. *Nation Builders: Barnardo Children in Canada.* Toronto: Dundurn Press, 2002.

Knowles, Valerie. *Forging Our Legacy: Canadian Citizenship and Immigration, 1900–1977.* Ottawa: Citizenship and Immigration Canada, 2000.

———. *Strangers at Our Gates: Canadian Immigration and Immigration Policy, 1540–1997.* Ottawa: Citizenship and Immigration Canada, 1997.

Obee, Dave. *Destination Canada: A Guide to 20th Century Immigration Records.* Victoria: Dave Obee, 2004.

Woodham-Smith, Cecil. *The Great Hunger.* New York: Harper and Row, 1962.

Woodsworth, James S. *Strangers within Our Gates.* Toronto: University of Toronto Press, 1970.

ADDRESSES

Citizenship and Immigration Canada
Public Rights Administration
360 Laurier Avenue West, 10th Floor
Ottawa, ON K1A 1L1

Library and Archives Canada
395 Wellington Street
Ottawa, ON K1A 0N4

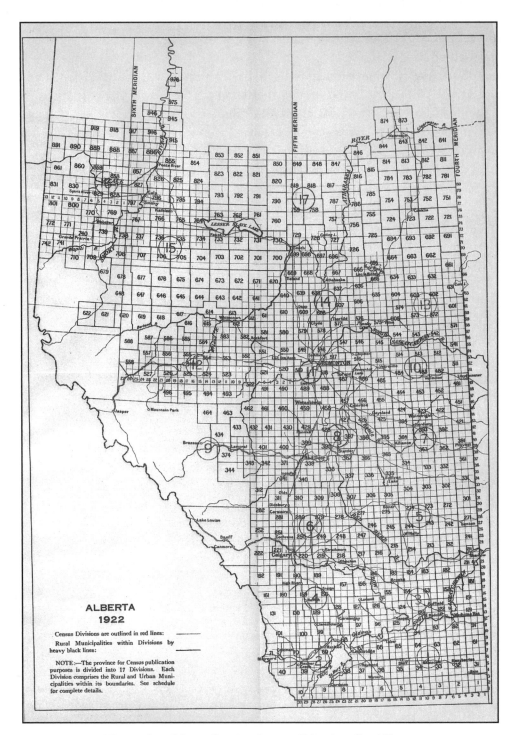

Figure 4-1. Map of 1921 Census Districts for Alberta
Image courtesy of Glenbow Archives (NA-3487-11)

CENSUS

4

Census returns are among the most important resources available to genealogists. The government enumerates the population to determine the state of a colony or country and to plan for the future. It uses this information to, among other things, assess economic health and draw electoral district boundaries. When census registers containing the names of those enumerated are preserved, these records are of inestimable value for family history.

Canadian censuses from the French regime up to 1911 can be consulted by the public. Most records are held by Library and Archives Canada (LAC) and are widely available in several formats; some returns have been digitized and indexed. Censuses have also been taken by provinces, cities, parishes, seigneuries, and captains of coastal vessels in Newfoundland. Check with local archives for locations, dates, and content.

The first census taken in Canada was carried out in New France in 1666 and recorded 3,215 people. A second census the following year found 3,918 people. French authorities conducted about a dozen more over the next one hundred years. Some of the early censuses included every person living in the French communities, although many included only the names of the heads of households.

After the area came under British control, censuses were not taken as consistently as had been done under the French. Unlike the French lists of inhabitants, the British censuses generally listed only heads of households. Also, there were format differences between censuses in all of the colonies.

Censuses became more comprehensive and more frequent in the 1800s. In 1851 and 1852, censuses were taken in Ontario, Quebec, New Brunswick, and Nova Scotia, although again formats differed between the areas.

Nova Scotia wanted the names of heads of household only. New Brunswick asked for the year of arrival. Ontario and Quebec wanted to know if each person was part of a family but did not ask that the person specify which family. Also, the census in Ontario and Quebec was taken in January 1852, months after the censuses in Nova Scotia and New Brunswick were completed.

Confederation in 1867 brought consistency to Canadian censuses, and this spread as the country grew. The new Dominion's first census was taken in 1871 and included Ontario, Quebec, New Brunswick, and Nova Scotia. The next national census, in 1881, enumerated most of present-day Canada. All three Maritime Provinces are there, along with Ontario, Quebec, British Columbia, and the three Prairie Provinces under Manitoba and the Northwest Territories.

The rush of immigration to the Prairies at the start of the twentieth century led the federal government to conduct an extra census of the region in 1906, the first to use modern names for all three provinces. Special Prairie censuses were also taken in 1916, 1926, 1936, and 1946.

Since 1951 a national census has been taken every five years. The 1951 census was also the first Canadian census to include Newfoundland and Labrador, which joined Confederation in 1949. Nine colonial enumerations were held in Newfoundland between 1836 and 1945, and all are open to public research. This has allowed people with roots in Newfoundland to get a head start on the rest of the country.

By law, federal census returns are to be opened ninety-two years after they are compiled, so every five years, more information will be made available to family historians. The 1916 Prairies census will be opened for research in 2008, and the 1921 national census is due to be released in 2013.

Censuses have also been taken on a local and provincial basis, including returns for cities such as Calgary. Check with local archives for regional censuses in your area.

CONTENT

The number and types of questions asked in a census return have varied widely over the years. Some of the pre-Confederation censuses were remarkably detailed. In 1842 in Canada West (today's Ontario) and in 1851 in New Brunswick, for example, people were asked for the year they arrived in Canada.

Generally, you can expect to find names, ages, and occupations on a census return. From 1891 forward, you will find out a person's relationship to the head of household. The 1901 census asked for date and year of birth and year of immigration to Canada.

The special censuses taken on the Prairies in the first half of the twentieth century did not include as many questions as the national ones of the same era. In 1971 the government introduced the "short form" of the census, with fewer questions than the regular one. The descendants of those millions of people "lucky" enough to get the short version will surely be disappointed at the lack of detail.

If your ancestors worked the land, be sure to check the 1851 and 1861 censuses. They include an agricultural schedule with details such as location, land under cultivation, cash value of implements, and the like. In some areas nominal returns were lost, but the agricultural returns have survived.

SOME CENSUS QUESTIONS IN 1851/52:

Name
Occupation
Birthplace
Age next birthday
Religion
Sex
Married or single
Number of Negroes
Number of Indians
Whether a member of a family
Members of the family who are absent
Residence if out of limits
Number of deaf and dumb
Number of blind
Number of lunatics
Number attending school
Births during census year
Deaths during census year
Cause of death
Details about the house
Remarks

The 1871 census also asked for extra information on agriculture, including full details on a wide variety of crops. If your ancestor was farming that year, you will be able to learn how many bushels of barley, oats, and peas, among other crops, he or she produced. The census also asked for information on fishing, mining, and forest ventures. As an added bonus, the 1871 census includes a list of deaths within the previous twelve months.

All of the original paper census returns have been destroyed, leaving only microfilm copies. Unfortunately, the microfilming rarely included all of the schedules compiled by the enumerators, and much information has been lost.

GENEALOGICAL USE

Information in a census return can help you identify individuals, origins, family relationships, and people's movements over many years and long distances. Many census indexes and returns are on the Internet, making this great resource more useful than ever before.

Most Canadian census returns identify birthplaces, which can be used to confirm where a family originated. The birthplaces of children can be used to trace the family's location over several years. And if there are grandparents living with the family, the birthplaces shown could push research back another generation, even if they don't specify an exact parish or village.

The date of birth is usually shown and, whether exact or just the year, can guide you to a birth record and the parents' marriage. Birth information can be inconsistent from one census to the next, so check every available census and look for the birth record.

The census returns from 1901 and 1911 also include the year of immigration to Canada. Again, don't treat the date as the absolute truth because our ancestors rounded dates up or down and sometimes didn't remember exactly.

Canadian returns give each person's religion. This can be used to confirm that the correct person has been found or to help you find church records.

Land information makes it easy to find out how much property a person had and the size of a house. The precise location can help point to other sources, such as directories and land records.

While the census is supposed to represent a snapshot taken on a single day, the actual enumeration sometimes dragged on for days, weeks, or months. You might find a relative listed twice, with two addresses, giving you a clue about when he or she moved.

Extracting information from a census is easier if you use forms with categories already identified. Downloadable forms are available on the Ancestry website.

LOCATING CENSUS RETURNS

Canadian census returns are easy to find. They are available on microfilm through Library and Archives Canada (LAC), at many large libraries across the country, and at the Family History Library (FHL). It is important to note that the FHL holds

SOME CENSUS QUESTIONS IN 1871:

Name
Occupation
Birthplace
Racial origin
Married within the previous twelve months
Ability to read and write

Ancestry.ca

1911 Canadian Census Form

SCHEDULE NO. 1. POPULATION BY NAME, PERSONAL DESCRIPTION, ETC.

FIFTH CENSUS OF CANADA, 1911

Province _____   District No. _____   S. District No. _____   Enumeration District No. _____   in _____ _____ (City, town, village, township, or parish.)

Page _____   Nominal return of living persons by _____   Enumerator.   Page _____

NUMBERED IN THE ORDER OF VISITATION
1 — Dwelling House
2 — Family, Household or Institution

RESIDENCE AND PERSONAL DESCRIPTION
3 — Name of each person in family, household or institution
4 — Place of Habitation (Township or parish, city, town or village. Range or concession and cadastral number if in township or parish. Street and house number in city, town or village. Or other description)
5 — Sex
6 — Relationship to head of family or household
7 — Single, Married, Widowed, Divorced or legally separated
8 — Month of birth
9 — Year of birth
10 — Age at last birthday

CITIZENSHIP, NATIONALITY AND RELIGION
11 — Country or place of birth (If in Canada specify province or territory)
12 — Year of immigration to Canada, if an immigrant
13 — Year of naturalization, if formally an alien
14 — Racial or tribal origin
15 — Nationality
16 — Religion

PROFESSION, OCCUPATION, TRADE OR MEANS OF LIVING
17 — Chief occupation or trade
18 — Employment other than at chief occupation or trade, if any
19 — Employer
20 — Employee
21 — Working on own account (See instructions)

WAGE EARNERS
22 — State where person is employed, as "on farm," "in woolen mill," "at foundry shop," "in drug store," etc.
23 — Weeks employed in 1910 at chief occupation or trade
24 — Weeks employed in 1910 at other than chief occupation or trade, if any
25 — Hours of working time per week at chief occupation
26 — Hours of working time per week at other occupation, if any
27 — Total earnings in 1910 from chief occupation or trade
28 — Total earnings in 1910 from other than chief occupation or trade, if any
29 — Rate of earnings per hour when employed by the hour -- Cents

INSURANCE HELD AT DATE
30 — Upon life $
31 — Against accident or sickness $
32 — Cost of insurance in census year $

EDUCATION AND LANGUAGE OF EACH PERSON FIVE YEARS OF AGE AND OVER
33 — Months at school in 1910
34 — Can read
35 — Can write
36 — Language commonly spoken
37 — Cost of education in 1910 for persons over 16 years of age at College, Convent or University $

INFIRMITIES. Specify age when infirmity appeared
38 — Blind
39 — Deaf and dumb
40 — Crazy or lunatic
41 — Idiotic or silly

copyright © 2005 MyFamily.com, Inc.

For more family history charts and forms, visit http://MyFamily.com/charts/canadacensus.aspx

Figure 4-2. 1911 Canadian Census Form
Available at Ancestry.ca

microfilm copies of all censuses up to and including the 1906 Prairie census but not the national returns for 1911. Also, more and more census records are being placed online, complete with indexes.

The Ancestry website has indexes to the 1851, 1901, and 1911 national censuses, as well as the 1906 Prairies census. Indexes are linked to images of the census pages at the LAC website.

Other indexes to the censuses of 1901, 1906, and 1911, compiled by volunteers across the country, are at Automated Genealogy. Stephen Morse offers another way to search census indexes with his One-Step Webpages site.

Census images can be viewed at the LAC website. The site is not indexed, and you will need a place-name in order to browse the appropriate segment. Consult a map and search the place-name or that of a larger place nearby and refer to the introduction to each census at the website as well as to the online edition of *Catalogue of Census Returns on Microfilm 1666–1901*. The catalogue also indicates what returns survive for each district.

The LAC website includes images of the 1851 census (images only), which must be browsed by place, and an index to the heads of families in Ontario in the 1871 census.

An index to the 1881 census can be found at FamilySearch.org. Another index, with expanded search options, is available on CD-ROM from The Church of Jesus Christ of Latter-day Saints.

For other years, you will need to consult local and regional indexes, both online and in printed form. Many returns have not yet been indexed, while other areas have been indexed by provincial archives, societies, and individual volunteers. Advice on finding these options is found in the provincial chapters in this book.

The book *French-Canadian Sources: A Guide for Genealogists* (Geyh et al., 2002) includes details of every census in the provinces from Ontario eastward. The section on the census includes dates, coverage, and whether the census includes everyone in the household or just the head.

SPECIAL CONSIDERATIONS

Comprehensive indexes on the Internet make it tempting to speed through your census research, but be warned: Indexes are not always accurate. It is easy to misread or misinterpret entries.

Be careful when dealing with census districts. Many of their boundaries changed between enumerations, and often the names used in the census had little connection to the local area. Some names were used just for the census and for federal elections, and some local place-names are duplicated elsewhere.

When using the census, look for place-names that are familiar to you, and keep an atlas handy for reference. The 1880 *Illustrated Atlas of the Dominion of Canada*, available on microfilm through the FHL, shows census district boundaries. The 1895 *Electoral Atlas of the Dominion of Canada*, on the LAC website, shows electoral boundaries, which were generally the same as census boundaries.

SOME CENSUS QUESTIONS IN 1891:

Relationship to the head of the household
Birthplace of mother
Birthplace of father
Construction of the home
Number of floors
Number of rooms

The census shows subdistricts within the census districts, and some returns list addresses as well. These details can help you determine the precise location for your ancestor. Plot the location of your family on a map; then see if other relatives lived in the area. Also look for schools, churches, stores, and transportation systems. All of these things had an impact on their lives.

Census records can help us gain a better understanding about the lives of our ancestors. Look at the community as a whole. Were your ancestors surrounded by people of the same ethnic background? The same religion? Were they the only Albanians in a sea of Scots? Factors such as these would have influenced their daily lives.

ALTERNATIVE AND SUPPORTING SOURCES

While the census is one of the key sources available to genealogists, it won't answer all of your questions. Sometimes you cannot find a person, and sometimes a family moved several times between enumerations. Census substitutes, including newspapers and directories, are described in the next chapter.

Some of these additional sources are more than substitutes. They can enhance what you learn from a census, make it easier to find people, or help you fill in the gaps between the census years. You might consult a directory, for example, to supplement information found in a census. The census might give a person's occupation, but the directory will give the person's employer as well.

WEBSITES

Ancestry.ca: <www.ancestry.ca>
Automated Genealogy: <www.automatedgenealogy.com>
Catalogue of Census Returns on Microfilm, 1666–1901:
    <www.collectionscanada.ca/archivianet/020121_e.html>
Library and Archives Canada: <www.collectionscanada.ca>
Steve Morse's One-Step Pages: <stevemorse.org>

BIBLIOGRAPHY

Geyh, Patricia Keeney, et al. *French-Canadian Sources: A Guide for Genealogists.* Orem, UT: Ancestry, 2002.
Obee, Dave. *Back to the Land: A Genealogical Guide to Finding Farms on the Canadian Prairies.* Victoria: Dave Obee, 2003.
Statistics Canada. Census reports, various years.

SOME CENSUS QUESTIONS IN 1901:

Sex
Color
Relationship to the head of the
    household
Marital status
Date and year of birth
Age last birthday
Country or place of birth
Year of immigration to Canada
Year of naturalization
Racial origin
Nationality
Religion
Profession or occupation
Employment
Months at school
Whether can read or write
Whether can speak English or
    French
Mother tongue

VITAL RECORDS—CREATED BY GOVERNMENTS

5

The term *vital records* may refer to any records of birth or christening, marriage, and death or burial. They are among the first resources used by genealogists and the logical starting point when working back from known individuals alive for some or all of the last 150 years.

In Canada the collection of civil vital records has been a responsibility of the provinces and territories since the country was founded in 1867. Prior to Confederation some of the colonial administrations started recording vital events, but collection may have lapsed and resumed some years after the region became part of Canada. The year a province or territory joined Canada is not necessarily the year provincial civil records started. The period between the two dates may be a year or two or decades.

Some records included in this category, such as marriage bonds, may appear to be church records and predate government records, but they were submitted to a civil office, and today they are usually made available with collections of vital statistics.

CONTENT

In spite of many different offices generating and looking after these records, there are similarities in content across the country. All provinces note the type of event, the date it took place and where, the principal people involved, and the date the event was registered. Records may also contain additional details, such as occupation, name of the informant, witnesses, one or both parents, or cause of death.

Marriage license records are usually found among civil record collections in the Atlantic region. These records begin in the 1700s. Existence of a marriage license or bond indicates the intention to marry but does not prove a marriage took place. Usually a bond was completed when a license was obtained. The bond was a guarantee,

CONTENT OF RECORDS

Birth Record:

Generally includes full name of child, sex, date of birth, place of birth, name of father, name of mother.

May include mother's maiden name, name of informant, occupation of the father, hospital, place of residence if different from place of birth.

Marriage Record:

Generally includes name of bride, name of groom, date, place, marital status of the parties (e.g., bachelor, spinster, widowed), witnesses, name of officiating minister or registrar.

May include age of the bride, age of the groom, names of their fathers or of both parents, occupations, places of residence.

Marriage Bond and License:

Includes the names of the bride and groom and may include the name of the bondsman, amount of the bond, when and where the marriage could take place.

Death Record:

Generally includes name of deceased, occupation, date of death, place, age, informant.

May include place of residence, place of burial, spouse, parents, cause of death.

a promise to pay a sum of money should a reason emerge that prevented a marriage from taking place. Requirements for licenses and bonds varied, and some bond amounts were large: in New Brunswick the amount was set at £500.

Several provincial governments sought information about events that predated their own records and collected either church record information or details from individuals and churches. In addition, individuals sometimes needed a birth record, perhaps to collect a pension, but no such record existed. These two situations mean that collections of early records and individual retrospective entries may be found within regular vital records. *Retrospective* means the record was created long after the fact and usually validated by the declaration of a relative.

GENEALOGICAL USE

Birth, marriage, and death are the major events of a life history and essential details for understanding family relationships. They reveal many useful pieces of information, such as the ones in this list. Always record every detail in case a strange name turns out to be a relation.

- Accurate facts about when and where an event occurred
- Names of immediate family members of the same generation
- Names of immediate family members of an older generation
- Maiden names of brides, wives, or mothers
- Names of witnesses and informants who may be collateral relations
- Clues or facts to facilitate using other avenues of enquiry
- Clues about work and social status

Vital records can be used to sort out families of the same name. Dates and places, names of witnesses, or the father's occupation may help you recognize ancestors. In addition, all the facts in vital records help you reconstruct families, with people placed in the proper generations and relationships recorded accurately. Some genealogical problems are solved by collecting the vital records of all family members and carefully studying the details.

LOCATING VITAL RECORDS

Older records of birth, marriage, and death are generally accessible across the country. Modern privacy legislation determines the cutoff dates separating publicly available records from those with restricted access. Original records for each province or territory are usually in the capital city and, depending upon privacy legislation, are in some way divided between the archives and the department responsible for vital statistics.

Quebec is unique because its civil records were created from copies of church records. This makes their provincial vital records the longest running and most complete in Canada. Newfoundland is another special situation because it joined Canada in 1949, so its records start later than those in other provinces.

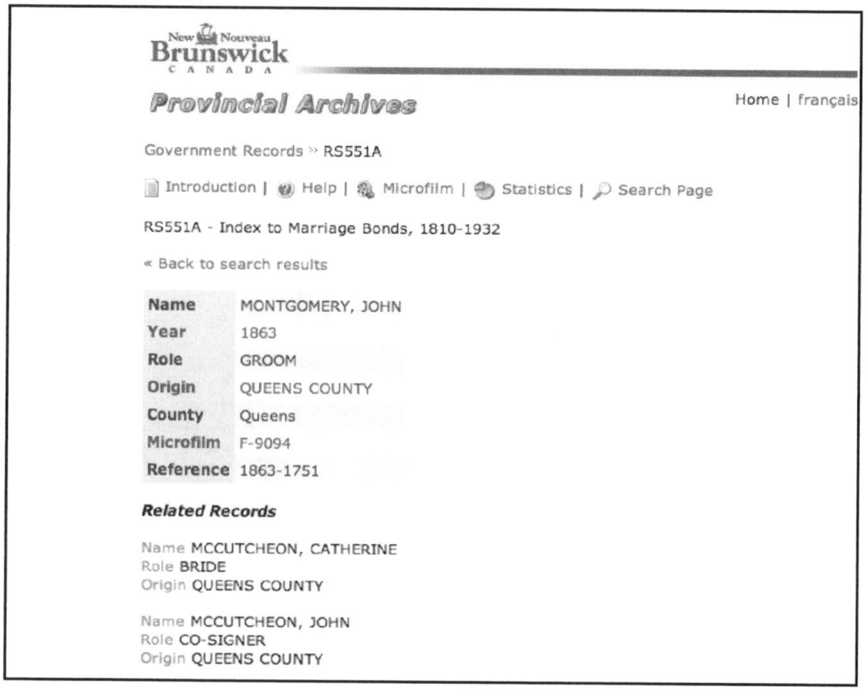

Figure 5-1. A New Brunswick Marriage Bond Index Search Result
Marriage bonds were required when banns were not read or when the clergyman did not know both the bride and groom. They provide the names and residences of the couple intending to marry and the cosigner(s). The indexes do not give exact locations, but more information appears in the records.
<http://archives.gnb.ca/APPS/GovRecs/RS551A/Details.aspx?L=EN&Key=15507>

Some parts of the country have moved to digital records and to providing Web-based search tools; some also offer images or an image ordering service online. The Canadian Genealogy Centre has a central access point for information on vital statistics records, with links to the provincial offices and to sources for events that occurred outside of Canada.

In some cases historic records may be available through paid genealogical data services operated by either the government or a commercial provider.

In addition to checking provincial archives and online resources, you should check the collections of the Family History Library (FHL), using the online catalog at FamilySearch.org. Anything they have filmed can be accessed through local Family History Centers.

You can be confident of a thorough search if you go through this checklist before beginning your search:

- Discover the year records begin.
- Find out if there are gaps in the records.
- Find out about other records now treated as official and how they are indexed.
- Learn the regulations regarding access.

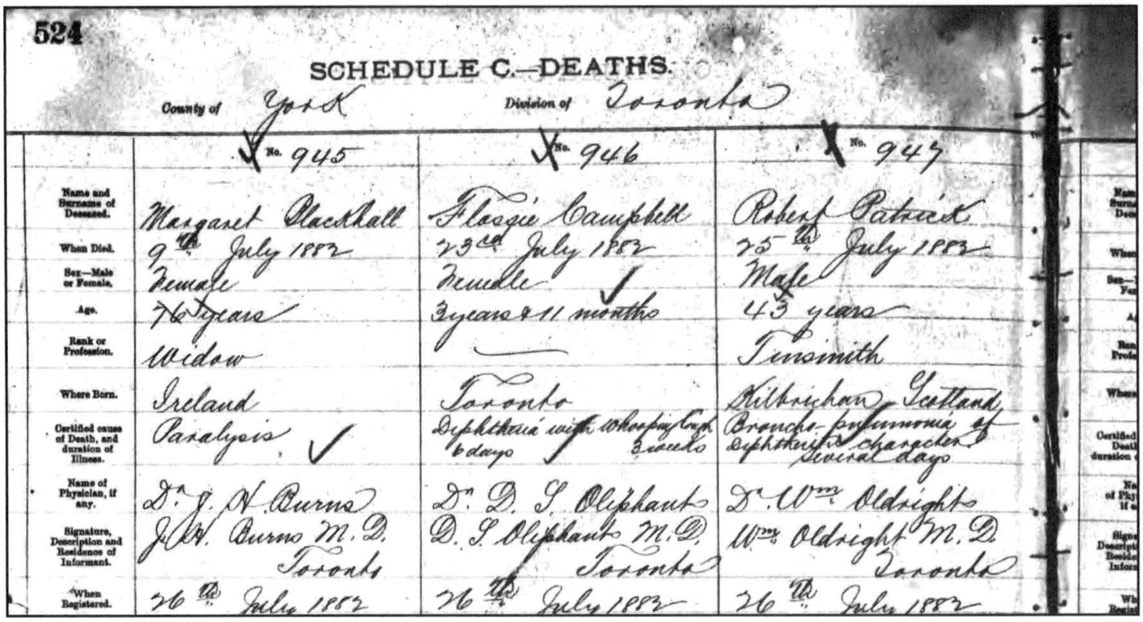

524

SCHEDULE C.—DEATHS.

County of York Division of Toronto

	No. 945	No. 946	No. 947
Name and Surname of Deceased.	Margaret Blackhall	Flossie Campbell	Robert Patrick
When Died.	9th July 1882	23rd July 1882	25th July 1882
Sex—Male or Female.	Female	Female	Male
Age.	76 years	3 years & 11 months	43 years
Rank or Profession.	Widow	—	Tinsmith
Where Born.	Ireland	Toronto	Kilbrechan Scotland
Certified cause of Death, and duration of Illness.	Paralysis	Diphtheria with whooping cough 6 days 3 weeks	Broncho-pneumonia of diphtheritic character several days
Name of Physician, if any.	Dr. J. H. Burns	Dr. D. S. Oliphant	Dr. Wm. Oldright
Signature, Description and Residence of Informant.	J. H. Burns M.D. Toronto	D. S. Oliphant M.D. Toronto	Wm. Oldright M.D. Toronto
When Registered.	26th July 1882	26th July 1882	26th July 1882

Figure 5-2. Top Half of a Page of Civil Death Records—Ontario

The record shows the variety of detail that may appear for place of birth and religious denomination of the deceased. Ontario Death Records 1882, County of York, District of Toronto, page 524.

Available at Ancestry.ca

- Check for online indexes and images.
- Check for microform indexes and images.
- Discover how to order copies of records.

A provincial vital statistics or archives website may recommend the purchase of a register photocopy rather than a certificate because it may contain the most information.

DIVORCE

Divorce was a civil matter in Canada, and before the mid-twentieth century it was both uncommon and expensive. Fewer than 900 divorces were granted in all of Canada between 1867 and 1913—not surprising when it required an act of Parliament in most regions. Divorces granted by the federal government can be identified using the database at the Canadian Genealogy Centre website.

Three provinces had their own divorce courts before World War I: British Columbia, New Brunswick, and Nova Scotia, which has case files starting in 1759. Manitoba, Saskatchewan, Alberta, and the Northwest Territories created their own courts by 1919, Ontario did so in 1930, and Quebec and Newfoundland waited until 1968.

Records of divorce provide the names of both parties, and this includes the maiden name of the wife. There is a date for the divorce, and usually you can learn who initiated the action.

RESEARCH CONSIDERATIONS

Any family that moved about is harder to find in civil vital records, and this is especially true if a move happened at a time when one region had records and another did not. Ontario had centralized civil records from 1869, but records for the province of Manitoba do not begin until 1888; these years correspond to a time when many in Ontario were moving west. In those circumstances, alternate sources for dates of birth, marriage, and death must be found.

The later starting dates for Canadian records can mean some facts important for picking up the trail in a different country of origin may be difficult or impossible to find. As for people moving back and forth across the U.S. border, the United States also lacks a central registration system. In the United States, civil records over the last 150 years have been collected by cities, counties, and states. If two provinces or two countries figure in your research, be sure to check and compare civil registration records in both.

Migration is one possible source of trouble when using vital records. More information on common genealogical pitfalls can be found in appendix B.

ALTERNATIVE AND SUPPORTING SOURCES

If you think about the information you need, you can probably come up with a list of likely alternative records. A death is a good example. The event could generate some or all of these records:

- the official civil record
- a notice in the newspaper
- the funeral home file
- a grave marker
- church burial record
- probate court record

There are other related records, too, because after a death, a house may be sold or at least have new occupants. The name of the deceased would also disappear from directories and electoral rolls.

WEBSITES

Ancestry: <www.ancestry.ca>
Canadian Genealogy Centre: <www.collectionscanada.ca/genealogy/>
FamilySearch: <www.familysearch.org>
Provincial vital statistics offices and archives: See individual provincial chapters.
Online finding aids for each province: See individual province chapters.

BIBLIOGRAPHY

Tracing Your Ancestors in Canada. Ottawa: Library and Archives Canada, 2006. (available as a booklet and online at the Library and Archives Canada website as a PDF file)

ADDRESSES

Look in the individual provincial chapters for the addresses of provincial departments of vital statistics.

VITAL RECORDS—
CHURCH REGISTERS

Immigrants to Canada brought their religions with them, and they built churches, missions, and meetinghouses where they settled. The inhabitants of New France were almost all Catholic, and in the earliest British colonies the place of worship was usually Church of England. However, with immigration, the number of religions grew, changed, and reflected the origins of the newcomers.

By 1800 three other Protestant denominations were firmly established: Presbyterian, Methodist, and Lutheran. In 1901, except for the addition of Baptist to the list, the pattern of church membership did not look much different from one hundred years before. About 230,000 of Canada's 5.4 million people, roughly 4 percent, belonged to a religion other than the six predominant Christian faiths.

The Roman Catholic faith arrived first with the earliest French settlers and was closely linked to French colonial authority. The Anglican Church of Canada came about one hundred years later and until 1959 was known as the Church of England in Canada.

The Baptist, Congregational, and Lutheran Churches were in Nova Scotia in the middle of the eighteenth century and Methodists about a generation later. These religions moved west with settlement, and new faiths came with new immigrants from central Europe. The first Orthodox Church in Alberta was founded in the 1890s, and the Lutheran Church also had congregations in the West by that time.

Not all of the different religions were unified amongst their own followers. The splits amongst Presbyterians and Methodists in the United Kingdom were reflected in Canada, but following Confederation some put their differences aside.

In 1874 the Methodist Church of Canada was formed from six groups: Methodist Episcopal, Wesleyan Methodist Church in Canada, Wesleyan Methodist Conference of Eastern British America, New Connexion, Primitive Methodist, and Bible Christian.

The Presbyterian Union in 1875 brought together the Church of Scotland, Free Church of Scotland, Macdonaldite churches, Reformed Presbyterian congregations, and the congregations of the United Presbyterian Synod in Ontario. The Congregational Union of Canada was founded in 1908. In 1925, the United Church of Canada was formed by the union of most Methodists, most Congregationalists, and approximately 70 percent of Presbyterians.

Religion	1871	1881	1891	1901	1911	1921	1931
Anglican	504,392	589,599	661,608	689,540	1,048,002	1,410,632	1,639,809
Baptist	244,773	297,891	307,103	319,234	384,152	422,312	447,944
Jewish	1,233	2,443	6,501	16,493	74,760	125,445	155,766
Lutheran	38,226	46,653	66,151	94,110	231,883	286,891	394,920
Roman Catholic	1,536,733	1,814,055	2,009,201	2,238,955	2,841,881	3,399,011	4,289,839
United, Presbyterian, Methodist, Congregational	1,182,503	1,456,637	1,660,373	1,800,889	2,240,304	2,612,486	2,904,131
Other Denominations	71,922	117,532	122,302	212,094	385,661	531,172	544,377

Major Religious Groups in Canada, 1871 to 1931
Statistical tables in the census reports for 1931 indicate the membership and growth of major Christian religions in Canada. The reports contain similar details for each province and figures for many other religious groups. The population of Canada in 1871 was 3,689,257, and in 1931 it was 10,376,786.

The large numbers of immigrants in the early twentieth century brought many more religions to Canada, and the statistical reports of the censuses begin to mention them. By 1921 the eight religious groups with the most followers were Roman Catholic, Anglican, the Presbyterian/Methodist/Congregational grouping, Baptist, Lutheran, Greek Orthodox, and Jewish. Some religions had concentrations in particular areas. These included about 19,000 Mormons in southern Alberta and about 60,000 Mennonites in southern Ontario and Manitoba. More than 32,000 individuals either stated they had no religion at all or failed to respond to the question in the census.

There were 501 Jews in Canada in 1851, with the largest number arriving between 1900 and 1920, mainly from eastern Europe. The census numbers for Greek Orthodox included those attending a variety of Orthodox churches from different eastern European countries such as Russia, Romania, Bulgaria, and Ukraine.

CONTENT

Information in church register entries varies according to the denomination or the inclination of individual ministers. However, there are some details you can be sure of:

- Baptism: name of child, surname, first names of one or both parents, date and place
- Marriage: names of bride and groom, name of bride's father, witnesses, date and place
- Burial: name of deceased, date and place, age appears in many, and if a child, the name of the father is likely to appear

Additional details that may have been recorded include occupation, maiden name of a child's mother, names of godparents, and full names of both parents of bride and groom.

Christenings, marriages, and burials may be together in a single volume, perhaps year by year, or there may be different parts of the book for different events. In a populated parish there may be separate volumes for each event.

Figure 6-1. A Country Church in Manitoba
Photo courtesy of Canada Science and Technology Museum

For some faiths baptism came at an older age, and other records, such as confirmations, can be as important in providing facts. Ages can be found in Sunday school lists as well. Presbyterians generally carried a letter of recommendation from one church to another. Some of these different but equally useful records survive.

GENEALOGICAL USE

Dates, places, names of principal people involved, and names of other participants, such as witnesses and relations, are all important details to be gleaned from registers. These facts help build families and provide the evidence of direct bloodlines and collateral relationships. Information about where and when baptisms, marriages, and burials occurred is important to planning research and taking a family line further back in time.

Browse through church records. Even if an entry is found in a detailed index, look at the record or a copy to verify the facts and check for unindexed notations. If you browse further you can catch errors and omissions in the index and read burial entries, often left out of indexes.

LOCATING CHURCH RECORDS

Your search begins with two questions: What church recorded the event, and where might that record be today?

There are several ways to find out where a christening, marriage, or burial took place. Look at contemporary maps, and consult books of local history, gazetteers, and town directories to learn when churches were built and their denominations. You may find the name of the church in a family Bible or in a note about a photograph.

Sometimes a family worshipped several miles away. They went to hear a good preacher, to attend a particular denomination, or because nothing was close by.

Locating records, originals or copies, will be easier in some provinces. Quebec offers few difficulties because of the predominance of one religion and the system of record keeping. In New Brunswick a majority of surviving church records are in the provincial archives. Elsewhere you will not be so fortunate, and for some religions you will find that records are in local or regional church archives, in museums and libraries, or still with the church. Always check with the provincial archives for records and information, but be prepared to search in other places.

Remember that church records are not government records. They generally remain the property of individual churches or congregations or of a larger church organization. It is important to understand the history and administration of the religious denomination to which your ancestors belonged, then and now.

There are databases to try, but there is no comprehensive national index to Canadian church records or even for one denomination. French-Canadian Catholic records come closest at present, with many finding aids and large marriage indexes. Resources for French-Canadian research will soon improve even more; images of the Drouin Collection can now be browsed at the Ancestry website and indexes will be added (see chapter 24).

The International Genealogical Index for Canada is made up predominantly of submissions from members of The Church of Jesus Christ of Latter-day Saints. There are more microfilm copies of records of eastern Canadian churches in the Family History Library (FHL), but because the library has many published transcripts and indexes, you should always check the catalog. In addition, the FHL has copies of any church records held by Library and Archives Canada (LAC).

Resources on the Internet for other denominations are mixed. Those for Jewish research, for example, are good, including finding aids, background information, and society websites. Generally you will be using genealogical gateway sites such as GenWeb to direct you to locally produced databases, but you should check provincial archives early in your search because some have online indexes. Using these steps as a guide should help you turn up available online indexes or transcripts:

- Identify the church where the event occurred, or churches near the place where your ancestors lived if you do not know the church.
- Check if the church still exists (see Canadian Church Directory online).
- Check GenWeb.
- Check provincial archives for any indexes.
- Check the publications of provincial and local family history societies.
- Use the list of websites at the end of the chapter to locate denominational archives.
- Use a search engine (keyword search, place and name of church, or place and the word *church*).

The Internet can help you locate church records held by archives and libraries. You can search the catalogs of LAC, provincial archives, community libraries, the FHL in Salt Lake City, and university libraries. Websites of family history societies list their publications. Some universities hold extensive collections of church records, though these may not include registers. If records remain with a church or congregation, look for a website. Some church sites provide a detailed history, including mention of members of the congregation.

The church archives of different denominations hold varying numbers of local records. For the Anglican Church, check with their regional archives; some of them have published guides. Information about Catholic records and archives can be obtained from diocesan offices, which can be identified using a search engine or the website of the Canadian Council of Catholic Bishops.

The United Church of Canada has published a guide to its holdings, and online you can find websites for its regional archives. The Presbyterian Church has information online for genealogists, and their archives hold records relating to roughly four hundred churches across the country. The Lutheran and Baptist Churches also have collections and provide details online. Mormon records are at the FHL.

To track down the locations of original records or copies, follow these steps:

- Check on the Internet for a church office and for national or regional archives.
- Consult the LDS Family History Library Catalog (FHLC).
- Consult catalogs of archives and libraries for the province and community.
- Check the collection of church records at Library and Archives Canada.

Title Details	FAMILY HISTORY LIBRARY CATALOG	THE CHURCH OF JESUS CHRIST OF LATTER-DAY SAINTS

View Film Notes

Title	Church records, 1770-1870
Authors	Dutch Reformed Church (Lunenburg, Nova Scotia) (Main Author) Presbyterian Church (Lunenburg, Nova Scotia) (Added Author)
Notes	Microfilm of typescript in possession of the Public Archives of Canada, Ottawa, Ontario. Contains communions, baptisms, 1770-1819, marriages, 1770-1818 and burials, 1771-1818 for the Dutch Reformed Church (translated from German), and baptisms, 1837-1870, marriages, 1837-1855, and burials, 1837-1854, for the Presbyterian Church. The Dutch Reformed Church in Lunenburg became a Presbyterian Church in 1837.
Subjects	Nova Scotia, Lunenburg, Lunenburg - Church records
Format	Manuscript (On Film)
Language	English
Publication	Ottawa, Ontario : Central Microfilm Unit, Public Archives of Canada, 1967
Physical	on 1 microfilm reel ; 35 mm.

For a printable version of this record click here then click your browser's **Print** button.

© 2002 Intellectual Reserve, Inc. All rights reserved.

Figure 6-2. Church Record Entry in the Family History Library Catalog

The Family History Library Catalog can be searched several different ways. The Place and Keyword searches are best for finding entries for individual churches. This result for Lunenburg, Nova Scotia, was located using the Place search; Lunenburg is repeated in the Subject line because it is the name of the town and the county.

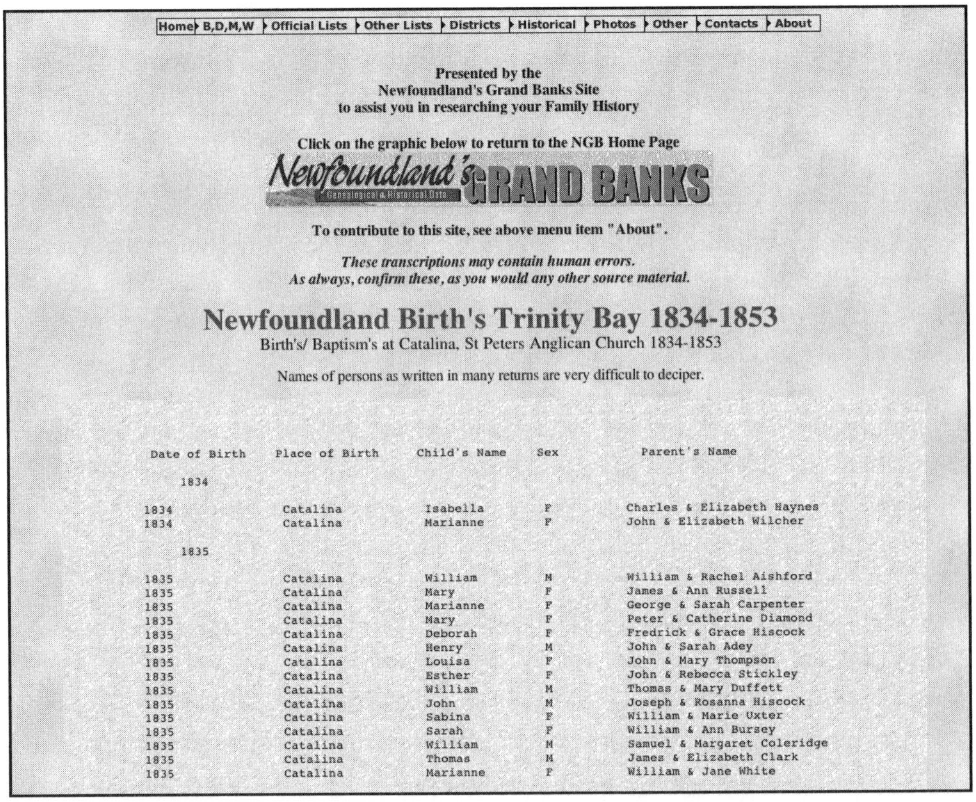

Home B,D,M,W Official Lists Other Lists Districts Historical Photos Other Contacts About

Presented by the
Newfoundland's Grand Banks Site
to assist you in researching your Family History

Click on the graphic below to return to the NGB Home Page

Newfoundland's GRAND BANKS
Genealogical & Historical Data

To contribute to this site, see above menu item "About".

These transcriptions may contain human errors.
As always, confirm these, as you would any other source material.

Newfoundland Birth's Trinity Bay 1834-1853

Birth's/ Baptism's at Catalina, St Peters Anglican Church 1834-1853

Names of persons as written in many returns are very difficult to deciper.

Date of Birth	Place of Birth	Child's Name	Sex	Parent's Name
1834				
1834	Catalina	Isabella	F	Charles & Elizabeth Haynes
1834	Catalina	Marianne	F	John & Elizabeth Wilcher
1835				
1835	Catalina	William	M	William & Rachel Aishford
1835	Catalina	Mary	F	James & Ann Russell
1835	Catalina	Marianne	F	George & Sarah Carpenter
1835	Catalina	Mary	F	Peter & Catherine Diamond
1835	Catalina	Deborah	F	Fredrick & Grace Hiscock
1835	Catalina	Henry	M	John & Sarah Adey
1835	Catalina	Louisa	F	John & Mary Thompson
1835	Catalina	Esther	F	John & Rebecca Stickley
1835	Catalina	William	M	Thomas & Mary Duffett
1835	Catalina	John	M	Joseph & Rosanna Hiscock
1835	Catalina	Sabina	F	William & Marie Uxter
1835	Catalina	Sarah	F	William & Ann Bursey
1835	Catalina	William	M	Samuel & Margaret Coleridge
1835	Catalina	Thomas	M	James & Elizabeth Clark
1835	Catalina	Marianne	F	William & Jane White

Figure 6-3. Records of Individual Churches Can Be Found Online

Part of the list of births extracted from the records recorded at St. Peter's Anglican Church, Trinity Bay, Newfoundland, found at the Grand Banks website within the Parish Records section.

<http://ngb.chebucto.org/Parish/trin-cat1d.shtml>

- Look for printed records, including published lists of entries in church newspapers.
- Contact the church.

The collection of church register copies at the FHL is quite extensive, though not equally good for every province. Do not use the content, or lack of it, in the International Genealogical Index as a guide; use the FHLC and find out for yourself. For some areas they have good collections, such as Quebec Catholic registers. It is important to know what you can accomplish using microfilm copies at a Family History Center.

RESEARCH CONSIDERATIONS

There are unique religious and ecclesiastical situations in many parts of Canada. Some religions were in only one location, in other areas people were married by justices, and some groups had views about sacraments that influenced their records. Dipping into church and local history will reveal the story of local development, including the history of churches.

For example, you may have to explore the history and records of another denomination. Your ancestor may have had little choice about which church would be the place of baptism. It is also possible that there was no church, an itinerant minister christened the child, and no record survives.

It is important to take your time and not stop a search too soon; you might miss the record. A complete search depends upon careful work and looking in every possible place for finding aids, copies, or original records. It is a good idea to create a checklist of what should be done and to think twice about the dates, places, and names chosen for the search.

ALTERNATIVE AND SUPPORTING SOURCES

In some places the details of baptisms, marriages, and burials can be checked against civil or legal records—for example, marriage bonds and licenses or the marriage contracts found in notarial records in Quebec.

Newspaper reports of weddings or funerals may give greater detail than a marriage or burial record, and you should find out when papers begin to publish brief entries for these events. If your church record entry occurred near the time of a census, compare the facts in both records.

Burial records should send you off in search of tombstone inscriptions and probate records. In addition, you may be able to use records such as directories or lists of voters to confirm when and where someone was residing shortly before an event occurred.

Some people came to Canada with a church leader. Others became involved as lay people in building and supporting a place of worship. Some became ministers. For all these reasons, watch for the names of church leaders around the time and place your ancestor lived, and look for them in the *Dictionary of Canadian Biography*, which is online at LAC.

The previous chapter pointed out that some civil records originated with churches, predate civil registration, and can be found in provincial archives and in online databases. Make sure any search for church registers includes a check for related civil records.

WEBSITES

Anglican Church of Canada: <www.anglican.ca> (to find their archives, type the word *archives* into the space for searching the site)

Anglican Church of Canada (links to dioceses): <www.anglican.ca/about/diocese. htm>

Canadian Baptist Archives: <www.macdiv.ca/students/baptistarchives.php>

Canadian Church Directory:

Canadian Conference of Catholic Bishops: Catholic Church in Canada: <www.cccb.ca/site/content/blogcategory/64/1075/lang,eng/>

Canadian Encyclopedia Online:

Canadian Genealogy Centre: <www.collectionscanada.ca/genealogy/>

Canadian Genealogy Centre Guide to Religious Archives:
<www.collectionscanada.ca/genealogy/022-806-e.html>
Dictionary of Canadian Biography: <www.biographi.ca/EN/index.html>
FamilySearch: <www.familysearch.org>
Jewish Genealogical Society of Canada (Toronto):
<www.jgstoronto.ca/Links.html>
Jewish Heritage Centre of Western Canada:
Lutheran Church Canada Central District Archives:
Lutheran Church Canada East District Archives: <www.lcceastdistrict.ca>
Lutheran Historical Institute: <www.lccarchives.ca>
Mennonite Heritage Centre Archives:
<www.mennonitechurch.ca/programs/archives/>
Presbyterian Archives Genealogical Resources: <www.presbyterian.ca/archives/genealogy.html>
United Church of Canada Archives Network:
<www.united-church.ca/archives/>

BIBLIOGRAPHY

Anglican Church of Canada. Province of British Columbia and Yukon. *Guide to the Holdings of the Archives of the Ecclesiastical Province of British Columbia and Yukon.* Toronto: Anglican Church of Canada, General Synod Archives, 1993.

Anglican Church of Canada. Province of Ontario. *Guide to the Holdings of the Archives of the Ecclesiastical Province of Ontario.* Agincourt, ON: Generation Press, 1990.

Bowker, John, ed. *The Concise Oxford Dictionary of World Religions.* Oxford and New York: Oxford UP, 2000. (also available within Oxford Reference Online)

Committee on Archives and History. *Guide to Family History Research in the Archival Repositories of the United Church of Canada.* Toronto: Ontario Genealogical Society, 1996.

Livingstone, E. A., ed. *The Concise Oxford Dictionary of the Christian Church.* 2nd ed. Oxford and New York: Oxford UP, 2006. (also available within Oxford Reference Online)

MacDonald, Wilma. *Guide to the Holdings of the Archives of the Ecclesiastical Province and Dioceses of Rupert's Land.* Winnipeg, MB: St. John's College Press, 1986.

ADDRESSES

The Anglican General Synod Archives
80 Hayden Street
Toronto, ON M4Y 3G2

Canadian Baptist Archives
McMaster Divinity College
1280 Main Street West
Hamilton, ON L8S 4K1

Canadian Conference of Catholic Bishops—Catholic Church in Canada
2500 Don Reid Drive
Ottawa, ON K1H 2J2

Jewish Heritage Centre of Western Canada
Suite C116 - 123 Doncaster Street
Winnipeg, MB R3N 2B2

Library and Archives Canada
395 Wellington Street
Ottawa, ON K1A 0N4

Lutheran Church—Canada
Central District Archives
1927 Grant Drive
Regina, SK S4S 4V6

Lutheran Church—Canada East District
Malinsky Memorial Archives
470 Glenridge Avenue
St. Catharines, ON L2T 4C3

Lutheran Historical Institute
7100 Ada Boulevard
Edmonton, AB T5B 4E4

Ontario Jewish Archives
4600 Bathurst Street
Toronto, ON M2R 3V2

Presbyterian Church in Canada
Archives and Record Office
50 Wynford Drive
Toronto, ON M3C 1J7

United Church of Canada/Victoria University Archives
73 Queen's Park Cres. East
Toronto, ON M5S 1K7

Figure 7-1. A Grave Site in Quebec
Photo courtesy of Canada Science and Technology Museum

7

CEMETERY RECORDS

Inscriptions on tombstones and monuments have special meaning. When you find a grave and the marker, you feel close to your ancestor. In addition, tombstone inscriptions often provide significant genealogical information.

Cemeteries are interesting places, and volunteers have been transcribing details from burial markers for a very long time. There are collections old and new, in print and online, for thousands of church and community graveyards, and you may even find a cemetery picture gallery on the Internet.

There is an excellent chance your ancestors were buried in a cemetery and that you can find some record of this. As recently as 1973, 90 percent of deceased Canadians were buried in a cemetery.

Many cemeteries and burial sites were established along religious and ethnic lines. The name of the cemetery often reveals this because it includes the name of the religion, the race or nationality, the name of the town, or the type of occupation. Browsing lists of cemeteries reveals defining terms like these: *military, Fort Saskatchewan, Lutheran, Greek Orthodox,* and *Norwegian.* Some small burial plots, for one or two families, were on private property. Unfortunately, locations for some of these may be unknown.

Overall responsibility for the management of funeral homes, cemeteries, and crematoria is vested in the provincial governments. This does not mean the government has any records, only that the government monitors them. Some archives have received collections of graveyard inscriptions, and some special burial sites are cared for by the government. Today cemeteries are owned by churches, synagogues, other religious organizations, municipalities, nonprofit trusts, and private entities. The burial locations of those who died in the major conflicts of the twentieth century are in the care of the Commonwealth War Graves Commission, which means some cemeteries have two agencies involved in upkeep and management (see chapter 9).

CONTENT

The information found on grave markers and tombstones ranges from brief and useless to detailed and significant. Several factors influenced what was carved on markers and what has lasted to the present. Religious and ethnic traditions played a part. Finances did as well—longer inscriptions were more expensive. Letters carved in soft stone wore away in wind and rain. Fashion was a factor, and for a time in the nineteenth century, people wanted lasting and elaborate memorials.

Cemetery records may include plot books (registers of where and when burials occurred) as well as transcriptions of gravestone inscriptions. In all records you can expect to find the name of the deceased and date of death. It is quite likely that an

Figure 7-2. Not Every Inscription Is Useful
Not much on the grave marker, but more can be found in the cemetery records.
Photo courtesy of Dave Obee

inscription states the age at death or the years of birth and death, and for a child, the names of parents are often included. Additional possibilities in transcriptions and plot books include country of origin, occupation, year of immigration, mention of spouse or other family members, and the cause of death. Some markers have symbols or abbreviations signifying membership in an organization or service in one of the armed forces.

GENEALOGICAL USE

The inscription on a grave marker is sometimes the only record of when and where a death occurred. Inscription details should be compared to what is found in other records such as civil registration and church registers. Protestant burial entries are generally less informative than Catholic, but for anyone of any religion there may be differences between register entries and gravestone inscriptions.

In some instances the tombstone inscription is found first and leads to other records. The grouping of individuals in a cemetery, or added memorials to others on existing monuments, tells something about relationships and can contribute to sorting out families and generations.

Clues to an ancestor's origin can be found in a symbol (such as a harp for Ireland) or a bit of text about the mother country, or they can emerge from studying the markers of others in the graveyard. If you take time to look around for the origins of others and to read local history, you may get some ideas for further research.

There is no way to predict what you will find in a cemetery register or on a gravestone, which is part of the fun. There is the potential for valuable family facts as well as humor and sadness. Perhaps a cemetery connected to your family has a place in a published collection of amusing, even insulting epitaphs.

LOCATING CEMETERY RECORDS

Begin with background information. Use directories, gazetteers, and local histories to locate cemeteries and learn when they were established. You may need to gather information about several possible places of burial.

Cemetery data is ideal for putting into databases, and there are excellent resources online. Interment.net is one site that tries to be broadly inclusive, calling itself a cemetery transcription library. Its Canadian section is far from comprehensive, but it may contain something that interests you.

At GenWeb there is a national burial index in progress. Each province has a section, and volunteers are encouraged to add information about names and locations of cemeteries and details from markers in those cemeteries. Progress in building this data collection is slow and varies considerably from province to province. In addition, you need to be aware to what extent the information in the Canada GenWeb project differs from what can be found within the GenWeb sites of individual provinces. Always look at both.

Many online cemetery sites for Canada are specific to a province, city, town, or even a single cemetery. Follow a number of stages in your search, from the broad to the specific, to make it as complete as possible. Start with Interment.net, GenWeb, Cyndi's List, and a search engine. After that try the following steps:

- AVITUS (use the option to browse by topic, choose Burials, or choose Cemeteries)
- Provincial archives website
- Provincial or local family history society website
- District, county, or municipality administration website

Transcriptions can be found in books, on microfilm, and in manuscripts. Libraries and archives, museums, and historical societies are all places where collections may be

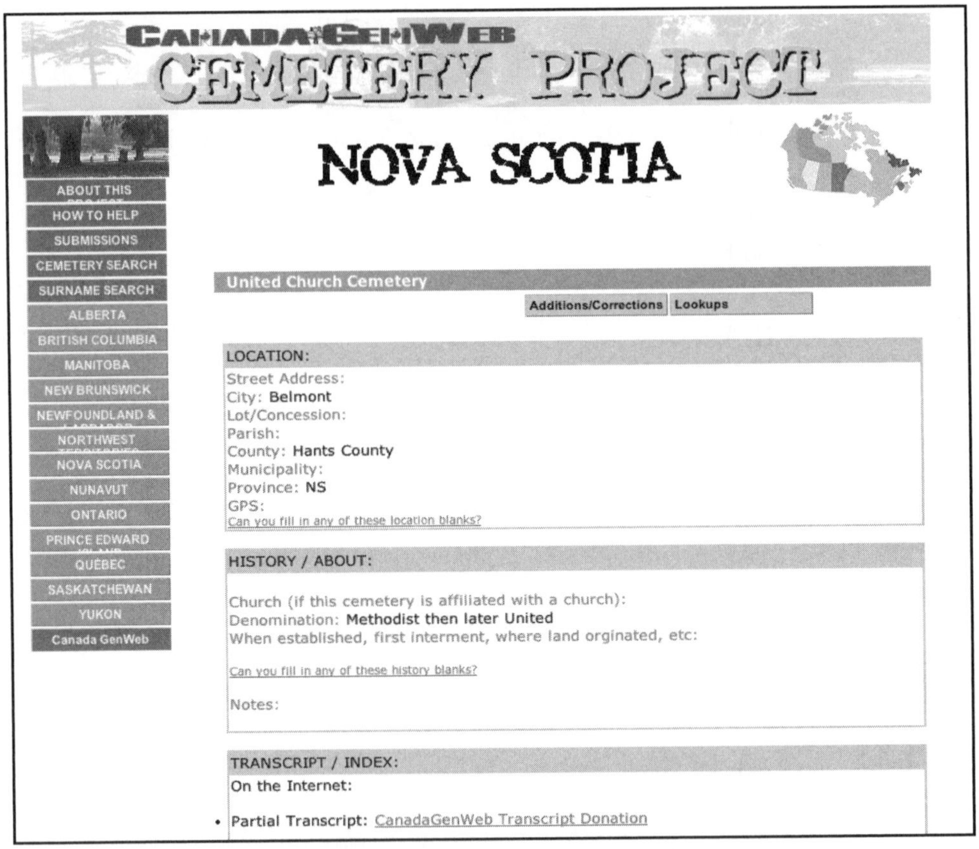

Figure 7-3. The Canada GenWeb Cemetery Project
The Nova Scotia cemetery listings include this one for Belmont United Church. There is a photograph of each transcribed headstone.
<http://continue.to/cgwcem>

located. At the Library and Archives Canada home page, in the Search box, select only Library resources, and you will be able to check their holdings; a large number of cemetery transcription publications have been deposited with them. The Family History Library also has a large collection of Canadian cemetery inscriptions, and their catalog should be consulted, too.

RESEARCH CONSIDERATIONS

Not everyone is buried in what to you seems the logical place. Here are several situations that may make a burial location hard to find:

- The person died away from home, and there were neither resources nor interest in returning the body for burial.
- The individual left a special, unknown request to be buried at a particular place or with a particular person, and neither connection is apparent.
- The individual was buried at public or charity expense by an agency that no longer exists.

- The individual is buried in a family plot or cemetery for which the location is unknown.
- The individual was buried in one location and moved sometime after to another burial ground, possibly far away.

Cemetery inscriptions are only as reliable as the information available to the person who carved the stone. Death date, age, year of birth, and place of origin, even personal names could be wrong.

ALTERNATIVE AND SUPPORTING SOURCES

Cemetery records are more likely to be used in a supporting role. If a death record is found in civil records or in the church burial records, then you naturally want to find the cemetery, the marker, and the inscription, or you want to read a transcription and hopefully see a photograph.

When a death or burial record cannot be found among civil or church records, you need to search for the cemetery record as another possible source for a death date. Newspapers are another place to find death and burial information that can help you find a tombstone or a date of death. Funeral home records are sometimes available, and these are another way to locate gravestones and collect family information. Some funeral home records have been indexed, and long-established businesses can sometimes help with finding records of a burial. Use city directories to find out the names of undertakers in business at the time of an ancestor's death.

WEBSITES

Canada GenWeb: <www.rootsweb.com/~canwgw/>
Canada GenWeb Projects Page:
    <www.rootsweb.com/~canwgw/projects/index.html>
Cyndi's List, Canada: <www.cyndislist.com/canada.htm>
FamilySearch: <www.familysearch.org>
Interment.net: <www.interment.net>
Library and Archives Canada: <www.collectionscanada.ca>
Library and Archives Canada, AVITUS: <www.collectionscanada.ca/
    genealogy/022-501-e.html>

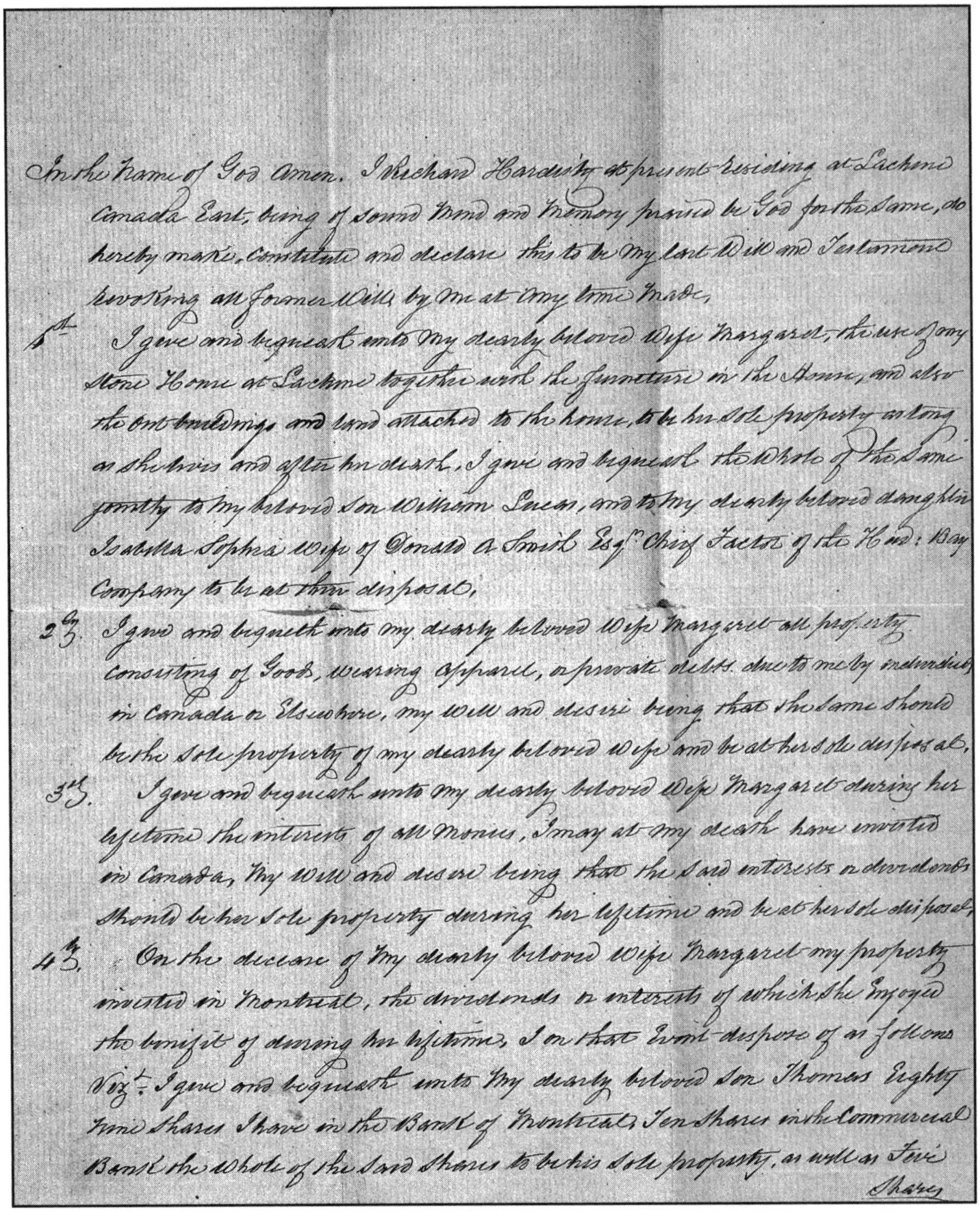
In the Name of God Amen. I Richard Hardisty at present residing at Lachine
Canada East, being of Sound Mind and Memory praised be God for the Same, do
hereby make, constitute and declare this to be my last Will and Testament
revoking all Former Wills by me at any time Made,
1st. I give and bequeath unto My dearly beloved Wife Margaret, the use of my
Stone House at Lachine together with the furniture in the House, and also
the out buildings and land attached to the house, to be her Sole property as long
as She lives and after her death, I give and bequeath the Whole of the Same
jointly to My beloved Son William Lucas, and to my dearly beloved daughter
Isabella Sophia Wife of Donald A Smith Esqr. Chief Factor of the Hud: Bay
Company to be at their disposal,
2d. I give and bequeath unto my dearly beloved Wife Margaret all property
consisting of Goods, wearing apparel, or private debts due to me by individuals
in Canada or Elsewhere, my Will and desire being that the Same Should
be the Sole property of my dearly beloved Wife and be at her sole disposal,
3d. I give and bequeath unto my dearly beloved Wife Margaret during her
lifetime the interests of all Monies, I may at my death have invested
in Canada, My Will and desire being that the Said interests or dividends
Should be her Sole property during her lifetime and be at her sole disposal,
4th. On the decease of My dearly beloved Wife Margaret my property
invested in Montreal, the dividends or interests of which She Enjoyed
the benefit of during her lifetime, I on that Event dispose of as follows
Viz: I give and bequeath unto My dearly beloved Son Thomas Eighty
Nine Shares I have in the Bank of Montreal, Ten Shares in the Commercial
Bank the whole of the Said Shares to be his Sole property, as well as Five
Shares

Figure 8-1. Page from the Last Will and Testament of Richard Hardisty, Lachine, Quebec

Image courtesy of Glenbow Archives (NA-4216-2)

PROBATE RECORDS

There are three strong reasons for looking at probate records. First, in many areas probate records begin long before government records of births, marriages, and deaths or census enumerations. Secondly, probate records can and do reveal valuable information about the deceased person, family, and associates. Finally, probate records are public documents that are not affected by privacy legislation.

A will is an individual's legal declaration directing the disposal of his or her estate after death. The person who makes the will is called the testator. According to English Common Law, a will could be made by anyone of sound mind, legal age, and not in prison. The process that proves a will to be the last wishes of the deceased person and confirms the executor(s) of those wishes is called probate. If an individual dies without a will, a court issues letters of administration to an administrator to settle the estate. In some cases a named administrator dies before the testator or refuses to act, and then someone else would have to apply to be the estate's administrator.

Several records were generated by probate or letters of administration. The usual documents found in a file are the petition for probate (if there was a will) or administration (if there was no will), the oath taken by the executor or administrator (could be more than one), and an inventory of the deceased's assets.

From the middle of the 1700s most of Canada followed the legal practices of the United Kingdom. The exception was Quebec, which from 1626 registered all contracts through notaries, including matters relating to the estates of deceased persons. The French civil code was retained when Quebec became a British Crown Colony.

Although the basis of law was the same in most of Canada, probate matters were a responsibility of each colony and later, each province. Genealogists researching in more than one province will find differences with regard to process and court structure. The names and the number of courts varied, subdivisions might be counties or judicial districts, and larger urban areas might have their own unique jurisdictions.

The earliest probate court of the English form was established in Halifax, Nova Scotia, in 1749. Other areas in the Maritimes also had courts before 1800, but for the rest of Canada outside Quebec, records began in the 1800s.

Not everyone made a will, and, as the assets of many people were few, probate was often unnecessary. Merchants, professionals, and other more prosperous men, particularly in towns, made wills. Women, farmers, and working class people seldom did. There are not many wills in Quebec because civil law stipulated how assets were divided. However, there is usually a probate record among notarial documents.

If you are interested in learning more about regulations affecting probate at a particular time, consult an almanac or provincial year book. Library and Archives Canada has a large collection and provides selected, detailed listings at its website. The Family History Library (FHL) has some almanacs on microfilm, and you may find others in local libraries or on the Web.

CONTENT

Many details are common to all wills: the name of the deceased, date the will was made, name of the executor, date of probate, name of the beneficiaries, and the value of the estate. You may also find place of residence at the time the will was made, occupation, witnesses to the will, date of death, place of death, relationship of beneficiaries to the deceased, names of guardians of underage children, and an inventory of assets. There may be mention of debts owed, debts due, and other information about the business and community connections of the deceased.

Sometimes wills included instructions for alternative legacies should someone not outlive the testator or should a beneficiary fail to meet certain conditions. The actual record of probate added a few additional points: date probate was granted, or to whom administration was granted, and the amount of the bond to be paid should the executor or administrator fail to carry out the obligation.

If your ancestor died intestate, meaning without a will, there may be a record of a grant of administration. The value and nature of the estate could determine whether probate was necessary; for example, a creditor could have gone to the probate court for administration of an estate as a means of ensuring a debt was paid. The documents are less informative, but they can offer helpful clues and so are worth searching for.

Probate did not always happen immediately, and in some cases the delay was significant. You should always search up to three years after a death and be prepared to look as many as ten years after. Modern computer indexes make this easy to do.

GENEALOGICAL USE

Nothing is potentially more revealing of family relationships, likes, and dislikes than the directions contained in a will. You also learn the value of all that the testator owned at the time of his or her death.

The majority of people did not leave a probate record, a factor that may deter you from making the search. It is better to take the view that there may be a will than to

In the Surrogate Court of the *County of York*

In the Goods of   *Charles Blackhall*

Inventory and Valuation of the Personal Estate and Effects, Rights and Credits of the said deceased

<u>GENERAL DESCRIPTION OF PROPERTY</u>

Household goods and furniture	**$75.00**
~~Farming Implements etc.~~	
~~Stock in Trade~~	
~~Horses~~	
~~Horned Cattle~~	
~~Sheep and Swine~~	
Book Debts and Promissory Notes	**$42.00**
Money Secured by Mortgage *principal and interest to date of deceased's death*	
	$745.97
~~Moneys Secured by Life Insurance~~	
Books	**$25.00**
~~Bank Shares and Other Stocks~~	
Wearing Apparel and Jewellry	**$36.00**
~~Securities for Money~~	
~~Cash on Hand~~	
~~Farm Produce of all Kinds~~	
~~Other Property not before mentioned (if any)~~	
	$923.97

I *Maria C. Blackhall of the City of Toronto in the County of York Widow*_____

Make oath and say THAT I am *the person applying for Administration of the personal estate and effects of Charles Blackhall, deceased*

That the above is, to the best of my knowledge, information and belief, a true Inventory and Valuation of the Personal Estate and effects of the said deceased at the time of his death so far as I can at present ascertain.

To the best of my knowledge and belief the only lands owned by said deceased at the time of his death was an . . . . . in fee simple in lands situate on the north side of Shuter Street in the City of Toronto after a life interest therein for my life owned by me. The fee simple of said lands was purchased in March one thousand eight hundred and eighty four for Sixteen hundred and fifty dollars.

Sworn at the City of Toronto
in the ———— *County of York*
the *Twenty fifth* ———— *day*   (signature) Maria C. Blackhall
of *October* ———— A.D. 1886
before me   (signature) A. J. Williams

Figure 8-2. The Inventory of the Estate of Charles Blackhall, 25 October, 1886

Charles Blackhall died without a will, and administration was granted to his widow, Maria C. Blackhall; Edward Henry Boddy of Toronto, Painter, and Anne Mara of Toronto, Widow. These connections and the information about the value of the estate and the land are valuable genealogical information.

Facsimile from record in Ontario Archives, GS 1, reel 1003, #6201

assume otherwise and miss a valuable resource. You have no way of knowing whether or not your ancestors appear in probate records, and you could pick up clues by finding them named as testators, beneficiaries, creditors, and witnesses in the records of others.

Wills and probate administration records are especially useful in verifying family connections. In most cases family members named are the same age or younger than the testator; they are rarely of an earlier generation. This is different from most other records and can be vitally important when piecing together family structure from vital records and census returns.

LOCATING PROBATE RECORDS

Records, including those of the colonial period, can be found in the appropriate province or territory—though there are some wills in the archives of the Hudson's Bay Company that are from a wide area of Western Canada.

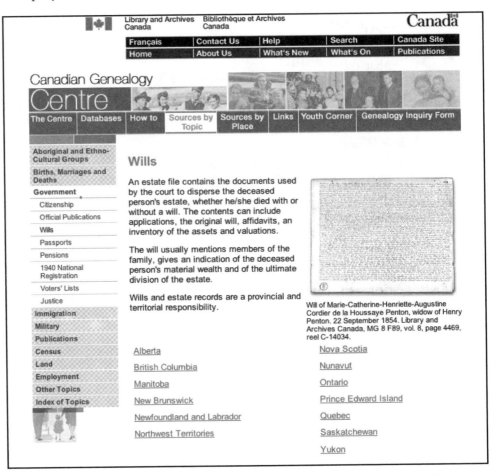

Figure 8-3. The Canadian Genealogy Centre Information on Wills
The links for the provinces and territories take you to contact information for the appropriate courts and archives.
<http://www.collectionscanada.ca/genealogy/022-907.003-e.html>

Online finding aids for probate records are something of a patchwork across the country. Begin your search at the website of the provincial archives and with the appropriate GenWeb page. Where online records exist, you should make sure you understand how much is accessible.

At the start of any search you need to check for a cutoff date dividing records held by the archives and those still within the files of the provincial probate court system. In addition it is important to understand probate divisions within the colony, province, or district. You may have to know boundaries of divisions contemporary to the time of an ancestor's probate and at the present in order to figure out where the record was filed originally and where it could be now. Modern databases might eliminate such problems, but if you are unsure about boundaries, contact the archives or the probate court office for help.

A significant proportion of probate records have been filmed by the FHL in Salt Lake City. Check their online catalog under the name of the province and the topic of Probate as a standard step in looking for records.

RESEARCH CONSIDERATIONS

If research for a probate record fails to produce a result, think about why this might be and whether you can discover the record of a relation. You should reexamine the date range selected and any name variations in the search. Perhaps the finding aids consulted do not exactly match the period you want to cover, or you have missed checking for someone dying intestate and therefore having a record of administration.

Not all testators named all of their children, a detail that may leave you uncertain about having found the right record. The eldest son could be omitted from a will if he was already in possession of the family farm. Other children may have been given a portion in advance, and in other cases family disputes meant children or siblings were ignored.

There could also be other unexpected factors, such as a second marriage you know nothing about.

Sometimes you may want to search beyond your ancestor and his or her immediate family. If you know of other close associates, look for their records, and in small communities check for wills of everyone dying in the same period. Your ancestor could turn up as a beneficiary, a witness, or a creditor.

ALTERNATIVE AND SUPPORTING SOURCES

Where no will exists, check the land records. Change of ownership was recorded here, and this includes when land changed hands because of death and inheritance. Some probate records were deposited with land registry offices.

You have probably checked vital records before your probate search, but make sure this was done thoroughly. In addition, cross-check between vital records, census returns, and probate records. This combination of information is an excellent source of proof that your research conclusions are valid.

Sometimes the survivors were at odds over the terms of a will and ended up taking their disagreement to court; if this seems likely, talk to the provincial archives about the records of civil disputes.

WEBSITES

Canada GenWeb: <www.rootsweb.com/~canwgw/>
Canadian Genealogy Centre: <www.collectionscanada.ca/genealogy/>
FamilySearch: <www.familysearch.org>
Library and Archives Canada: Selected Almanacs Listing: <www.collectionscanada.ca/2/20/index-e.html>

BIBLIOGRAPHY

Dukelow, Daphne, and Betsy Nuse. *Dictionary of Canadian Law*. Scarborough, ON: Carswell, 1995.

MILITARY RECORDS

9

Wars have shaped Canada's history. Many of these conflicts took place on Canadian soil, where the English and the French fought intermittently for 150 years for control of North America. That period ended in 1763, when the Treaty of Paris resulted in France ceding Canada to Britain.

During the French years, local militia units were responsible for defense. The regular French army was on Canadian soil only twice—from 1665 to 1668 and from 1755 to 1761.

British regular military and naval forces, supported by local volunteer units, protected Canada during the American Revolution and for almost one hundred years after it. Defense plans assumed that the United States posed the greatest threat to Canada's national security. Those fears were borne out in conflicts such as the War of 1812 and the Fenian Raids of 1865 through 1871.

There was fighting within Canada as well, including rebellions in both Upper Canada and Lower Canada in 1837 and in the Red River region of Manitoba in 1870. The latter conflict marked the last time that British forces fought beside Canadian volunteers on Canadian soil.

British forces were garrisoned in fortifications such as those found in Quebec, Kingston, and Halifax and could be augmented from time to time by reinforcements from Britain in response to war scares, rebellion, and war itself. Permanent bases for the Royal Navy were maintained in Halifax from 1749 until the creation of the Canadian navy in 1910 and at Esquimalt, on Vancouver Island, from 1862 to 1905.

In 1871 the Treaty of Washington created a lasting peace between Canada and the United States, and the last British regular soldiers were withdrawn from Canada. Canada's first regular units were formed that year to complement the militia units that had been around for decades.

The North West Rebellion of 1885 was the first campaign that Canadians fought without British assistance. Fourteen years later, more than 7,300 Canadians, including twelve nursing sisters, served in South Africa during the Boer War. This was the first time that Canada dispatched troops to an overseas war.

At the start of the First World War in 1914, Canada had only 3,000 permanent members of the armed forces. By the time the war ended four years later, more than 600,000 Canadians had signed up to fight. They were quickly disbanded at the end of the war, and twenty-five years later, at the start of the Second World War in 1939, there were 4,000 full-time service personnel, armed with First World War weapons. Canadians again answered their country's call, with 1 million people volunteering before the war's end in 1945.

Members of Canada's armed forces have fought in countries such as Korea and Afghanistan and have served as United Nations peacekeepers around the world. In all, more than 1.6 million Canadians have served in conflicts around the world since 1899. More than 116,000 have died in wars, and their graves are found in seventy-five countries.

Figure 9-1. Soldiers Outside Battalion Recruiting Office, Ontario
Photo courtesy of Glenbow Archives (NA-3496-2)

CONFLICTS OVER THE YEARS

Your veteran ancestor was not acting alone; he was part of an army regiment or a ship's company or an air force squadron, and Canadian units fought closely with those of other countries. Your military ancestor may have been a nursing sister, been a member of home defense, or served in hundreds of wartime occupations open to women. To tell the story adequately you need to reflect on every aspect of service life. Also, think of the impact on the family at home in Canada.

BEFORE CONFEDERATION

Many early militia records consist of only lists of names on a muster roll or pay list. Records from the French era are in archives in France, although copies have been provided to Library and Archives Canada (LAC) as well as Bibliothèque et Archives nationales du Québec.

British military and naval records up to and including the First World War are in the custody of The National Archives in England, in the War Office and Admiralty series. The book *British Army Pensioners Abroad, 1772–1899* (Crowder, 1995) lists many people who lived in Canada; it is available on Ancestry.

Library and Archives Canada has copies of some records of regiments that served in Canada. The British Military and Naval Records series covers the period from the American Revolution to the mid-1800s. It includes documents relating to the British army in Canada, Loyalist regiments, the War of 1812, the Canadian militias, etc. A nominal/subject card index and the actual records are available on microfilm.

Early Canadian military records consist mainly of muster rolls and pay lists, with little or no personal information. Most are not indexed, and you need the name of a regiment before attempting a search. If you know your ancestor's place of residence, you might find references to his service in the militia rolls for that county.

THE NORTHWEST TERRITORIES, 1870 AND 1885

Information on soldiers who fought in the Red River Rebellion of 1870 might be in the *Red River Register of Service*, available on microfilm from LAC.

There is no official list of the men who served in the North West Rebellion of 1885. An honor roll of officers, noncommissioned officers, and men in the North West Field Force was published in a book, *A History of Riel's Second Rebellion and How It Was Quelled* (Haultain, 1885), which is on the Peel's Prairie Provinces website. LAC also has medal registers and land grant information.

Between the two conflicts, the federal government created the North West Mounted Police, now known as the Royal Canadian Mounted Police, with the assignment of bringing law and order to the Canadian West.

SOUTH AFRICAN (BOER) WAR, 1899–1902

Service files generally contain an attestation paper, with a physical description of the recruit, a service history, a medical report, a discharge certificate, and a notation on medals awarded. Some files also contain correspondence relating to pensions, land grants, and medals.

Library and Archives Canada holds 5,935 of 7,300 service files from the Boer War; the others no longer exist. The existing files have been digitized and are available online at the LAC website.

Under the Volunteer Bounty Act of 1908, veterans of the South African War were entitled to 320 acres of Dominion land. LAC has the land-grant applications, two-page forms that include the name of the applicant, place of residence, and service summary. Veterans could also receive sixty dollars in payment rather than a land grant or sell their land-grant entitlement to a "substitute."

The Canadian government recruited, equipped, and transported two contingents of volunteers to serve with the British forces in South Africa for the Boer War from 1899 through 1902. The British War Office paid all other costs, including pay and return transport. Later contingents were financed completely by the British War Office, with the exception of one recruited and paid for by Lord Strathcona.

FIRST WORLD WAR, 1914–1918

Personnel records can provide the date and place of birth, name and address of next of kin, previous military service, and occupation.

Library and Archives Canada has a database that will help you find the basic information in the files of those who served in the army. It is linked to images of the attestation papers and enlistment forms, the key documents in the files. You can order an entire set of documents from Library and Archives Canada.

The personnel files do not generally include information on exact postings or battles. It is possible, however, to learn more about military operations by consulting the war diaries on the LAC website. These provide information on the day-to-day movements of the regiments and occasionally include reports on individuals.

The official history of the Canadian army in the First World War is *Canadian Expeditionary Force, 1914–1919* (Nicholson, 1962). It is available as a free download on the Veterans Affairs Canada website. There are also histories of individual regiments, often with information on the travels of the men and the battles in which they fought, in print form as well as on the Internet.

The Canadian navy was established in 1910 but had only two ships at the time the First World War started. The decision was made to concentrate on the army instead. Still, the navy had 5,500 personnel by the end of the war and contributed 3,000 officers and men to the Royal Navy.

Many Canadians served in British forces such as the Royal Flying Corps. Their personnel records, if they still exist, are in the custody of the National Archives in England. A list of Canadians who served with the British flying services is on the website of the Air Force Association of Canada.

SECOND WORLD WAR, 1939–1945

Personnel files for Second World War veterans are available from LAC. Because of privacy regulations, you cannot access them via an online database, but it is still possible to get copies of the key documents from your ancestor's file.

Files include documentation about enlistment, discharge, and military units. The files may also contain personal evaluations, medical history, and details of medals awarded.

To obtain these records, use the application form found on the Canadian Genealogy Centre website. You will need to provide the person's name, date of birth, and service number or social insurance number. Other information, such as the names of next of kin and place of enlistment, can help the staff at LAC to identify the proper file. Be sure to ask for the "genealogy package," which includes only the documents central to the individual's service.

Files for those killed in action are available to the public with no restrictions. A file for a living person will not be released without that person's consent. If a person has been dead for less than twenty years, limited information will be released to the immediate family after proof of death and relationship has been provided. There are no restrictions on access to the file of a person who has been dead for more than twenty years, but proof of death is required.

Canada's merchant navy played a vital, dangerous role keeping a supply line across the Atlantic. Seventy-two ships were lost, with 1,600 Canadians killed. A database listing the dead is on the website of Veterans Affairs Canada.

Databases with information on air force veterans, including honors received, are on the website of the Air Force Association of Canada.

KOREAN WAR, 1950–1953

A total of 26,791 Canadians served in Korea in the early 1950s, and 516 of them were killed. A list of the casualties appears on the website of the Korea Veterans Association of Canada. For information, contact the Personnel Records Unit at LAC.

OTHER SOURCES

Commonwealth War Graves Commission

The commission's website features a database of the 1.7 million men and women of the Commonwealth forces who died during the two world wars and of the 23,000 cemeteries, memorials, and other markers where they are commemorated. The database also includes 67,000 Commonwealth civilians who died as a result of enemy action in the Second World War.

The commission has supported the construction of 2,500 war cemeteries and plots, erecting headstones over graves and, in instances where the remains are missing, inscribing the names of the dead on permanent memorials. More than 1 million casualties are commemorated at military and civil sites in some 150 countries.

Canadian Virtual War Memorial

This federal government website contains a registry of information about the graves and memorials of more than 116,000 Canadians and Newfoundlanders who died in service. It includes the memorials of more than one hundred service personnel who have died since the Korean War in peacekeeping and other operations. The site also contains digital images of photographs and personal memorabilia about individual Canadians.

Legion Magazine

Since 1928 *Legion Magazine* has printed short death notices for Royal Canadian Legion members with military backgrounds, Canadian war veterans, and Legion members with police service. An online database has more than 100,000 names and dates back to the early 1990s. The database is expanded twice a year with new entries as well as ones taken from earlier issues.

> More than 1 million Canadians and Newfoundlanders served in the Second World War. More than 45,000 of them were killed, and another 55,000 were wounded.

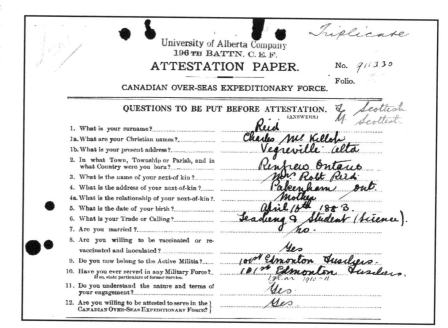

Figure 9-2. Attestation Papers of Charles M. Reid
<http://data2.archives.ca/cef/ren3/051318a.gif>

Passenger Lists

These records, on microfilm and on the LAC website, show soldiers' returns to Canada after the First World War. The records are often made up of typed sheets that were apparently pasted on regular passenger lists. The lists include the soldier's name and number.

Community Memorials and Cemeteries

A cenotaph in the soldier's hometown will probably have his name if he died in the conflict. If he died later, check for his grave. Veterans were often buried in military sections of cemeteries, but even if he is on his own, you might find information on his service on the memorial marker.

Many museums in Canada will help you gain a better understanding of the Canadian war experience. They commemorate service in the army, navy, and air force. Some links to help you start your search are included at the end of this chapter.

Local Printed Sources

Check newspapers for contemporary accounts. Depending on the size of the community, newspapers might have had references to local men signing up, regiments leaving for war, promotions, or letters home from people serving with your ancestor. Deaths and injuries were usually reported as well, with additional information about the soldier's prewar life in the community. There are often facts you would not find in the personnel file.

Most local histories have photographs of the people from the community who served in the military. In some cases there are photographs or transcripts of a soldier's cenotaph.

WEBSITES

Air Force Association of Canada: <www.airforce.ca>
Canadian Genealogy Centre:
    <www.collectionscanada.ca/genealogy/index-e.html>
Canadian Military Heritage Project: <www.rootsweb.com/~canmil>
Canadian Military History Gateway: <www.cmhg.gc.ca>
Canadian Naval Memorial Trust, HMCS Sackville:
    <www.hmcssackville-cnmt.ns.ca>
Canadian Navy of Yesterday and Today: <www.hazegray.org/navhist/canada>
Canadian Virtual War Memorial: <www.virtualmemorial.gc.ca>
Canadian War Museum: <www.warmuseum.ca>
Commonwealth War Graves Commission: <www.cwgc.org>
Interactive History of the Canadian Navy: <collections.ic.gc.ca/navy>
Juno Beach Centre: <www.junobeach.org>
Korea Veterans Association of Canada: <www.kvacanada.com>
Land Forces of Britain, the Empire and the Commonwealth: <regiments.org>

Legion Magazine: <www.legionmagazine.com>
Library and Archives Canada: <www.collectionscanada.ca>
National Defence Directorate of History and Heritage:
    <http://www.forces.gc.ca/dhh/engraph/home_e.asp>
Peel's Prairie Provinces: <peel.library.ualberta.ca/index.html>
RCMP Highlights: <www.rcmp-grc.gc.ca/history/history_e.htm>
Royal Canadian Air Force Memorial Museum:
Veterans Affairs Canada: <www.vac-acc.gc.ca/general>
Veterans Affairs Memorials/Museums/Military Collections: <www.vac-acc.gc.ca/
    general/sub.cfm?source=links#4>

BIBLIOGRAPHY

Crowder, Norman K. *British Army Pensioners Abroad, 1772–1899*. Baltimore: Genealogical Publishing, 1995.

Haultain, Theodore Arnold. *A History of Riel's Second Rebellion and How It Was Quelled*. Toronto: Grip Print and Publishing, 1885.

Hitsman, J. Mackay. *The Incredible War of 1812*. Toronto: University of Toronto Press, 1965.

An Index to Canadian Service Records of the South African War (1899–1902) Held at the National Archives of Canada. Ottawa: British Isles Family History Society of Greater Ottawa, 1999.

Nicholson, G. W. L. *Canadian Expeditionary Force, 1914–1919*. Ottawa: Government of Canada, 1962.

Shipley, Robert. *To Mark Our Place: A History of Canadian War Memorials*. Toronto: NC Press, 1987.

Tyler, Grant. *Drab Serge and Khaki Drill: The Foreign Service, Universal Service, Battle and Combat Dress Jackets of the Canadian Army, 1899–2003*. Ottawa: Parks Canada, 2003.

ADDRESSES

Personnel Records Unit
Library and Archives Canada
395 Wellington Street
Ottawa, ON K1A 0N4
Fax: (613) 947-8456

Figure 10-1. John Beam's Homestead, Cochrane, Alberta
Photo courtesy of Glenbow Archives (NA-1130-10)

10

LAND RECORDS

Land records, the paper trail created through the buying, selling, or leasing of land, can provide key information that will help you gain a better understanding of your family. While these documents were designed to minimize the risk of disputes about the identity of the real owner or occupier of a piece of property, they can also help today's genealogical researchers.

Some land records were created for the transfer of land from a government to a private owner, while others record the transfers between two private owners. Lease documents record the conditions under which someone could occupy or use land belonging to someone else.

Before land could be assigned to an owner, it had to be accurately surveyed. In Canada, the first surveying of land boundaries came soon after the first European settlement, during the French regime from 1608 to 1758. That surveying resulted in the creation of seigneuries, long strips of land owned by the king of France and managed by landlords.

After Quebec came under British control, surveying of land for new settlement was changed to a township system, with rectangular or square lots. However, the seigneurial system was not completely done away with until 1854, and evidence of it remains in aerial photographs and on maps.

Large-scale surveying of the Prairie Provinces did not begin until after 1870, when the region became part of Canada. Before that, only a few small lots near rivers had been surveyed, generally into plots of land stretching back from the rivers. The original survey work is still evident in the Winnipeg area, which doesn't have the strict township system seen elsewhere on the Prairies.

The wide differences in land settlement across Canada underscore the value of local knowledge. Learn what you can about settlement patterns in your area of interest in order to better understand the land systems used and the availability of records.

MAPS

Using land records is easier if you use can visualize the property. Local maps will help you do that. Several different types of maps showing the names of landowners have been published throughout Canada over the years. For example, an excellent series of maps for Alberta, Saskatchewan, and Manitoba was produced by the Cummins Map Company between 1917 and 1922, with another set for Ontario created about 1924. They are on microfilm at Library and Archives Canada (LAC) and at relevant provincial archives. Online you can consult county-by-county atlases published in Ontario in the late 1800s.

Some county maps show the names of landowners. There are modern ones as well as historic ones, which would need to be obtained from an archive or library in the area in question. These local maps are often the best source of information on local roads and landmarks.

Check maps for the location of the property and pay special attention to the physical features shown. This will help you visualize the property; very likely it was not a flat piece of prairie or a treeless, open space.

Natural Resources Canada has published two series of Maps of the National Topographic System of Canada, in 1:250,000 scale and 1:50,000 scale. These don't show the names of individual landowners, but you can use them to familiarize yourself with the lay of the land.

Library and Archives Canada has a selection of digitized maps on its website. Search the database of maps, plans, and charts, limiting the search to results with digitized images. Coverage is strongest for the Maritimes, Quebec, and Ontario.

NATIONAL DIFFERENCES

If you are used to the United States Public Land Survey, Canada's Dominion Land Survey might seem a bit odd. The two systems follow the same basic philosophy, with one key difference.

In both countries, a township consists of thirty-six one-mile-square sections, stacked in six rows of six. These sections are numbered in a zigzag pattern from one to thirty-six.

In the United States, the first section is in the northeast corner of the township, and the thirty-sixth is in the southeast corner. In Canada, they are reversed, with the first section in the south-east and the thirty-sixth in the northeast.

31	32	33	34	35	36
30	29	28	27	26	25
19	20	21	22	23	24
18	17	16	15	14	13
7	8	9	10	11	12
6	5	4	3	2	1

Figure 10-2. Sections in a Township

CONTENT

Land records include the names of the buyer and seller, or owner and lessee, as well as a description of the land and the date of the transaction. Also look for land petitions, in which individuals tried to convince authorities that they should be granted property. Family information is often found in petitions, as well as in transfer documents within families in the seigneurial system.

If land was granted because of military service, the records will include evidence of that service. Beyond that, land grant documents consist of little more than the grantee's name, the date, and a description of the land.

Homestead records are not all the same. Some might include little more than a person's name, the date of entry on the land, and the date the land was given to someone else. A more extensive file could include the names of the applicant's spouse and children as well as biographical information, such as the date of arrival in the area.

GENEALOGICAL USE

The knowledge you glean from land records might help point you toward other sources. With luck, land records will help you confirm the names of spouses or children, or pin down the date of a move to or from an address.

The records might also indicate relationships between people or at least show who owned land jointly. This could help you sort out which person belongs to which family. Sometimes land changed hands as part of an estate, and it is possible that probate records could indicate the relationship between the deceased person and the beneficiary.

With homestead records, be sure to look for people who failed to complete their requirements as well as those who were successful. Files on the unsuccessful homesteads often include letters from the farmers giving reasons why things weren't going quite as well as they had hoped. Failures can be far more interesting than successes.

Also, look for a second attempt after a failed one. Many people tried again in another area.

LOCATING LAND RECORDS

Land records are usually open for genealogical research, although you might have to pay for access. They are found in two places: land titles offices, which have the land transaction documents, or archives, if the land titles offices have turned them over.

Check the websites of provincial archives for guides to land records. These will usually tell you which records are in the archives and provide clues regarding the location of the records that are not there.

Access varies by jurisdiction, although all records of land transactions must conform to laws covering planning, registry, land titles, and municipal acts.

In both Upper Canada (today's Ontario) and Lower Canada (today's Quebec), many military or civilian settlers submitted petitions to the governor in order to obtain Crown land. Those petitions are at LAC. Petitions for the Maritimes are found in the provincial archives; Nova Scotia and New Brunswick have online databases.

A database of homestead grants in Western Canada is on the LAC website. It includes only those people who successfully obtained title to their farms.

British Columbia, Alberta, and Saskatchewan have homestead indexes online that include everyone who applied for a homestead, not just those who gained ownership. Comprehensive indexes are available on microfilm at provincial archives. Some indexes

---

SAMPLE LAND DESCRIPTION

In Western Canada, the location of a farm is described like this: NE 29-12-6-2.

To read the description, start with the last number, which refers to the meridian. In this case, it tells you that the property in question is west of the second meridian, which is close to the Saskatchewan-Manitoba border.

The 6 means range. It tells you that this land is in the sixth township west of the meridian—in other words, it is thirty to thirty-six miles west.

The 12 is the township number, counted north from the U.S. border. In this case, the property is sixty-six to seventy-two miles north of the border.

The 29 locates the section within the township, and NE specifies that the farm is in the northeast corner of the section.

are also available on microfilm through the Family History Library (FHL) in Salt Lake City and Family History Centers.

The federal government granted land to the Canadian Pacific Railway and the Hudson's Bay Company for them to sell to settlers. A database of the railway sales is on the website of the Glenbow Archives; the actual records have little more than is shown on the Web. An index to the Hudson's Bay land deals is in the Hudson's Bay Company archives in Winnipeg.

Land descriptions, specifying quarters and sections, might appear on civil registration documents. When babies were born on farms, for example, the land description appears on the birth certificate. Local histories often refer to the locations of individual farms.

ALTERNATIVE AND SUPPORTING SOURCES

Directories, voters lists, and some census returns might help you identify locations where your ancestors lived. By comparing these records over several years, you will be able to estimate when your ancestors moved to or from an address. That will make it easier for you to pursue other land documents, including the records in archives or land titles offices.

You should also look for property tax records, which are available locally. Probate records will tell you if property changed hands as part of an estate. If you are working in Quebec, check for notarial records, private agreements that include leases, wills, and sales; they have been filmed by the FHL. And, of course, local maps are vital to your research into land records.

WEBSITES

Canada GenWeb: <www.rootsweb.com/~canwgw>
FamilySearch: <www.familysearch.org>
Glenbow Archives: <www.glenbow.org>
Hudson's Bay Company Archives:
    <www.gov.mb.ca/chc/archives/hbca/about/hbca.html>
Land Records, Canadian Genealogy Centre:
    <www.collectionscanada.ca/genealogy/022-912-e.html>
Library and Archives Canada: <www.collectionscanada.ca>

BIBLIOGRAPHY

Harris, Richard Colebrook. *The Seigneurial System in Early Canada: A Geographical Study*. Kingston and Montreal: McGill-Queen's University Press, 1984.

McGregor, James G. *Vision of an Ordered Land: The Story of the Dominion Land Survey*. Saskatoon, SK: Western Producer Prairie Books, 1981.

Obee, Dave. *Back to the Land: A Genealogical Guide to Finding Farms on the Canadian Prairies*. 3rd ed. Victoria: Dave Obee, 2004.

Spry, Irene M., and Bennett McCardle. *The Records of the Department of the Interior and the Research Concerning Canada's Western Frontier of Settlement.* Regina, SK: Canadian Plains Research Centre, University of Regina, 1993.

Thomson, Don W. *Men and Meridians: The History of the Surveying and Mapping of Canada.* 3 vols. Ottawa: Queen's Printer, 1966–1969.

Tyman, John Langton. *By Section, Township and Range: Studies in Prairie Settlement.* Brandon, MB: Brandon University, 1995.

Figure 11-1. The *Daily Free Press* (Winnipeg), 1875

Available at Ancestry.ca

NEWSPAPERS

11

Newspapers represent an important source for family history researchers. They help you put the lives of your ancestors into a local context, and they sometimes clarify or correct an official record. A wise researcher will, however, look to newspapers for much more than basic vital statistics. They can provide a level of detail not available from other sources. Obituaries help us fill in gaps and find descendants; stories of local celebrations and anniversaries sometimes relate the family's history and mention everyone present.

The first newspaper published in what is now Canada was the *Halifax Gazette*, founded by John Bushell on March 23, 1752. Twelve years later, William Brown started the *Quebec Gazette*. The *Montreal Gazette*, first printed in 1778, is the oldest continuously published newspaper in North America.

Early newspapers contained government announcements and small news items, including international news that had arrived by ship. These newspapers were rarely larger than four pages.

In the nineteenth century, many newspapers were established in the population centers of Canada. Some of the newspapers dating from this period include the *Bytown Packet*, which evolved into the *Ottawa Citizen*, and the *Toronto Globe*, now the *Globe and Mail*. Both have been in print since 1844. As the western provinces were settled, new newspapers were established, including the *British Colonist* in Victoria in 1858, the *Winnipeg Free Press* in 1874, and the *Calgary Herald* in 1885.

The number of daily newspapers peaked at 138 in 1938. Today, about 100 dailies are published in Canada, along with about 700 newspapers that publish one, two, or three times a week.

Canada has also had hundreds of ethnic and religious newspapers printed in dozens of languages. They are often a better source of information on Canadians who did not speak French or English.

CONTENT

Daily newspapers generally have much more national and international news than weekly newspapers, which tend to emphasize local coverage. Dailies were usually published in the larger towns and cities, while weeklies were found in villages and small towns.

Typical items of genealogical interest include

- birth, marriage, and death announcements;
- local celebrations and social events;
- news stories on significant events such as major economic changes, disasters, and the deaths of prominent people;
- stories about crimes, court cases, and the activities of the coroner;
- lists of names. These were published after events such as school graduations, sports events, or fall fairs, or simply indicated who was staying in the local hotels. You might also find petitions or the names of contributors to a relief fund;
- advertisements, important if your ancestor owned a business;
- legal notices, including notices to creditors, divorces, and changes of name.

The type of information included in newspapers has changed dramatically over the 250 years they have been published in Canada. Before the late 1800s, newspapers were quite small, so not many words were given to any one topic unless it caught the fancy of the editor.

GENEALOGICAL USE

Newspapers can bridge the gaps in official records and enhance or corroborate what you learn from other sources. They can provide information not available anywhere else. For example, if someone who should be in a census cannot be found, check the social notes in the newspaper. It could be that the person was out of the area at the time the census was taken and the newspaper mentioned the trip.

Newspapers in port cities often ran lists of some of the passengers on recently arrived ships. These lists supplement the information available in passenger lists. Also, you might find information about the voyage taken by your ancestor—maybe a famous person was on board, or possibly the trip was hampered by especially rough seas.

Weekly newspapers will often be the best choice if you're looking for information on local people. Also, if you're looking in weeklies rather than dailies, you'll have fewer rolls of microfilm to go through.

Church publications and newspapers published in different languages might include information that you won't see in the regular newspapers.

Expect to find more references to men than women, a bias that did not start to change until the latter half of the twentieth century. You are also more likely to see the names of community leaders—business owners, council members, and so on—than laborers, unless those laborers got in trouble with the law.

Look for both a paid death announcement and a news story, especially if a death record mentions an accident. The information offered might be different in the two references. And remember that death notices may help fill in gaps in civil registration documents, when people died outside the province, for example. A notice to creditors published a few weeks after a person died could indicate that a will was being probated.

LOCATING NEWSPAPERS

Some early newspapers are on websites such as Ancestry and NewspaperArchive.com. Every edition of the *Toronto Star*, Canada's largest newspaper, from 1894 through 2002 is on the Internet. Selected libraries have online access to historic editions of the Toronto *Globe and Mail* dating back to 1844. A project in Alberta is putting newspaper titles from many communities online.

A comprehensive list of Canadian newspapers is on the Library and Archives Canada (LAC) website. Lists of newspapers in provincial collections are often found on the websites of provincial archives and legislative libraries. Also check the *Union List of Canadian Newspapers*, available at most libraries in Canada in print form or on microfiche.

If your newspaper of interest is not on the Internet, you will probably need to use microfilmed collections. If the specific titles you need are not available at your local library, they can be brought in through interlibrary loan.

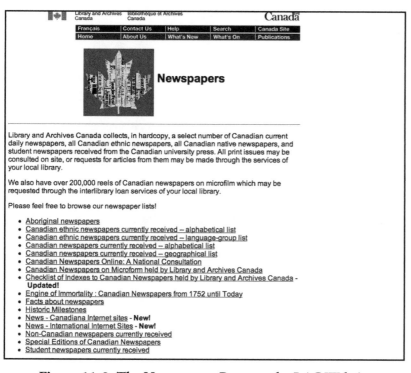

Figure 11-2. The Newspapers Page on the LAC Website

<http://www.collectionscanada.ca/8/16/index-e.html>

The largest collection of newspapers in Canada is at LAC in Ottawa. Every province has a library with a substantial newspaper collection. Check major city libraries, university libraries, reference libraries, and archives for newspapers on microfilm.

Many early newspapers have been indexed by newspaper staff, local libraries, or by volunteers, and some of these indexes are being posted on the Internet. Check the provincial GenWeb, genealogical societies, local archives, the Family History Library Catalog, and public and university libraries for indexes of birth, marriage, and death notices from local newspapers.

Library and Archives Canada has several newspaper lists, including Checklist of Indexes to Canadian Newspapers Held by Library and Archives Canada. You can also search for *newspaper* using AVITUS.

MODERN NEWSPAPERS

Many newspapers have websites that often provide access to obituaries from the past few years. The largest newspapers are included in online libraries such as FPInfomart. Searches are free, with full stories available for a fee. These online libraries are more comprehensive than newspaper websites and cover more years. Paid obituaries are not normally found in online libraries, but they might be on the newspaper websites.

Obituary Daily Times, on the Rootsweb site, includes references to death notices from several Canadian cities. Search by keyword, using both the surname and the place of residence—for example, "Jones Winnipeg."

You might also contact the newspaper in the area where your ancestors lived. Some will publish letters from people seeking information on family members who lived in the town, and others will require that you place an advertisement.

WEBSITES

Ancestry: <www.ancestry.ca>
Canadian Genealogy Centre: <www.collectionscanada.ca/genealogy/>
Checklist of Indexes to Canadian Newspapers Held by Library and Archives
    Canada: <www.collectionscanada.ca/8/16/index-e.html>
FPInfomart: <www.fpinfomart.ca>
Newspaper Archive: <www.newspaperarchive.com>
Obituary Daily Times: <www.rootsweb.com/~obituary>
Toronto Star, 1894–2002: <thestar.pagesofthepast.ca>

BIBLIOGRAPHY

Taylor, Ryan. *Researching Canadian Newspaper Records*. Toronto: Heritage
    Productions, 2002.
Union List of Canadian Newspapers. Ottawa: National Library of Canada, 1993.
    (microfiche)

12

OTHER WAYS TO FIND PEOPLE

Do not stop just because you have checked all of the usual sources for information about your family—there is much more that can be done. Alternative sources might help you find a family member who has gone missing. They help you bridge the gaps between censuses and can help make up for records that have been lost.

DIRECTORIES

Canada's first city directories were published in Quebec City in 1790 and 1791, commissioned by the government as a form of census. Directories did not become a regular feature in Canada, however, until commercial publishers revived the idea several decades later. Directories were designed to help businesses, churches, schools, and government agencies. They contained addresses and key information about people that made it easier to determine property ownership or target selective marketing.

By the middle of the nineteenth century, many communities had several competing directories, although over the years these businesses were generally consolidated into one or two major publishers. Only one publisher was left at the end of the twentieth century. In 2000 that company, R. L. Polk, abandoned the Canadian market, effectively bringing an end to the directory business more than two centuries after the first ones appeared.

At first directories listed business and civic leaders only. In time they were expanded to include most of the adult males in a community and then all males and females over the age of eighteen. But coverage never included everyone. Some people did not want to be listed, and some—including those in the poorest areas and those who did not speak the language of the enumerators—were not even asked.

Some directories covered wide areas. Directories for all of British Columbia, as an example, were published until 1948. However, the scale of these directories might not help today's researchers. Listing every adult would have made them too large, so the listings included only a small percentage of the residents. In general, the wider the area covered by a directory, the less comprehensive it was.

Typically, a city directory includes an alphabetical list of inhabitants, and each entry states the surname, given name or initial, occupation and employer, the name of the spouse (generally after 1945, unless they worked outside the home), and address. The alphabetical list usually includes businesses, with the name of the owner or manager. Most directories also have advertisements, a description of the community, and street-by-street listings, which help in identifying neighbors.

To make the most effective use of directories, look for

- more than one reference to an individual: a business owner, for example, could be listed as an individual and with the business;
- children: people usually had to be at least eighteen to appear in a directory, so watch for children after they move to their own homes;
- disappearing wives: this could be due to death or because a man has remarried;
- disappearing single women: if a woman is in the directory one year but gone the next, check the address for the second year. It is possible she is living in the same house with a new husband;
- spelling variations: this is especially important when looking for recent immigrants from non-English-speaking countries.

Be sure to have a map of the community as you go through the directory. Use it to plot a person's residence and place of employment, as well as nearby churches and schools. That will help narrow your search for church registers and school records.

Directories are on the Web; significant collections include the Who Was Where database at Library and Archives Canada (LAC), Peel's Prairie Provinces at the University of Alberta, and the Lovell collection at Bibliothèque et Archives nationales du Québec. Several provincial archives have placed finding aids to a few directories within their online resources, and you can find transcripts and extracts of directories within sections of Canadian GenWeb. Ancestry and OurRoots also have some directories on the Internet.

There are Canadian directories on microfilm and microfiche at the Family History Library. You will find them listed in the Family History Library Catalog under the province, city, or town.

VOTERS LISTS

Early lists of voters, which were needed for elections and referendums, included only adult males who held property. Gradually, the electoral process was opened to more and more people, including women in 1918, Canadians of Asian ancestry in the 1940s, and registered Indians living on reserves in 1960.

URBAN VS. RURAL

Federal voters lists made a distinction between rural and urban areas, with urban voters listed by address and rural ones listed alphabetically by surname. The urban lists are not as easy to use, but they are much more complete than the rural lists. That is because the government allowed rural residents who were not on the list to cast ballots if registered voters vouched for them. Urban residents, on the other hand, had to be included on the list, or they were not allowed to vote.

Voters lists have been compiled by all three levels of government: local, provincial or territorial, and federal. Through the years, different rules have been applied in different jurisdictions, and until 1920, federal eligibility was determined by provincial rules. The federal government used provincial lists until the 1935 election, when it created its own.

These federal lists, covering elections from 1935 through 1980, are the easiest to find. They are available on microfilm from LAC. They are grouped by election, then by province, then by electoral district, then by polling division. Almanacs or the Library of Parliament website will help you determine the electoral district.

Provincial voters lists cover an earlier time period than the federal ones but can be tougher to locate. They have generally been turned over to provincial or territorial archives and, unlike the federal ones, are not available through interlibrary loan.

Local lists, including those for municipalities and school districts, have usually been retained locally in libraries or archives. A few old poll books are on the Canadiana. org website.

An entry on a voters list confirms that the person was alive and gives the address and occupation at the time the enumeration was taken. These facts are reference points for several records, such as vital events and probate records.

OTHER SOURCES

• The Canadian Genealogy Index, 1600–1900, was published on CD-ROM in 1996. It's also available on Ancestry.ca and was sold as part of the Canadian version of *Family Tree Maker*. It was based on four sets of books: *Atlantic Canadians, 1600–1900*; *French Canadians, 1600–1900*; *Central Canadians, 1600–1900*; and *Western Canadians, 1600–1900*. Information in the index was drawn from directories, historical atlases, and other sources.

• The records collected by the National Registration Program, from 1940 through 1946, are available to researchers. There was a war on, so the government required Canadians to identify themselves, provide information on their birthplaces, and, if they were immigrants, the year of immigration.

To access these records, you will need to provide Statistics Canada with the name of the person in question, where he or she lived in 1940, and proof that the person has died. You'll also need to provide payment; the fee is $45 plus tax.

• School records have lists of children. Check provincial archives for class lists for schools in your research area. These lists show names and grades, which can help you determine the ages of the children in a family.

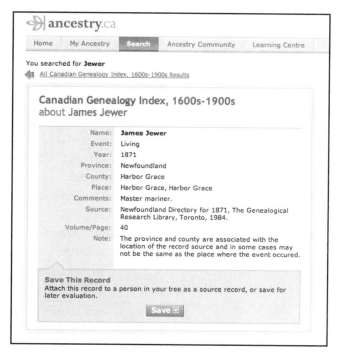

Figure 12-1. Selection from the Canadian Genealogy Index, 1600s–1900s

Available on Ancestry.ca.

- Occupations could provide valuable clues. Check lists of professionals, such as doctors and lawyers. Check for trade associations. The census, obituaries, and, in urban areas, directories can help you determine your ancestor's employment.

- You might find lists of people in unusual places, so don't hesitate to check every source. Government publications often mentioned people by name. You could find lists of civil servants, teachers, people declaring bankruptcy or changing their name, and even people given permission to buy alcohol. Family sources, such as Bibles, could also provide valuable clues.

WEBSITES

Ancestry: <www.ancestry.ca>

Canada GenWeb: <www.rootsweb.com/~canwgw/>

Canadiana.org: <www.canadiana.org>

Canadian Directories, Who Was Where, Library and Archives Canada: <www.collectionscanada.ca/canadiandirectories/index-e.html>

Canadian Genealogy Centre—Employment: <www.collectionscanada.ca/genealogy/022-913-e.html>

FamilySearch: <www.familysearch.org>

Library and Archives Canada: <www.collectionscanada.ca>

Lovell Directories, Bibliothèque et Archives Nationales du Québec: <bibnum2.banq.qc.ca/bna/lovell>

Our Roots: <www.ourroots.ca>

Peel's Prairie Provinces: <peel.library.ualberta.ca/index.html>

Statistics Canada—Searches of the National Registration File of 1940: <www.statcan.ca/bsolc/english/bsolc?catno=93C0006>

BIBLIOGRAPHY

Bond, Mary E. *Canadian Directories, 1790–1987: A Bibliography and Place-name Index.* Ottawa: National Library of Canada, 1989.

Canadian Institute for Historical Microreproductions. *Pre-1900 Canadian Directories.* Ottawa: Canadian Institute for Historical Microreproductions, 1988.

Obee, Dave. *Federal Voters Lists in Ontario, 1935–1979.* Victoria: Dave Obee, 2004.

———. *Federal Voters Lists in Western Canada, 1935–1979.* Victoria: Dave Obee, 2003.

Ryder, Dorothy E. *Checklist of Canadian Directories, 1780–1950.* Ottawa: National Library of Canada, 1979.

13

THE ABORIGINALS

RECORDS OF FIRST NATIONS AND MÉTIS

The Aboriginal people of Canada (originally called Indians, more recently Native people and First Nations) had a long history of their own before Europeans arrived. Four hundred years ago, before any European settlement, the most heavily populated region was the Pacific coast, and the principal Native groups were the Coast Salish and Haida. The largest area inhabited by one nation was that of the Ojibwa; their lands included part of southern Ontario and Wisconsin and stretched west to Saskatchewan and Montana. In the east, around the Great Lakes and the St. Lawrence River, were the Algonquian and Iroquois nations. Native territories crossed the boundaries that were later created by English, French, and Spanish agreements.

The first of many alliances with Europeans occurred in 1615 when Champlain allied New France with the Huron. The Iroquois and Huron were already in conflict, and the addition of European alliances created a complex situation. There was to be another hundred years of fighting involving the Dutch, French, and British.

At the outbreak of the Seven Years' War (French and Indian War) in 1756, the French had strong alliances with the Algonquians, and the British were allied with the Iroquois. Twenty years later, during the American Revolution, the Algonquians were loyal to the British, and the loyalty of the Iroquois split. Many of both nations settled in areas along the St. Lawrence River and Lake Ontario.

The War of 1812 between Britain and the United States also involved an alliance of First Nations on the British side. The British commander, General Isaac Brock, recognized the need for help to counter American attacks. He and Chief Tecumseh had great mutual respect, which was an important factor in the defense of Canada. The Americans were determined to take the colony, but the combined leadership of Brock and Tecumseh held them back. The war was an inconclusive conflict, but it marked the last time that Natives fought in a British conflict.

Close contact with Europeans meant that French and English records began to include Indians. The instances were haphazard at first, in church records and colonial papers. Government record keeping began in 1829, and references increase after that.

Contact between Europeans and Native people of the Plains happened through the fur trade. The fur trade was one of three things that changed the Native people's lives; the other two were horses and firearms. The major period for the fur trade was 1730 to 1870. As the fur trade declined, settlement increased at a time when violence in the American West was increasing and spilling north over the border. In response, the North-West Mounted Police were established in 1874.

On the west coast, contact with Europeans happened later. Settlement came later as well, and it was the 1857 gold rush on the Fraser River that brought large numbers of white people to what became British Columbia.

At all places and in all historical periods, contact between Native people and white men led to liaisons and marriages and the birth of children of mixed blood. The French changed their stance on these relationships from initial acceptance, and even encouragement, to disapproval. At first, the Hudson's Bay Company did not allow employees to marry Native women, but eventually they had to accept it.

In the West the people of mixed blood (called Half-breed or Métis, which means "mixed") became a strong group with their own identity. They were a mix of French, Scots, English, and Native but were predominantly French speaking and Catholic. By the time the struggles between the North West Company and the Hudson's Bay Company ended in 1821, the Red River Colony was overwhelmingly populated by people of mixed descent. The disaffection of the Métis population led to events in the 1870s and 1880s in Saskatchewan and Manitoba that culminated in the Riel Rebellion of 1885.

As tensions were increasing, the young country of Canada faced two related issues. One was the negotiation of land deals prior to building the transcontinental railway, and the other was the acquisition of all the territory of the Hudson's Bay Company. Both meant that new agreements had to be reached with Native peoples. The negotiations started the Numbered Treaties, a series of eleven agreements signed between 1870 and 1921.

The Canadian government made no change in Native policy in the first half of the twentieth century; the long-standing expectation of eventual assimilation remained. Attitudes shifted after World War II, in part because six thousand Natives served in the military. Part of the significance of the Indian Act of 1951, which affects so many of the records, lies in the fact that it was the first time Native people were included in the discussions about legislation. Nine years later, in 1960, they were given the vote.

About Records of First Nations

Starting Point

The records of the Department of Indian Affairs, known as Record Group 10 (RG 10), are the administrative records of the federal government from 1872 to the 1950s concerning Aboriginal people. Other important resources, all at Library and Archives

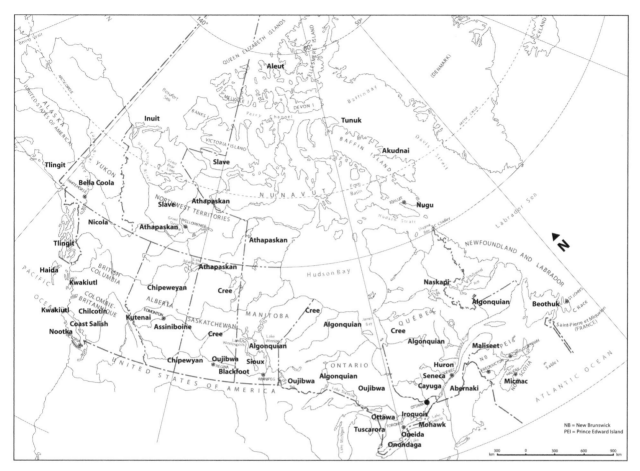

Figure 13-1. Canadian Tribal Territories

Canada (LAC), include a large collection of maps and online special exhibits, many with searchable text and or indexes.

Provincial archives, university libraries, museums, and societies hold records about First Nations, and some offer data, guides, or exhibits online. Not all parts of Canada are represented in federal government records, which is why it is important to check resources held by other repositories and organizations.

You should also read guides that focus on Native and Métis research. The LAC website includes *Researching Your Aboriginal Ancestors at Library and Archives Canada* (2005). A useful recent book is *Tracing Your Aboriginal Ancestors in the Prairies: A Guide to the Records and How to Use Them* (Hanowski, 2006). Other titles are in the bibliography at the end of this chapter.

Important Facts

Location information is essential. Begin by searching for all places of residence and of any reserves associated with your ancestors. Published resources include the *Schedule of Indian Bands, Reserves and Settlements* (1972) and the *Atlas of Indian Reserves and*

Settlements of Canada (1972). At the website of the Saskatchewan Office of the Treaty Commissioner is a key map indicating treaty areas in that province. Selecting a treaty area on the key map leads to a larger map with names and locations of reserves as well as more about the treaties.

You also need to know whether ancestors were treaty or non-treaty Indians, whether they were status or non-status, and whether or not they were Half-breed or Métis. If they were treaty, then knowing the treaty date and number is going to be useful. Perhaps the most important piece of information is the name of the band the ancestors belonged to. Records are usually arranged according to band, agency, or district; members of bands received a band number or ticket, which was a government-issued identification number.

Band names were not static, and the name used in records could be different from the name members of a band used—changes occurred because of amalgamation, surrender of treaty rights, or a simple name change. LAC has an online guide to help you research RG 10 records that shows the relationship between field offices and the Native bands they administered. The resources within the Aboriginal Peoples topic at the LAC website also contain a map database for Indian Reserves in Western Canada.

Finally, determine a time period for your search. It will help you sort out records and individuals within them if you have dates of major life events or at least some idea of the lifespan of an ancestor.

Pitfalls

Pay attention to how names were recorded and indexed. Some people had only one name, which could be in English or in the native form, and it could be indexed as a

DEFINITIONS

Band: an Aboriginal community officially recognized as an administrative unit by the Crown (government).

Tribe: a large group of Aboriginal people sharing language, culture, and way of life; can be made up of several bands (the term is not used much in Canada).

Half-breed: An English term for those of mixed Aboriginal and white descent.

Métis: A French term for those of mixed Aboriginal and white descent.

Status Indian: one legally defined as an Indian according to the Indian Act; may be treaty Indians or registered Indians (those who lived in areas where there were no treaties).

Non-status Indians: Indians who have lost their legal status either by intermarriage with whites or by abandoning it and are not granted status under the Indian Act.

Treaty: formal agreement between the Crown and an Indian band or bands covering issues and benefits that may relate to land, money payments, fishing rights, etc.; no treaties were made in Newfoundland and Labrador, Quebec, parts of the Maritimes, most of British Columbia, the Yukon, Northwest Territories, and Nunavut.

first name or as a surname, with the other part of the name left blank. Some indexes will have to be searched twice to get around this problem.

Natives were not included in the provincial and federal records for some time. You may not find records of birth, marriage, and death within provincial vital statistics. However, in some cases the records are held in a separate set. Federal census takers made no effort to enumerate Native people until 1901. Those of mixed blood were included in censuses but not necessarily identified as such. You must rely on birthplace to spot them.

Major Resources at Library and Archives Canada

Pay Lists

The federal records are for status Indians, both treaty Indians and registered Indians. The first treaties were signed about three hundred years ago in the Maritimes. These early agreements made between the 1690s and 1790s usually did not involve land. In Ontario, treaties were signed from the 1780s after the coming of the Loyalists and again for the northern Great Lakes areas in the 1850s. Ontario and the West figure in the series known as the Numbered Treaties signed between 1870 and 1921.

The terms of some treaties involved payment of annuities to members of Indian bands, and these account records are informative. Individuals who received payments appear in lists found under two headings: *Treaty Annuity Pay Lists, 1850 to 1982*, and *Interest Distribution Pay Lists, 1856 to 1982*. The pay lists are available on microfilm to 1910.

Treaty Annuity Pay Lists exist for bands that signed treaties. During the first forty-three years, the lists indicate heads of families only. The records are arranged by treaty number. Information in the records includes name, band name, date of birth, date and place of payment, amount, and name of the agent.

Interest Distribution Pay Lists were created for bands that had money in the care of the federal government and who distributed interest payments to their members. The records are arranged by band name. Information includes names, band name, date and place of payment, amount, and name of the agent.

Quebec is not a treaty area, but the Abitibi Dominion Band and the Abitiwinni are listed among those that obtained annuity payments.

Registers

Library and Archives Canada holds the Indian Register from its inception in 1951 up until 1984. It is still maintained by the government and is a national record of every known person entitled to Indian status under the Indian Act. The Indian Register contains the names of everyone with Indian status or who has acquired Indian status since the time the act was passed. Additional information includes vital events, family relationships (parents, spouse, children), religion, and band number. There are restrictions concerning access to these records, and members of the general public should contact the government for more information.

For a period before 1951 the government prepared community lists that were posted publicly. This gave the records their name, Posted Lists. The purpose for these lists was to give people an opportunity to raise objections over whether or not they were included in lists of status Indians. Access restrictions may also apply to these records.

A second group of pre-1951 records are called Membership Registers and Lists. They can be found among the records of different agencies and regional offices. Once again, there may be access restrictions.

Red and Black Series

In 1872 the Canadian government started to keep track of all correspondence and documents received and generated by the various departments that were responsible for Indian affairs over the years. The volumes, bound in red and black, were finding aids to millions of paper items, recording their dates, content summaries, and file numbers. Because of their distinctive binding, all the records are referred to as the Red and Black series.

At first everything was logged into volumes bound in red, but the mass of material for the West grew to the point that a new series of black volumes was started in 1882, recording material for the West and the Maritimes. In 1907 the Maritimes was moved back into the red books. The red volumes run from 1872 to 1923 and the black ones from 1882 to 1919. There is considerable variety and much of interest to family historians in these records.

Library and Archives Canada has an online search tool for all the text descriptions of the Red and Black series and has digitized a significant segment of the documents from the Red series. LAC intends to digitize completely both series, but this will take some time. Right now the search tool covers all the titles and summaries, and search results indicate whether or not images are available. It is a simple matter of clicking on a link to see the document. You can search according to keywords such as personal names, band names, and place-names. Some record restrictions may apply, but this is also indicated.

Other Records

Within federal records are some estate files for deceased Indians who were living on reserves on Crown land or who were living elsewhere but maintained an interest in land on a reserve. Probate files may reveal the details of heirs, next of kin, personal assets, land, names of creditors, and details of the probate record itself.

Another class of records containing family information is school records. You may be able to find such facts as name, age, band number, names of parents, religion, school grades, and level of school completed. These files may have restrictions.

Provincial archives websites should be checked for information. Two examples are Ontario and Nova Scotia. Ontario offers an online guide to records of Aboriginal peoples. The records are scattered among their holdings and relate to contacts between white groups and Natives from the 1760s and after. Some papers of the fur trade and missions refer to other parts of Canada.

Nova Scotia has the Mi'kmaq Holdings Resource Guide at the archives website. It should be consulted by anyone interested in Native research in Atlantic Canada. This guide is a combination of exhibits, tips on language and names, genealogical advice, and data. The database mentions over two thousand textual records, and the exhibit contains selected document images, maps, portraits, and photographs.

Other provincial archives websites with useful resources are Saskatchewan and Manitoba, which also houses the Hudson's Bay Company Archives. More is said about their collections later in the chapter.

The University of Saskatchewan has created a national database to all reported Native law case decisions from 1763 to 1978. You can carry out a surname or keyword search. In some cases genealogical information was entered as evidence. Official copies of proceedings may be available for purchase from the court where a case was heard.

Records of Métis

Manitoba Act and North-West Scrip Commission Records

Legislation of the 1870s created a system for ending Aboriginal title for Métis people by means of compensation that was known as scrip. It was necessary to claim scrip by application, and applicants had to meet certain requirements: residence in Manitoba or the Northwest Territories at 15 July 1870 or born before the end of December 1885.

The scrip was a type of certificate that entitled the person holding it to land or money. If it was for land, the amount was 240 acres, and if it was for money there were several denominations to a maximum of 240 dollars. Land was presumed to be worth one dollar per acre at the time.

When scrip was exchanged for land, the selection had to be made from areas allocated as homestead land. This could be a very long way from where a Métis family was living. As a result many people sold or traded their scrip because they had no intention of moving two or three hundred miles away. A black market developed, and the certificates were sold and traded, generally for less than face value. The only way to get full value was to redeem the scrip at a government lands office. Land speculators bought up scrip.

Scrip records may tell you date and place of birth, names of parents, spouse, and children. The time period stretches from 1870 to 1906 in two parts: 1870 to 1885 for Manitoba and 1885 to 1906 for the Northwest Territories (i.e., Saskatchewan and Alberta). The Manitoba Act scrip applications are online at LAC with a finding aid and record images. If the land was in Saskatchewan, the names of Métis who sold scrip and of those who purchased it appear in the Saskatchewan homestead database at the Saskatchewan Archives website. The North-West Commission records are to be added at a future date.

Census Records

Censuses were taken at Red River and other locations in Hudson's Bay Company territory by the company and by the government. There were several between 1827 and 1870, most in the 1830s and 1840s. The returns give the following facts about the

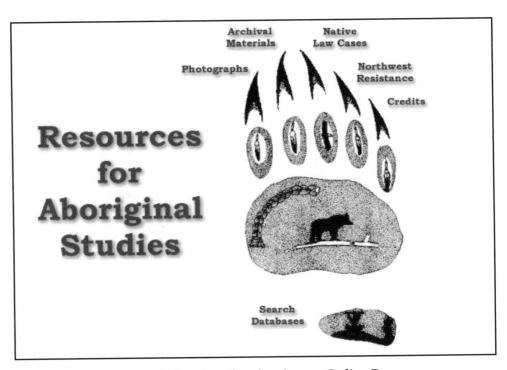

Figure 13-2. University of Saskatchewan Online Resources
From this page you can search five collections: an index to photographs related to aboriginal and Métis research, an index to materials in the aboriginal collections, the Canadian Native Law Cases Index (see page 88), and a database of materials on the Northwest Rebellion of 1885.
<http://library2.usask.ca/native/>

head of the household: name, age, country of birth, marital status, and details of his dependents but no names. There may be additional facts about buildings, livestock, and crops.

There are census enumerations for Company forts as well. They can be found at the Hudson's Bay Company Archives and at repositories in Saskatchewan and Alberta.

Company archives are within the Manitoba Archives. At their website is a list of the available Red River settlement records, and there is a finding aid to the censuses. Copies of records and an index are at the Family History Library (FHL) and can be viewed on microfilm at Family History Centers.

You can read about these censuses in *Biographical Resources at the Hudson's Bay Company Archives,* Volume I (Briggs and Morton, 1996).

Other Collections

Three collections need highlighting because of extensive holdings or helpful websites: the Glenbow Museum and Archives, Arthur S. Morton Collection at the University of Saskatchewan, and the holdings of the Société historique de Saint-Boniface.

The Glenbow Library and Archives, Calgary, holds the Charles Denney Métis Genealogy Collection; descriptions are at its website. Contents include censuses, church records, and the histories of over 1,200 families, including some Métis with Red River connections. The papers of Richard C. Hardisty, a Hudson's Bay Company factor, are also here.

The Société historique de Saint-Boniface in Manitoba holds many records of Western Canada and Quebec. There are parish, census, and scrip records and some notarial records. The library has its own database to select census and church records. Online there are indexes, in French, to Familles francophones et métisses de l'Ouèst canadien and to voyageurs. Members of the society can use resources without charge.

At the University of Alberta in the School of Métis Studies is the Métis Archival Project. It is an ambitious project and will gather many resources together. You can find out more at the website.

Look Elsewhere

There are some entries for Mi'kmaq people in early Acadian church records, and some appear later in Nova Scotia land records. The 1921 census of Newfoundland included Natives and specifically asked, "Are you a MicMac Indian?" Although Natives and Métis did not always appear in records created by the colonial and Canadian authorities, or cannot always be identified in them, it is important that you consider which of these records to consult and include them in your research.

WEBSITES

Archives of Ontario: <www.archives.gov.on.ca>
Archives of Ontario (guide to Aboriginal research):
   <www.archives.gov.on.ca/english/aborige/index.html>
Assembly of First Nations: <www.afn.ca>
Canadian Directory of First Nations, Métis and Inuit Library Collections:
   <http://library2.usask.ca/native/directory/english/index.html>
Canadian Encyclopedia:
Glenbow Museum Archives: <www.glenbow.org/collections/archives/>
Hudson's Bay Company Archives:
   <www.gov.mb.ca/chc/archives/hbca/index.html>
Library and Archives Canada: <www.collectionscanada.ca/index-e.html>
Library and Archives Canada Aboriginal Documentary Heritage:
   <www.collectionscanada.ca/aboriginal-heritage/index-e.html>
Library and Archives Canada Métis Scrip Records:
   <www.collectionscanada.ca/02/02010507_e.html>
Library and Archives Canada, Resources for Aboriginal Peoples:
   <www.collectionscanada.ca/aboriginal-peoples/index-e.html>
Manitoba Archives: <www.gov.mb.ca/chc/archives/>
Manitoba Archives Guide to Aboriginal Research:
   <www.gov.mb.ca/chc/archives/genealogy/gen_text/aborg_recmn.html>
Métis National Council (links to five regional organizations):
   <www.metisnation.ca>

Saskatchewan Archives (explanation of scrip):
<www.saskhomesteads.com/metis-scrip.asp>
Saskatchewan Archives Board: <www.saskarchives.com>
The Société historique de Saint-Boniface: <www.shsb.mb.ca/englishindex.htm>
University of Saskatchewan Major Special Collections:
<https://library.usask.ca/spcoll/major>
University of Saskatchewan Resources for Aboriginal Studies:
<http://library2.usask.ca/native/>

BIBLIOGRAPHY

Archives of Ontario. *Aboriginal Peoples in the Archives: A Guide to Sources in the Archives of Ontario.* Toronto: Ministry of Culture and Communications / Archives of Ontario, 1992. (online publication)

Barkwell, Lawrence J., Leah Dorian, and Darren R. Prèfontaine. *Resources for Métis Researchers.* Saskatoon and Winnipeg: Gabriel Dumont Institute of Native Studies and Applied Research and the Louis Riel Institute of the Manitoba Métis Federation, 1999.

Briggs, Elizabeth, and Anne Morton. *Biographical Resources at the Hudson's Bay Company Archives.* Vol. 1. Winnipeg: Westgarth, 1996.

Coates, K., *Aboriginal Land Claims in Canada.* Mississauga, ON: Copp Clarke Pitman Limited, 1992.

Collins, Richard. *Researching Your Aboriginal Roots at Library and Archives Canada.* Ottawa: Library and Archives Canada, 2005. (online publication)

Department of Indian Affairs and Northern Development Canada. *Atlas of Indian Reserves and Settlements of Canada.* Ottawa: Department of Indian Affairs and Northern Development, 1971.

———. *Schedule of Indian Reservations and Settlements.* Ottawa: Department of Indian Affairs and Northern Development, 1972.

Hanowski, Laura, ed. *Tracing Your Aboriginal Ancestors in the Prairies: A Guide to the Records and How to Use Them.* Regina, SK: Saskatchewan Genealogical Society, 2006.

Jenness, Diamond. *The Indians of Canada.* 3rd ed. Ottawa: National Museum of Canada. 1955.

McLean, Donald G. *Home from the Hill: A History of the Métis in Western Canada.* Regina, SK: Gabriel Dumont Institute, 1987.

Micmac-Maliseet Institute. *Maliseet & Micmac Vital Statistics from New Brunswick Church Records.* Fredericton, NB: Micmac-Maliseet Institute, 1998.

Morice, A.G. *Dictionnaire historique des Canadiens et des Métis français de l'Ouest.* 2nd ed. Québec: J.-P. Garneau, 1912.

Morin, Gail. *Manitoba Scrip.* Pawtucket, RI: Quintin Publications, 1996.

Peterson, J., and Jennifer. S. H. Brown, eds. *The New Peoples: Being and Becoming Métis in North America.* Manitoba Studies in Native History, No. 1. Winnipeg: The University of Manitoba Press, 1993.

Russell, Bill. *Records of the Federal Department of Indian Affairs at the National Archives of Canada: A Source for Genealogical Research*. Toronto: Ontario Genealogical Society, 1998.

ADDRESSES

Archives of Manitoba
200 Vaughan Street
Winnipeg, MB R3C 1T5

Archives of Ontario
77 Grenville Street, Unit 300
Toronto, ON M5S 1B3

Glenbow Museum and Library and Archives
130 - 9 Avenue SE
Calgary, AB T2G 0P3

La Société historique de Saint-Boniface
340 Provencher Boulevard
Saint-Boniface, MB R2H 0G7

Library and Archives Canada
395 Wellington Street
Ottawa, ON K1A 0N4

Nova Scotia Archives and Records Management
6016 University Avenue
Halifax, NS B3H 1W4

Saskatchewan Archives Board, Regina Office
University of Regina
Regina, SK S4S 0A2

Saskatchewan Archives Board, Saskatoon Office
Murray Building, University of Saskatchewan
3 Campus Drive
Saskatoon, SK S7N 5A4

Special Collections
University of Saskatchewan Library
301 Main Library, 3 Campus Drive
Saskatoon, SK S7N 5A4

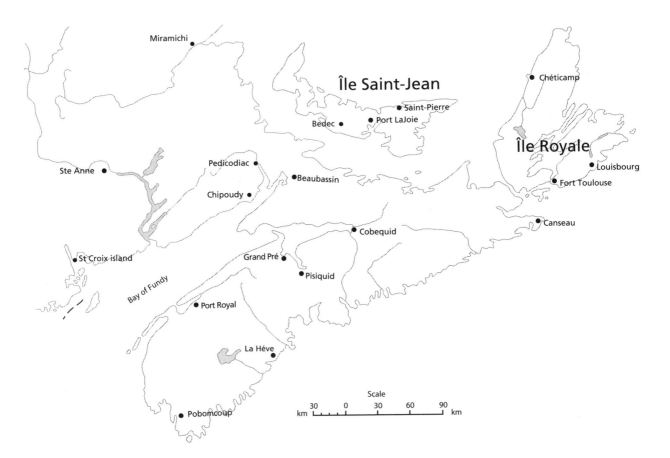

Figure 14-1. Acadia

The map indicates many of the Acadian settlements in the years between 1713 and 1750. At this time Ile Saint-Jean and Ile Royale were French possessions, other areas were British.

THE ACADIANS

The Acadians lived in the French territory known as L'Acadie, or Acadia, that stretched across present-day Nova Scotia, Prince Edward Island, eastern New Brunswick, and some of the state of Maine. This region was caught between French and British interests in the New World. From 1604 to 1713 it changed hands many times through conflicts and the treaties that ended them.

Almost all Acadians were French and Catholic; they were also good farmers and self-sufficient. They wanted to be left alone, but neutrality was not a choice; France expected them to be loyal, and Britain considered their declarations of neutrality suspect.

In 1713 a European peace treaty ceded most of the region to Britain. For a while longer, Île Saint-Jean (Prince Edward Island) and Île Royale (Cape Breton Island) belonged to France, but from 1713 the majority by far of the Acadian people lived under the authority of Britain. Thirty years of peace for the Acadians followed the treaty of 1713, and their numbers multiplied.

The rivalry between France and England continued in Europe, and the French decided to strengthen their North American colonies with a fortress at Louisbourg on Île Royale. It was finished in 1745 and shortly after was attacked by a group of volunteer soldiers from New England. The fortress was taken, but the treaty of 1748 returned it to France. As a counter to the continued presence of French forces in the region, Britain moved ahead with plans for a fortified town with settlers and a garrison, establishing Halifax in 1749.

Tension remained high and intensified prior to the resumption of fighting in 1756. The Acadians were ordered to take a full oath of allegiance to Britain and refused. Rather than be uncertain of their loyalty, the British governor decided to remove the problem, deporting the people and burning their farms. From 1755 to 1763 about ten thousand people were moved. Several thousand went only as far as Île Saint-Jean and Île Royale but were forced to move again. Acadians went elsewhere in the American colonies, as well as to the Caribbean, to England, and to France.

The Seven Years' War (or French and Indian War) ended in 1763, Île St-Jean and Île Royale were ceded to Britain, and the Acadians were permitted to return. A great many had died of disease or in shipwrecks, and many chose not to go back. Those who returned found their land occupied by New Englanders and new restrictions on where they could live. Some went to Cape Breton, others to the shores of the Gulf of St. Lawrence, and others inland into New Brunswick, where they worked in lumbering and fishing. Once again they were successful settlers, and by 1901 their descendents numbered over 100,000.

ACADIAN RESEARCH

Begin your work with background information on the history of the conflicts between France and England and about Acadia in particular. It is easy to begin online by visiting the Nova Scotia Archives and Records Management (NSARM) and Halifax Public Libraries websites. The archives will help you prepare for research, and the library will provide more links and a comprehensive bibliography.

Much work has been done to make Acadian research easier, and you should take advantage of the resources. Look at copies of original records whenever possible. Many records have not survived, and you may have to sort out problems with names and nicknames (known as *dit* names).

LISTS OF ACADIANS

The Canadian Genealogy Centre website includes a finding aid to Gaudet's *Notes*, an important starting point for research. Placide Gaudet was an employee of the Canadian Archives who took a particular interest in Acadian families. The finding aid summarizes all his notes, made over many years, about Acadians prior to 1755. Most of his sources are in the Library and Archives Canada collections, but some are housed in the United States, France, and the United Kingdom.

Bona Arsenault's *Histoire & Généalogie des Acadiens* (1965) is a useful compilation, available on microfilm and in print. You should also consult *Le grand arrangement des Acadiens au Québec: notes de petite histoire, généalogies: France, Acadie, Québec de 1625 à 1925* (Bergeron, 8 vols., 1981).

An ongoing work, and generally regarded as the best, is the *Dictionnaire Genealogique des Familles Acadiennes* by Stephen White (1999). The first part, in two volumes, covers the years from 1636 to 1714, using the date of marriage as the basis for inclusion. The work is in French, but an English supplement was published giving full translations of the supplementary text (though not the family histories) and of the bibliography.

CENSUS RECORDS

There is no shortage of censuses of the Acadian population. Charts and summaries appear in *French-Canadian Sources: A Guide for Genealogists* (Geyh et al., 2002). You can find many indexes and transcripts at Acadian GenWeb and Acadian-Cajun Genealogy. Also, resources specific to New Brunswick, Nova Scotia, and Prince Edward Island can be found at their GenWeb pages. Look also for websites of historical societies in areas of Acadian settlement. For example, the Kings Historical Society in Kentville, Nova Scotia, includes on its website a surname index to Acadians in early records at Grand Pré.

Heads of families were recorded on several occasions for Île Saint-Jean and Île Royale between 1713 and 1735. Nominal returns, naming everyone, were done in 1749 (Île Royale) and 1752 (Île Saint-Jean). Transcriptions of most of the Île Saint-Jean returns are online at the Island Register website.

The modern compilation *The Atlantic Canadians* (Elliot, 1994) includes entries for Acadians extracted from some eighteenth-century census records and secondary sources. This series first appeared in print and is now available at Ancestry.

The Family History Library (FHL) has microfilm copies of the census records held by archives in Paris and copies of published transcripts as well. The Centre for Acadian Studies (Centres d'études acadiennes) at the University of Moncton has collected together all census-type lists from earliest times to the first census of Canada in 1871.

CHURCH RECORDS

Surviving parish registers for Acadia are few in number. There are none for the period before 1700 and few between that date and 1755. Parishes that have surviving records include St. Jean-Baptiste Annapolis Royal, Beaubassin, and Grand Pré. Those for the parish of St. Jean-Baptiste Annapolis Royal are the most valuable because the parish was an important center, and the detailed entries cover more than fifty years, 1702–1755. The two volumes are available online at the NSARM site as fully searchable images. There are more than 3,500 entries; about 70 percent are christenings.

Check the Drouin Collection, which is now being added to the Canadian databases at Ancestry. There is a collection of Acadian French Catholic Church Registers, 1670–1946, within Drouin, and images can be browsed; indexes to personal names will be added soon.

Other online resources are either indexes or transcripts. You can locate these using the GenWeb and Acadian-Cajun websites.

Microfilm copies and/or published transcripts (not all collections are complete) can be found in several locations, among them the Center for Acadian Studies at Moncton, Centre d'archives de la Capitale in Quebec City, NSARM, and the FHL.

Acadian Church Records (1964) consists of five volumes of miscellaneous christenings, marriages, and burial records put together by Winston De Ville and others from records of churches and missions in Acadia, New Brunswick, and Gaspé. It is available on microfiche at the FHL.

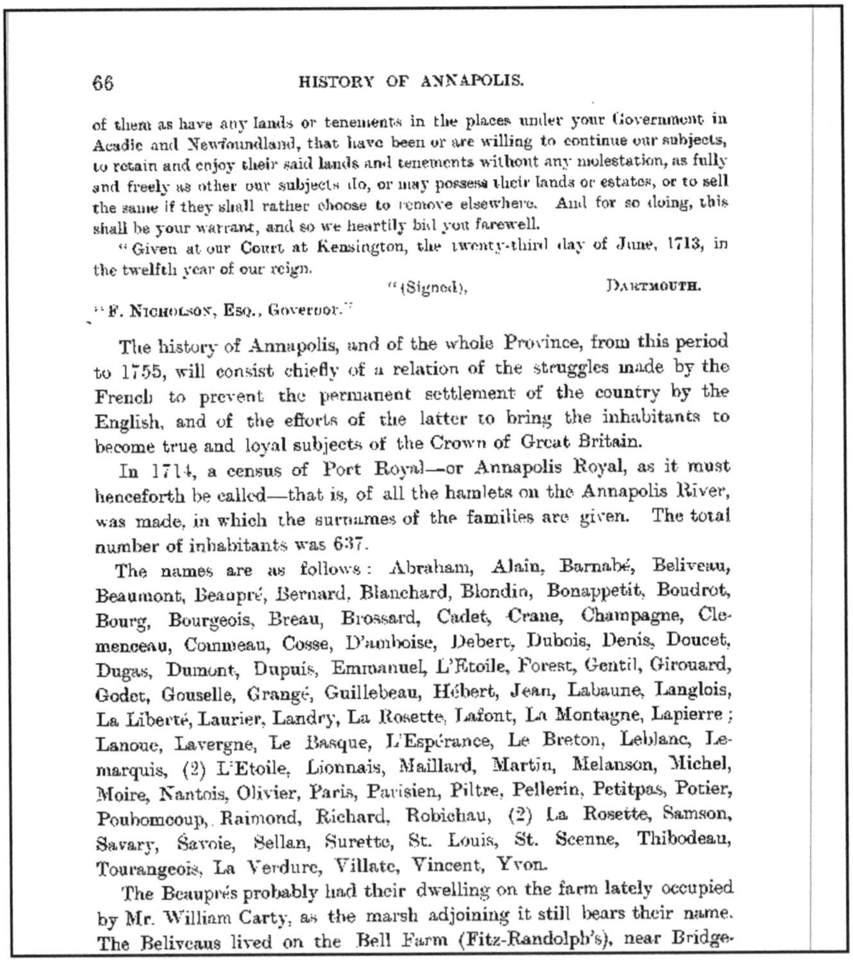

> 66   HISTORY OF ANNAPOLIS.
>
> of them as have any lands or tenements in the places under your Government in Acadie and Newfoundland, that have been or are willing to continue our subjects, to retain and enjoy their said lands and tenements without any molestation, as fully and freely as other our subjects do, or may possess their lands or estates, or to sell the same if they shall rather choose to remove elsewhere. And for so doing, this shall be your warrant, and so we heartily bid you farewell.
>
> "Given at our Court at Kensington, the twenty-third day of June, 1713, in the twelfth year of our reign.
>
>   "(Signed),   DARTMOUTH.
>
> " F. NICHOLSON, ESQ., Governor."
>
> The history of Annapolis, and of the whole Province, from this period to 1755, will consist chiefly of a relation of the struggles made by the French to prevent the permanent settlement of the country by the English, and of the efforts of the latter to bring the inhabitants to become true and loyal subjects of the Crown of Great Britain.
>
> In 1714, a census of Port Royal—or Annapolis Royal, as it must henceforth be called—that is, of all the hamlets on the Annapolis River, was made, in which the surnames of the families are given. The total number of inhabitants was 637.
>
> The names are as follows: Abraham, Alain, Barnabé, Beliveau, Beaumont, Beaupré, Bernard, Blanchard, Blondin, Bonappetit, Boudrot, Bourg, Bourgeois, Breau, Brossard, Cadet, Crane, Champagne, Clemenceau, Comneau, Cosse, D'amboise, Debert, Dubois, Denis, Doucet, Dugas, Dumont, Dupuis, Emmanuel, L'Etoile, Forest, Gentil, Girouard, Godet, Gouselle, Grangé, Guillebeau, Hébert, Jean, Labaune, Langlois, La Liberté, Laurier, Landry, La Rosette, Lafont, La Montagne, Lapierre; Lanoue, Lavergne, Le Basque, L'Espérance, Le Breton, Leblanc, Lemarquis, (2) L'Etoile, Lionnais, Maillard, Martin, Melanson, Michel, Moire, Nantois, Olivier, Paris, Parisien, Piltre, Pellerin, Petitpas, Potier, Pouhomcoup, Raimond, Richard, Robichau, (2) La Rosette, Samson, Savary, Savoie, Sellan, Surette, St. Louis, St. Scenne, Thibodeau, Tourangeois, La Verdure, Villate, Vincent, Yvon.
>
> The Beauprés probably had their dwelling on the farm lately occupied by Mr. William Carty, as the marsh adjoining it still bears their name. The Beliveaus lived on the Bell Farm (Fitz-Randolph's), near Bridge-

Figure 14-2. Families at Annapolis Royal in 1714

Names in the early census lists of Acadia are found in several places on- and offline, including the pages of history books. History of the county of Annapolis including old Port Royal and Acadia *(Calnek, 1897) is among the titles in the Local and Family Histories at Ancestry.*

NOTARIAL RECORDS

Notarial records contain anything that had to be legally registered. They include vital records, land transactions, marriage contracts, business contracts, leases, settlements to civil disputes, bequests, and wills and inventories.

Surviving notarial records for Acadia are available at the Center for Acadian Studies, Library and Archives Canada, and the FHL. Île Royale is better represented in these. *The Loppinot Papers, 1687–1710: Genealogical Abstracts of the Earliest Notarial Records for the Province of Acadia* (DeVille, 1991) contains abstracts created at the time.

It could be worthwhile to check notarial records for Quebec, as some Acadians used legal services there. Quebec notarial record finding aids are part of the Drouin

Collection within Ancestry's Canadian databases. Images are available now for searching by the name of the notary and for browsing; indexes will be added later.

OTHER RESOURCES

The Nova Scotia Legislative Library and NSARM offer several interesting online resources. There is a guide to The Évangéline Collection: Commemorating 400 Years of Acadian Settlement, which is held by the Legislative Library. At the NSARM website are two special exhibits within a feature titled Acadian Heartland.

The first is the Records of the Deportation and Le Grand Dérangement, 1714–1768. This is a digitized and fully searchable resource made up of primary-source documents relating to the deportation of the Acadians.

Also at Acadian Heartland are the Records of British Government at Annapolis Royal, 1713–1749. Minutes of council meetings and a detailed finding aid to letter books were selected for this resource. These were the earliest records of the British government in Nova Scotia. Digitized, with full search capability, they mention individual and family names and convey details of daily life, weather, economic activity, and justice.

Another online resource is at the Centre acadien de l'Université de Sainte-Anne. This is a database of information contained in the genealogies of seventy-four Acadian families. There are nearly 150,000 entries, and the information focuses on families whose present-day descendants live in Digby and Yarmouth counties in Nova Scotia.

WEBSITES

Acadian Cultural Society: <www.acadiancultural.org>
Acadian Museum and Archives:

American Canadian Genealogical Society:
    <www.acgs.org>
Ancestry.ca (for Drouin Collection and Canadian Genealogy Index): <www.ancestry.ca>
Canada GenWeb Acadian section: <www.geocities.com/Heartland/Acres/2162/>
Centre Acadien, Université de Ste anne:
    <http://centreacadien.usainteanne.ca>
Centres d'études acadiennes: <www.umoncton.ca/etudeacadiennes/centre/cea.html>
Halifax Public Libraries Acadian resources:
    <www.halifaxpubliclibraries.ca/infodesk/acadian.html>

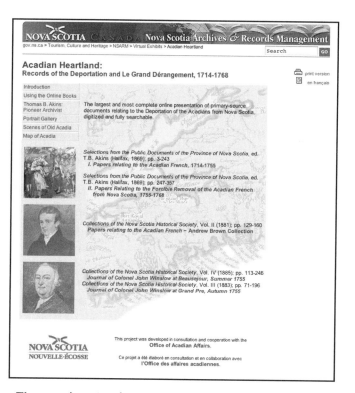

Figure 14-3. Acadian Records Online at Nova Scotia Archives and Records Management
The books and documents can be searched using keywords or phrases.
<http://www.gov.ns.ca/nsarm/virtual/deportation/>

Kings County Museum, Kentville, Nova Scotia:
Library and Archives Canada: <www.collectionscanada.ca>
Nova Scotia Archives and Records Management, Genealogical Research:NS Legislative Library (The Évangéline Collection): <www.gov.ns.ca/legislature/
    LIBRARY/digitalcollection/home.stm>
Our Roots: <www.ourroots.ca>
The Island Register (Prince Edward Island): <www.islandregister.com>

BIBLIOGRAPHY

Arsenault, Bona. *Histoire et généalogie des Acadiens.* 6 vols. 2nd ed. Montreal:
    Leméac, 1978.

Arsenault, Georges. *Historical Guidebook of the Evangeline Region.* Charlottetown,
    PEI: Ragweed Press, 1998.

———. *The Island Acadians.* Charlottetown, PEI: Ragweed Press, 1999.

Bergeron, Adrien. *Le grand arrangement des Acadiens au Québec: notes de petite
    histoire, généalogies: France, Acadie, Québec de 1625 à 1925.* 8 vols. Montreal:
    Éditions Élysée, 1981.

Calnek, W. A. *History of the county of Annapolis: including old Port Royal and Acadia,
    with memoirs of its representatives in the provincial parliament, and biographical
    and genealogical sketches of its early English settlers and their families; edited
    and completed by A. W. Savary.* Toronto: W. Briggs; Montreal: C.W. Coates;
    Halifax, N.S.: S.F. Huestis; London: Phillimore, 1897. (Reprinted Belleville,
    ON: Mika Publishing, 1973.

De Ville, Winston, trans. and comp. *Acadian church records: 1679–1757: being a
    compilation of miscellaneous baptismal, marriage, and funeral records ...* New
    Orleans: Polyanthos, 1975–<1984 >, c1964– , v. < 1–5 >; Reprint. Originally
    published: Mobile, AL.: W. De Ville, 1964.

De Ville, Winston, Milton P. Rieder, Norma G. Rieder, and David M. Rieder.
    Acadian Church Records. 5 vols. Mobile, AL: Winston De Ville, 1964. (also
    on microfiche, Family History Library)

Elliot, Noel M. *The Atlantic Canadians, 1600–1900: An Alphabetized Directory
    of the People, Places, and Vital Dates.* Toronto: Genealogical Research Library,
    1994. (part of the Canadian Genealogy Index 1600s to 1900s at Ancestry)

Gaudet, Placide. *Acadian Genealogy and Notes,* in *Report Concerning Canadian
    Archives for the Year 1905.* Ottawa: S.E. Dawson, 1906. (contains Gaudet's
    Notes, oaths of allegiance, and Île Saint-Jean census of 1752)

Geyh, Patricia Keeney, et al. *French-Canadian Sources: A Guide for Genealogists.*
    Orem, UT: Ancestry, 2002.

Griffiths, Naomi E. S. *The Contexts of Acadian History, 1686–1784.* Montreal:
    Published for the Centre for Canadian Studies, Mount Allison University by
    McGill-Queen's University Press, 1992.

Hebert, Timothy. *Acadian-Cajun Genealogy: Step by Step.* Lafayette, LA: Center for Louisiana Studies, 1993.

Jobb, Dean. *The Acadians: A People's Story of Exile and Triumph.* Mississauga, ON: John Wiley and Sons, 2005.

Kings County Historical Society. *Acadian Census, 1671–1758, and Acadie and Gaspésie, 1680–1757, Church Records.* Kentville, NS: Kings Historical Society, 2004. (CD-ROM)

Quintin, Robert J. *The "Dit" Name: French-Canadian Surnames—Aliases, Adulterations, and Anglicizations.* Pawtucket, RI: Quintin Publications, 1993.

Trahan, Charles C. *Acadian Census, 1671–1752.* Rayne, LA: Hebert Publications, 1994.

White, Stephen A., Brenda Dunn. *Patronymes acadiens/Acadian family names.* Moncton, NB: Éditions d'Acadie, 1992.

White, Stephen A., Hector-J. Hébert, Patrice Gallant. *Dictionnaire généalogique des familles acadiennes, "Première partie 1636 à 1714 en deux volumes."* Moncton, NB: Centre d'études acadiennes, Université de Moncton, 1999.

———. *English Supplement to the Dictionnaire généalogique des familles acadiennes.* Moncton, NB: Centre d'études acadiennes, Université de Moncton, 2000. (a complete translation of the introductory material, the bibliography, and the notes to the genealogies but not the genealogies themselves)

ADDRESSES

Acadian Cultural Society
PO Box 2304
Fitchburg, MA 01420

Acadian Museum and Archives
(#898 Highway 335)
PO Box 92
West Pubnico, Yarmouth County, NS B0W 3S0

American-Canadian Genealogical Society
PO Box 6478
Manchester, NH 03108-6478

Centre Acadien, Université de Ste anne
Université Sainte-Anne
Pointe-de-l'Église, NS B0W 1M0

Centres d'études acadiennes
Université de Moncton
Moncton, NB E1A 3E9
Halifax Public Library

Spring Garden Road Memorial Public Library
5381 Spring Garden Road
Halifax, NS B3J 1E9

The Kings Historical Society
c/o The Kings County Museum
37 Cornwallis Street
Kentville, NS B4N 2E2

The Legislative Library
2nd Floor, Province House
1726 Hollis Street
Halifax, NS B3J 2P8

Nova Scotia Archives & Records Management
6016 University Avenue
Halifax, NS B3H 1W4

THE LOYALISTS

A Loyalist was someone who resided in the American colonies in 1775 and served the British cause during the Revolutionary War. Most were of English background, but others came from all parts of the British Isles. Some descended from Dutch settlers and French Huguenots. Loyalists also included native peoples and blacks.

Other groups, such as German mercenary soldiers and pacifist Quakers, came at the same time but were not officially regarded as Loyalist refugees. In addition, some were "late Loyalists," who came later in response to relaxed qualifications for land grants and to escape continuing harsh treatment in the United States.

More than 70,000 Loyalists fled the American Colonies, and about 50,000 went to Nova Scotia and Quebec. The inflow of people was so great it prompted the subdivision of these colonies. New Brunswick, lying on the north side of the Bay of Fundy, was created from Nova Scotia because British authorities wanted to create a self-contained administrative unit for Loyalists. Upper Canada incorporated the western parts of Quebec, where large areas were set aside for settlement. Being some distance from the colony's capital, it needed its own government.

Sometimes soldiers of army units were disbanded together and granted adjacent lands. About 20,000 Loyalists had served in special volunteer forces, and many thousands of these received land grants. All Loyalists were entitled to compensation according to their service and their family needs.

Main routes of migration were by sea to Shelbourne and Halifax and overland following the waterways via Lake Champlain and the Richelieu River to Sorel in Quebec, which was one of several camps for refugees.

The new British North America forming within the two colonies of Nova Scotia and Quebec was profoundly influenced by this in-migration. British authorities faced a monumental task in resettling the refugees, and inhabitants of already settled areas were overwhelmed. Future attitudes toward America were forged by the experience.

In gratitude for their loyalty, Lord Dorchester, Governor of Quebec, granted Loyalists and their descendents, both male and female, the honor of putting the letters U.E. after their names to signify that they had supported the unity of the empire. One hundred years later this led to the formation of the United Empire Loyalists' Association, an organization that has done a great deal to preserve and collect records.

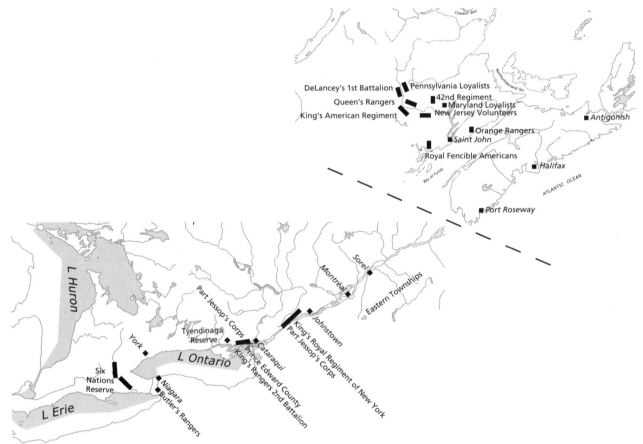

Figure 15-1. Some Regions of Loyalist Settlement (locations are approximate)

LOYALIST RESEARCH

Regardless of family traditions, take your research back through nineteenth-century records before getting deeply into Loyalist records. When your research has included all available census returns after 1840, that is a sensible point to review secondary sources—collected summaries of family histories such as *Loyalist Lineages of Canada, 1783–1983* (1983 and 1991) and volumes of local history, many of which relate family stories.

The most informative primary sources are land grants, military service records, returns of disbanded troops, compensation for losses papers, and early church records.

LISTS OF LOYALISTS

The authorities maintained lists of those entitled to assistance. These lists were revised from time to time, usually with some level of controversy from Loyalists or their descendants. The best known is *The Old United Empire Loyalists List*, which first appeared in 1885 as *The Centennial of the Settlement of Upper Canada by the United Empire Loyalists, 1785–1884*. It has appeared in books and reprints and is within the databases at Ancestry.

Other published lists include *The Loyalists in Ontario: The Sons and Daughters of the American Loyalists of Upper Canada* (Reid, 1973); *The Loyalists of Quebec, 1774–1825* (1989); and a collection of lists in *Names and Families from the Haldimand Papers* (Fitzgerald, 1984). Examples for the Maritime Provinces are *Loyalists and Land Settlement in Nova Scotia* (Gilroy, 1937) and *The Loyalists of New Brunswick* (Wright, 1955).

You may find other facts in these lists, such as the military unit, place of residence, and home in the thirteen colonies. Some include a reference to original records, and some are limited in scope, perhaps to one township or a disbanded regiment.

In addition to Ancestry, consult GenWeb sites and use a search engine. At GenWeb look at Canadian and U.S. sites; for example, Herkimer County, New York, includes Loyalist information. Cyndi's List has a topic specifically for Loyalists. Check the Family History Library Catalog (FHLC) for references to lists mentioned here and to browse for others.

FINDING HISTORY

You can begin reading about Loyalists in the Web version of the *Canadian Encyclopedia*. If your ancestors served under a famous commander such as John Butler or traveled with a prominent local leader such as Peter Van Alstine, look for those names in the *Dictionary of Canadian Biography*, online at Library and Archives Canada (LAC).

A place of settlement can also get you started. Check for county and township histories as full-text books online and in library catalogs. Our Roots is a good place to check for books, and *Early Settlement in Upper Canada* (Canniff, 1869) is at Ancestry. The LAC search tool AMICUS searches not only the national book collection but also the catalogs of other Canadian libraries. AMICUS and the FHLC will turn up even more titles.

LAND RECORDS

The lands designated for settlement in Nova Scotia and Quebec had to be surveyed. Sir Frederick Haldimand, governor and commander-in-chief at Quebec, estimated he needed twenty-one townships, each one of about 21,000 acres. He appointed Major Samuel Holland to oversee the survey; much of the work was done by former Loyalist soldiers.

Officials in London sent directions about land distribution. For every family member there was a grant of fifty acres, but amounts for heads of households were granted according to a scale. Heads of families or discharged private soldiers received

EASTERN TOWNSHIPS. 45

of a large and growing family were pressing, and, in connection with their heavy losses, caused serious embarrassment.

For one whole year after their return to Hinesburg, theirs was the only family in the town; their nearest neighbours on the one hand being at Burlington, ten miles, and on the other hand at Monkton, seven miles distant. After an ineffectual struggle of eleven years to rise above the depressing influences that seemed combined against them, Mr. Lawrence gave up thought of remaining there, and, at this juncture, having heard from a reliable source of the generous offers the British Government was ... settlement of Ca... there, it seeming ... in behalf of his ri... of availing himse... the country in 17... in Shefford, to w... following winter. ... ing two daughter... at this time only ... and three sons, ... the sons subsequ...

As has alrea... interests had be... of his first atte... of Vermont, so ... undertaken his ...

Library and Archives Canada — Bibliothèque et Archives Canada — Canada

Français | Contact Us | Help | Search | Canada Site
Library and Archives Canada | Université Laval | University of Toronto | Links
You are here: Home | Search Results | Biography Display

DICTIONARY OF CANADIAN BIOGRAPHY ONLINE

Show printable page

GRASS, MICHAEL, office holder; b. *c.* 1735 in Strasbourg, France; m. first Mary Ann – ; m. secondly Margaret Swartz, and they had at least six children; d. 25 April 1813 in Kingston, Upper Canada.

Michael Grass was part of the considerable emigration of Palatinate Germans to North America in the 18th century. He arrived on 22 Sept. 1752 at Philadelphia, Pa, where he remained for a while, earning his living as a saddler. He subsequently moved to Tryon County, N.Y., where lie operated a saddlery in addition to farming and thereby achieved a modest prosperity. A captain in the local militia, he refused to join the rebels after the outbreak of the American revolution. In 1777 he fled to New York City where he served as a lieutenant in the volunteer militia.

Grass's historical reputation derives from his connection with the settlement of loyalists at Cataraqui (Kingston, Ont.) after the revolution. Family tradition and popular lore accord him the position of founder. These accounts maintain that he had been a prisoner at the old French Fort Frontenac (Cataraqui) during the Seven Years' War, and thus, towards the end of the revolution, when the British commandant at New York City, Sir Guy CARLETON, asked him about the area he was in a position to recommend it. Grass may have had some familiarity with Cataraqui; there is, however, no evidence to corroborate this version of the settlement's founding.

A more plausible account is as follows. On 26 May 1783 Governor HALDIMAND ordered Surveyor General Samuel Johannes HOLLAND to Cataraqui to consider "the facility of establishing a settlement" there. Two months later, Major John Ross* was ordered to prepare the site for a military post. In the mean time, numbers of loyalist refugees, including Grass, were awaiting evacuation from New York City to Nova Scotia; on 12 June Grass had written on behalf of a group of them that "we cannot think of going to another place in the Universe for the many Benefits that will flow from that Settlement [Cataraqui] to the Settler." On 2 July he was given a temporary commission of captain for the second of the eight companies organized for transportation to Quebec. This group, many of whom were Associated Loyalists, probably numbered fewer than 500. Grass's transport *Camel* was the first of nine to reach Quebec, arriving there on 12 August. Three days later, Haldimand's military secretary, Robert MATHEWS, indicated to Ross the governor's intention to settle many of the New York exiles in the neighbourhood of Cataraqui. The actual decision, however, was not made until Haldimand had received reports indicating the suitability of the area for farming. In early September, while most of the New York loyalists prepared to winter at Sorel, Grass and 37 men ascended the St Lawrence River with a survey party to mark out the settlements at Cataraqui. When he returned to Sorel in late fall he found there another company from New York led by Major Peter Van Alstine. The presence of a new group led to jealousy and factionalism; Grass and several other captains complained of persons who "Presume to Place themselves at our head without our consent or Approbation."

In January 1784 Grass and others petitioned Haldimand for large-scale assistance in setting up their farms. They also indicated their preference for a "Form of Government . . . similar to that which they Enjoyed in the Province of New York in the year of 1763." Haldimand informed them that their requests were impossible to meet and reminded them that if they were not happy with his plans he could provide them passage to Nova Scotia. Several months later the governor was angered by Grass's seeming claim on behalf of himself and his

---

Figure 15-2. There Are Many Places to Look Online for Biography and History

Check for people and place-names whenever possible.

Top: From *Pioneers of the Eastern Townships*, available at Ancestry.ca.

Bottom: <http://www.biographi.ca/EN/ShowBio.asp?BioId=36552&query=grass>

one hundred acres. Discharged noncommissioned officers received two hundred acres. Field officers were awarded one thousand acres, captains received seven hundred acres, and other lower-ranking officers got five hundred acres each.

The colony of Quebec was not split into Upper and Lower Canada until 1791, and as a result, land records made prior to that date in Upper Canada are among those for Quebec/Lower Canada. In Nova Scotia the split to create the colony of New Brunswick happened earlier, in 1784. Some early Loyalist records may be found among those for Nova Scotia, but there will also be a second grant in New Brunswick.

Most interesting among land documents are the petitions for grants or leases of land because of what they reveal about individuals and families. They contain a petitioner's reasons for needing land and details of his service to the Crown. Family members are often mentioned, as well as details of life before the Revolution and a summary of military service. Petitions from sons and daughters of Loyalists include the name of the father and perhaps some facts about him. Land petitions for Upper and Lower Canada are held by LAC, but records for the Maritimes are in provincial archives. Consult the appropriate provincial chapter for additional information.

You may want to take a further step and look for the oaths of allegiance taken by those who received a land grant. When a record of the oath was made, the occupation, place of residence, and place of origin were recorded. These are preserved with the land petition records; they are not indexed.

MILITARY RECORDS

The British forces during the Revolutionary War were made up of regular army regiments, units of German mercenary soldiers, and Loyalist militia corps. Nearly 20,000 Loyalists served in such forces as the New Jersey Volunteers, the Queen's Rangers, and the King's American Volunteers.

The British military authorities kept track of soldiers on muster rolls and pay lists, organized by regiment. Muster rolls were lists of soldiers within regiments taken at regular intervals and were used to create pay lists. When a man's name dropped off the list, a reason was usually recorded, such as killed, transferred to duty elsewhere, or deserted. All regular British army units mustered, but this was not true for every volunteer Loyalist unit.

Of the existing Loyalist muster rolls, over half are at LAC, divided between two collections: the Ward Chipman Papers (regiments disbanded in NB) and the "C" Series of Record Group 8. The filmed records of Loyalist Militia 1775 to 1783 are actually copies of records in the United Kingdom. There are finding aids to the records, including a detailed database for the Ward Chipman Papers, at the LAC website.

Microfilm copies of muster rolls can be consulted through Family History Centers and some other Canadian archives, such as the Archives of Ontario. There are also records in the Loyalist Collection at the Harriett Irving Library, University of New Brunswick.

The Haldimand Papers, which are also in the UK, contain several muster rolls, including local militia units. The documents are available on microfilm at LAC, at the

FHL, and at the Archives of Ontario. *Loyalist Lists: Over 2,000 Names and Families from the Haldimand Papers* (Fitzgerald, 1984) is a partial index.

The Online Institute for Advanced Loyalist Studies has created a list that guides users to some muster rolls available on the Web, along with details such as where a unit was raised and the name of the commanding officer. It does not claim to be complete, but it makes a good starting point. Check Ancestry, which has some miscellaneous military lists in Loyalists in the American Revolution; refer to provincial GenWeb pages; and browse the Loyalist information at the Olive Tree Genealogy website.

If you know a regiment, studying the history of that unit can help you learn other things about an ancestor, such as where the man may have lived before the Revolution and where he took up residence in British North America. Without a regiment's name, see what you can learn from working in the other direction, searching for which regiments were disbanded near where the ancestor settled.

CLAIMS FOR LOSSES

The British government promised to compensate Loyalists for their losses, and from 1783 to 1786 a claims commission heard evidence. However, not many made claims because the Loyalist or an agent had to appear before the commission in Halifax, Saint John, Quebec, Montreal, or London. Those whose claims were upheld were entitled to a pension and other forms of assistance.

Original records of the commission are in the papers of the Audit Office at The National Archives in the UK. You may find the evidence of witnesses, supporting documents, and the memorials (petitions or applications) of those requesting compensation. Information is likely to include names, former places of residence, size of family, sometimes names of dependents, military service, residence at time of claim, and a summary of what was lost. There are also official transcripts of the hearings. Audit Office records have been microfilmed and are readily available in Canadian archives and libraries and the FHL. Some are in the Library of Congress.

The Second Report of the Bureau of Archives of Ontario for 1904 (Fraser, 1905) contains a transcript of evidence presented to the commissioners, but it leaves out any evidence they rejected. The report is indexed and available at Ancestry, where its database heading is United Empire Loyalists, Parts I–II. It is also on film at the FHL. Another publication, *Loyalist Settlements, 1783–1789: More Evidence of Canadian Loyalist Claims* (Antliff, 1985), contains the evidence left out of the *Report*.

CHURCH RECORDS

Registers of christenings, marriages, and burials may survive from an early date in Loyalist settlements. Detailed histories have been written of many early churches.

Loyalists belonged to many religions, not just the Church of England. There were Moravians, Presbyterians, Calvinists, and Lutherans among them. Books such as *The Trail of the Black Walnut* (Reaman, 1957) have been written about particular religious groups.

Provincial chapters in the second part of this book explain how to search for church records.

COLLECTIONS OF PAPERS

The Harriet Irving Library at the University of New Brunswick in Fredericton has a unique collection of Loyalist material. It includes microfilm copies of British, North American colonial, and early Canadian primary sources from approximately 1760 to 1867. The online inventory of sources is detailed, containing personal and place-names, regimental names, and lots of historical background.

The Winslow Papers are in the same library. They have been digitized and can be viewed online. Edward Winslow was a witness to events of the Revolution and the Loyalist settlement of New Brunswick. The website includes images of the collection and informative articles on the flight of the Loyalists, partition of Nova Scotia, and the Black Loyalists.

WEBSITES

> AMICUS: <http://amicus.collectionscanada.ca/aaweb/aalogine.htm>
> Ancestry: <www.ancestry.ca>
> Archives of Ontario:
> CanadaGenWeb:
> <www.rootsweb.com/~canwgw/>
> Cyndi's List: <www.cyndislist.com/loyalist.htm>
> FamilySearch: <www.familysearch.org>
> Herkimer County at NY GenWeb: <http://www.rootsweb.com/~nyherkim/>
> Library and Archives Canada: <www.collectionscanada.ca>
> Loyalist Collection Harriet Irving Library University of New Brunswick:
> <www.lib.unb.ca/collections/loyalist/>
> Nova Scotia Archives and Records Management: <www.gov.ns.ca/nsarm/>
> Online Institute for Advanced Loyalist Studies: <www.royalprovincial.com/military/musters/musters.htm>
> Prince Edward Island Public Archives and Records Office:
> <www.edu.pe.ca/paro/>
> Provincial Archives of New Brunswick: <http://archives.gnb.ca/Archives/Default.aspx?L=EN>
> United Empire Loyalists' Association of Canada:
> Winslow Papers: <www.lib.unb.ca/winslow/index.html>

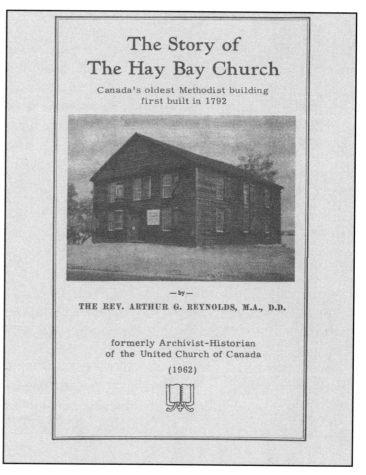

Figure 15-3. A Printed Church History
The Story of Hay Bay Church *includes the names of the first trustees and those who contributed to the building costs.*

BIBLIOGRAPHY

Antliff, W. Bruce. *Loyalist Settlements, 1783–1789: More Evidence of Canadian Loyalist Claims.* Toronto: Ministry of Citizenship and Culture, 1985.

Bunnell, Paul J. *Research Guide to Loyalist Ancestors: A Directory to Archives, Manuscripts, and Published Sources.* Bowie, MD: Heritage Books, 1990.

Canniff, William. *History of the Settlement of Upper Canada, with Special Reference to the Bay of Quinte.* Toronto: Dudley & Burns, 1869. (also at Ancestry.ca)

Chadwick, Edward M. *Ontarian Families: Genealogies of United Empire Loyalist and Other Pioneer Families of Upper Canada.* Toronto: Rolph, Smith & Co., 1894–98. (reprinted 1972 and 2001)

Coldham, Peter W. *American Loyalist Claims Abstracted from the Public Record Office, Audit Office Series 13, bundles 1–35 & 37.* Washington, D.C.: National Genealogical Society, 1980.

———. *American Migrations, 1765–1799: The Lives, Times, and Families of Colonial Americans Who Remained Loyal to the British Crown before, during, and after the Revolutionary War.* Baltimore: Genealogical Publishing Co., 2000.

Dubeau, Sharon. *New Brunswick Loyalists, a Bicentennial Tribute.* Agincourt, ON: Generation Press, 1983.

Fitzgerald, E. Keith. *Loyalist Lists: Over 2,000 Names and Families from the Haldimand Papers.* Toronto: Ontario Genealogical Society, 1984.

Fraser, Alexander. *Second Report of the Bureau of Archives for the Province of Ontario, 1904.* Toronto: L. K. Cameron, 1905. (also at Ancestry)

Fryer, Mary Beacock. *King's Men: The Soldier Founders of Ontario.* Toronto: Dundurn Press, 1980.

Gilroy, Marion, with D. C. Harvey. *Loyalists and Land Settlement in Nova Scotia.* Halifax: Public Archives of Nova Scotia, 1937. (reprinted many times)

Merriman, Brenda Dougall. *United Empire Loyalists: A Guide to Tracing Loyalist Ancestors in Upper Canada.* Toronto: Global, 2006.

Metz, Helmut. *The Hessians of Nova Scotia.* Hamilton, ON: German Canadian Historical Book Pub., 1994. (similar volumes on Upper Canada and Quebec published in 1997 and 2001)

Morgan, Lynn (ed.), and Toronto Branch, United Empire Loyalists' Association of Canada. *Loyalist Lineages of Canada, 1783–1983.* Agincourt, ON: Generation Press, 1984.

Rees, Ronald. *Land of the Loyalists: Their Struggle to Shape the Maritimes.* Halifax: Nimbus, 2000.

Palmer, Gregory. *A Bibliography of Loyalist Source Material in the United States, Canada, and Great Britain.* Westport, CT, and London: Meckler Publishing and the American Antiquarian Society, 1982.

Reaman, George E. *The Trail of the Black Walnut.* Scottdale, PA: Herald Press, 1957.

Reid, William D. *The Loyalists in Ontario: The Sons and Daughters of the American Loyalists of Upper Canada.* Lambertville, NJ: Hunterdon House, 1973.

Sabine, Lorenzo. *Biographical Sketches of Loyalists in the American Revolution*. Baltimore: Genealogical Publishing Company, 1979. Originally published 1864.

United Empire Loyalists' Association of Canada. Heritage Branch—Montreal. *The Loyalists of Quebec, 1774–1825: A Forgotten History.* Montreal: Price-Patterson, 1989.

Wilson, Bruce. *As She Began: An Illustrated Introduction to Loyalist Ontario.* Toronto: Dundurn Press, 1981.

Wright, Esther Clark. *The Loyalists of New Brunswick*. Fredericton, NB: 1955.

ADDRESSES

Archives of Ontario
77 Grenville Street, Unit 300
Toronto, ON M5S 1B3

Library and Archives Canada
395 Wellington Street
Ottawa, ON K1A 0N4

Nova Scotia Archives & Records Management
6016 University Avenue
Halifax, NS B3H 1W4

Prince Edward Island Public Archives and Record Office
Hon. George Coles Building
Richmond Street
PO Box 1000
Charlottetown, PE C1A 7M4

Provincial Archives of New Brunswick
Department of Supply and Services
Provincial Archives (Bonar Law—Bennet Building)
PO Box 6000
Fredericton, NB E3B 5H1

United Empire Loyalist Association of Canada
50 Baldwin Street, Suite 202
Toronto, ON M5T 1L4

University of New Brunswick, Fredericton
PO Box 4400
Fredericton, NB E3B 5A3

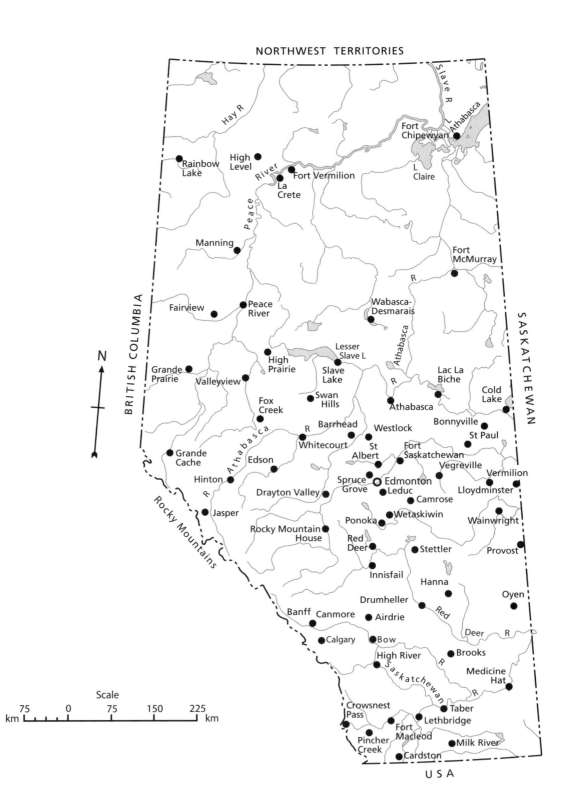

Figure 16-1. Alberta

ALBERTA

Other than fur traders and explorers, Alberta saw little European activity until the 1870s. Fort Calgary and Fort Macleod were founded by the North-West Mounted Police in that decade, and in 1882 the District of Alberta was created as part of the Northwest Territories. The district included Lethbridge, Calgary, and Edmonton but not Medicine Hat. It was much smaller than the modern province.

The Canadian Pacific Railway was completed in 1885, opening a regular transportation route to and from Alberta. The 1901 census recorded 73,022 people in Alberta, many of them working in mines or living on farms.

The following decade brought a dramatic increase in population, and the 1911 census recorded 374,295 people in Alberta. Even though the First World War brought a halt to immigration for five years, Alberta's population rose to 588,454 by 1921.

Alberta became a province in 1905. To create the province, the federal government took the old electoral district of Alberta and added the western part of Assiniboia West (including Medicine Hat) as well as part of the Athabasca District north of Edmonton.

The province provided a new opportunity to people from other Canadian provinces, the British Isles, continental Europe, and Asia. By the 1936 census, the most common birthplace for Albertans born outside the province was England, followed by the United States, Ireland, and Ontario.

After its late start, Alberta wasted no time catching up with the rest of the West. In the 1930s its population passed that of Manitoba, and in the 1940s it passed Saskatchewan as well. Today it has about 3 million people, with 2 million of them living in or near the two largest cities, Calgary and Edmonton. Its oil and gas industry has made it a leading economic force in Canada.

FINDING LOCALITIES

The late settlement of Alberta means there has been less time for name changes, so it is generally easy to find villages, towns, and cities. Some of the names have been changed, of course, but between the Canadian Geographical Names website and contemporary directories, most of the puzzles can be solved.

Several books listing Alberta's villages, towns, and cities have been published. The most comprehensive is *Over 2,000 Place Names of Alberta* (Holmgren, 1981).

Alberta has an extensive system of counties and municipal districts, but their boundaries are of little significance; most records helpful to family historians are province-wide. The landowner maps, published on a county-by-county basis, are an exception. They show rural areas in detail, including the names of the owners of farms.

The boundaries and names of Alberta's provincial and federal electoral districts have been changed many times, reflecting the province's rapid development in the twentieth century. These boundaries are used in census returns and voters lists, and you may have to check them carefully.

CENSUS

Every major federal census of Alberta open to researchers has been indexed. The province was included in the federal censuses of 1881, 1891, and 1901, all compiled using the old districts of the Northwest Territories. Alberta's modern boundaries were first used in the census of the Prairies taken in 1906. Further counts have been done every five years since then.

An index to the 1881 census is on the FamilySearch website. The 1891 census of the Alberta District has been indexed and published in book form by the Regina branch of the Saskatchewan Genealogical Society.

Indexes to the 1901, 1906, and 1911 censuses, and the census pages themselves, are on the Internet. The images without an index are on the Library and Archives Canada (LAC) website. Ancestry and a volunteer site, Automated Genealogy, have indexes, and results to searches are linked to the LAC images. A third index to the 1901 census was compiled by the Edmonton branch of the Alberta Genealogical Society. It is available on the Internet as well as in a series of books.

The Provincial Archives of Alberta and the large public libraries in Alberta have almost-complete collections of census microfilm. Censuses can also be consulted on microfilm using library and Family History Center loan services.

CIVIL REGISTRATION

Civil registration began in the late 1880s, when Alberta was still part of the Northwest Territories. Not all of the early births, marriages, and deaths were recorded, but there were scores of "late registrations" of events from before the start of the official registration program. Records up to 1905 have been indexed and published in two books, one by the Alberta Genealogical Society and the other by the Documentary Heritage Society of Alberta (now known as the Friends of the Provincial Archives of Alberta Society).

Extensive registers of births, marriages, and deaths, as well as some indexes, are in the Provincial Archives of Alberta in Edmonton. The most recent ones date from the 1980s. To use these sources, you should know the name of the district and—especially in larger communities—the most likely time frame. You will also find some registration documents, but there are tight restrictions on making photocopies. Be warned, however—the collection is not complete.

Any person can obtain from the provincial Vital Statistics department a copy of a birth registration after one hundred years, a marriage after seventy-five years, and a death after fifty years. Only close relatives are allowed to have copies of more recent registrations.

Figure 16-2. Mrs. Laura Gardiner Doing Family Laundry, Porcupine Hills, Alberta, 1896
Photo courtesy of Glenbow Archives (NA-2607-2)

The cost of getting a certificate depends on the length of the search needed to find it, so researchers should have as much information as possible before approaching Vital Statistics.

Divorce records from many districts dating from 1918 to about 1975 will also be found at the Provincial Archives of Alberta. To use these records, you will need to determine which court the couple was most likely to have used. Records are also held in courts throughout Alberta. The provincial archives also has a finding aid, as well as partial indexes to the divorce records.

CHURCH RECORDS

The late start of civil registration in Alberta, and the difficulty in obtaining the records, means many researchers should look for church registers. The earliest ones generally date from the 1870s, although the first missionaries were active in Alberta in 1838.

Anglican Church records from the northern part of the province are at the Provincial Archives in Edmonton, while registers from the southern part are in the University of Calgary Archives.

More than 500 United Church congregations have deposited records in the Alberta and Northwest Conference Archives, housed at the provincial archives. Lutheran records are at the Lutheran Historical Institute in Edmonton. For Roman Catholic registers, contact the church offices in Edmonton, Calgary, or St. Paul.

Some Anglican, Lutheran, Roman Catholic, and United Church registers are held in the provincial archives in Edmonton and the Glenbow Archives in Calgary. Some records are still held by local churches.

The Archives Society of Alberta website includes a searchable database that includes Anglican, United, Lutheran, Baptist, and Mennonite records. Under ANA (Archives Network of Alberta) Database, do a simple search for the name of your church of interest.

CEMETERY RECORDS

Burial records from hundreds of cemeteries throughout Alberta have been recorded by members of the Alberta Family History Society, based in Calgary, and the Edmonton-based Alberta Genealogical Society. Both societies have published them in booklet form. The AFHS has started producing a series of CD-ROMs. The two societies jointly produced a set of twenty-four microfiche that serves as a comprehensive index for deaths in Alberta. An updated version of the index is available at the AGS library in Edmonton.

A database of burials in the city of Edmonton's municipal cemeteries is on the city's website. A similar Internet index is available for Medicine Hat's Hillside Cemetery. Many smaller cemeteries have also been transcribed and placed online. Check the Alberta GenWeb for an up-to-date list.

WILLS AND PROBATE RECORDS

Records from some of Alberta's judicial districts have been transferred to the provincial archives, while other districts have retained them in local courthouses. Files less than thirty years old remain in the custody of the court. There are indexes for some of the deposited records.

Probate records are handled by the Court of Queen's Bench. There are eleven judicial districts, based in Calgary, Drumheller, Edmonton and Hinton, Fort McMurray, Grande Prairie, High Level and Peace River, Lethbridge, Medicine Hat, Red Deer, St. Paul, and Wetaskiwin. The Alberta Courts website has a guide that will help you quickly determine the court location for every community in the province.

LAND RECORDS

The paperwork resulting from property transactions is available through the land titles offices in Calgary and Edmonton. Historic searches are possible; you will need to provide information such as reference title numbers, legal description, and owner's name.

Land records most valuable to genealogists are those created by ancestors who had homesteads. These records often include basic biographical information and sometimes contain clues that could lead to other types of records, such as passenger lists or census returns. Check for your ancestors in homestead indexes even if you've never heard any talk of a homestead in the family. Many people signed up for a free farm but were unable to complete the work required to be granted the title.

Two indexes to Alberta homesteads are on the Internet, and a third is on microfilm at the Provincial Archives of Alberta. The online index compiled by the Alberta

Genealogical Society is the easiest to use and the most comprehensive. It includes people who successfully obtained title to their farms as well as those who did not. Another index, on the LAC website, includes only those people who obtained land grants. Both of these indexes include homesteads up to 1930.

The third index, on microfilm at the provincial archives, has later records. It can be cumbersome to use, as well as tricky; not every index reference will lead to a file. A person had to make a serious effort to farm the land, it seems, before paperwork was generated.

Homestead files are not available through the Family History Library. You will need to go to Edmonton to view the microfilms or contact the Alberta Genealogical Society, which offers a research service.

It's possible your ancestors obtained a farm by buying it directly from the Canadian Pacific Railway (CPR). The Glenbow Archives in Calgary has an online database of land sold by the CPR, which obtained the land as part of its agreement to build a railway across the country.

In Alberta, farmland descriptions end with W4, W5, or W6. The fourth meridian is the Alberta-Saskatchewan border, and the fifth runs through Calgary and west of Edmonton. Therefore, W4 refers to the eastern half of the province and W5 to much of the western half. The sixth meridian is west of Peace River and east of Grande Prairie; a land description that ends with W6 indicates that the land is in the northwest corner.

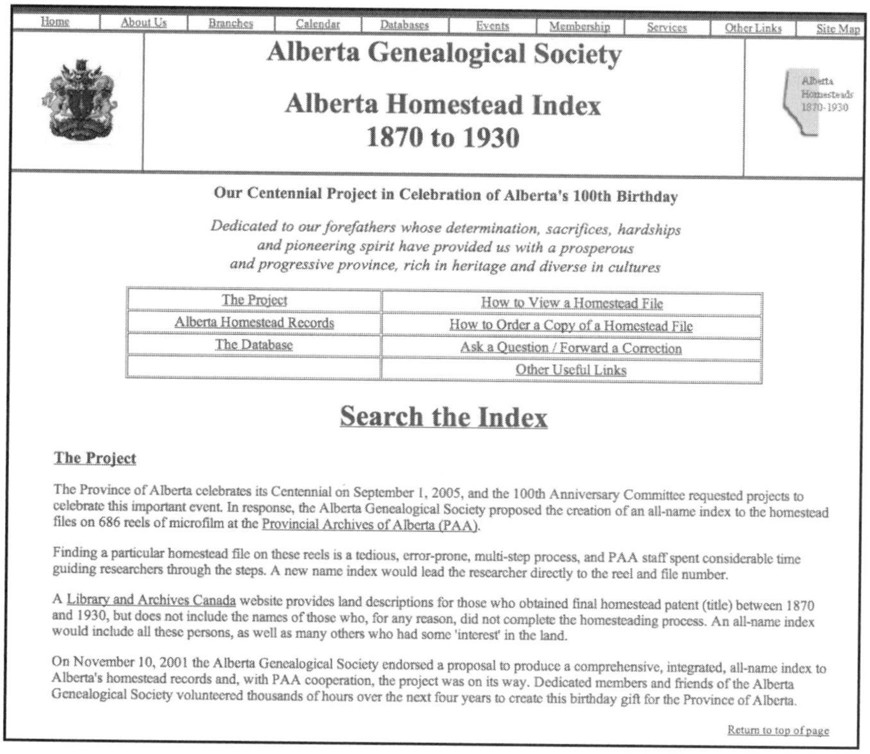

Figure 16-3. Website for the Alberta Genealogical Society's Alberta Online Homestead Index
<http://www.abgensoc.ca/homestead/index.htm>

NEWSPAPERS

More than one thousand different newspapers have been published in Alberta since 1880, covering virtually every community. The key dailies include the *Calgary Herald* (founded in 1883), the *Edmonton Journal* (1903), and the *Lethbridge Herald* (1905). The best guide to Alberta's newspapers is *Alberta Newspapers, 1880–1982: An Historical Directory* (Strathern, 1988).

Images of dozens of Alberta newspapers are available on the Internet. The Ancestry historical newspaper collection and NewspaperArchive.com both have incomplete runs of the *Lethbridge Herald* from 1938 to 1977. An index to obituaries in the *Lethbridge Herald* is also online.

The largest collection of online newspapers is found at the website of the Alberta Heritage Digitization Project. It includes many dailies and weeklies from 1885 through 2001, and the site will eventually include all of Alberta's early newspapers. While there is no index to the people mentioned in the newspapers, the site makes it possible to find a lot of information about your family. Search first for the newspaper of interest, then by date.

OTHER WAYS TO FIND PEOPLE

The first directories covering Alberta were published in Winnipeg in the 1880s and covered all three Prairie Provinces. Because of the large number of communities included, these directories generally had the names of only the most prominent people. These Prairie-wide directories continued until 1908.

Six directories covering all of Alberta were published between 1911 and 1928, but again, they included only the most prominent people. City directories designed to include every household were published in several cities until the late 1990s. They started in Edmonton in 1895, Calgary in 1908, Medicine Hat in 1913, Lethbridge in 1914, and Grande Prairie and Red Deer in 1967.

To find people in rural areas, check brand books, which listed the owners of cattle brands. An index to cancelled brands is on the website of the Stockmen's Memorial Foundation. Atlases showing the names of rural landowners were published between 1917 and 1930. Most counties and municipal districts in Alberta still publish similar maps.

Federal voters lists are available from 1935 through 1979. Municipal voters lists may also be available through local libraries and archives. Calgary's early voters lists, for example, are found in the main branch of the public library.

SPECIAL SOURCES

One of the most remarkable sources for Alberta genealogy is as close as your computer. The Alberta Heritage Digitization Project website includes scanned images of hundreds of local histories, which include biographies of most of the early families in rural areas. Better yet, the collection is fully searchable. If you are looking for all occurrences of a certain family name, you can have the information on your screen within seconds.

Figure 16-4. Home Page for the Alberta Heritage Digitization Project Website
<http://www.ourfutureourpast.ca/>

The digitization project also includes newspapers, legal documents, historic photographs, and more. Of special note is the collection of more than 30,000 aerial photographs showing the major population centers between 1924 and 1951.

Hudson's Bay Company records include information on early fur traders, including censuses. Company records are in Winnipeg. Another resource is the collection of the Glenbow Museum and Archives. More about both of these collections, in particular their documents on native people and the Métis, is in chapter 13.

WEBSITES

Alberta Courts:
Alberta Family Histories Society: <www.afhs.ab.ca>
Alberta Genealogical Society: <abgensoc.ca>
Alberta GenWeb: <users.rootsweb.com/~canab>
Alberta Heritage Digitization Project: <www.ourfutureourpast.ca>
Alberta Homestead Index 1870–1930: <www.abgensoc.ca/homestead/index.htm>
Alberta Vital Statistics: <governmentservices.gov.ab.ca/vs/genealogy.cfm>
Ancestry: <www.ancestry.ca>

Anglican Church Archives: <www.anglican.ca/about/departments/
General-Secretary/archives/archives-list.htm>
Anglican Diocese of Calgary: <www.calgary.anglican.ca>
Anglican Diocese of Edmonton:
Archives Society of Alberta: <www.archivesalberta.org>
Catholic Archdiocese of Edmonton: <www.edmontoncatholic-church.com>
Glenbow Archives: <www.glenbow.org/collections/archives>
Jewish Genealogical Society of Southern Alberta: <www.jewishgen.org/jgssa/>
Lutheran Historical Institute: <www.lccarchives.ca/lcc05a.html>
Mary's Genealogical Treasures: <www.telusplanet.net/public/mtoll>
Mennonite Historical Society of Alberta:
<www.mennonitehistory.org/index.html>
Peel's Prairie Provinces: <peel.library.ualberta.ca/index.html>
Provincial Archives of Alberta:
<www.cd.gov.ab.ca/preserving/paa_2002/index.asp>
Roman Catholic Diocese of Calgary: <www.rcdiocese-calgary.ab.ca>
Stockmen's Memorial Library:
United Church Alberta and Northwest Conference Archives:
<http://www.archivesalberta.org/walls/united.htm>

BIBLIOGRAPHY

Alberta, Formerly the Northwest Territories: Index to Registration of Births, Marriages and Deaths 1870 to 1905. Vol. 1. Edmonton: Edmonton Branch of the Alberta Genealogical Society, 1995.

Alberta, Formerly a Part of the North-West Territories: An Index to Birth, Marriage and Death Registrations Prior to 1900. Edmonton: Documentary Heritage Society of Alberta, 1999.

Holmgren, Eric J., and Patricia M. Holmgren. *Over 2,000 Place Names of Alberta.* Saskatoon, SK: Western Producer Prairie Books, 1981.

Lemieux, Victoria, and David Leonard. *Tracing Your Ancestors in Alberta.* Edmonton: Lemieux/Leonard Research Associates, 1992.

Main, Lorne W. *Index to 1881 Canadian Census of North West Territories and Algoma, Ontario.* Vancouver: L.W. Main, 1984.

Palmer, Howard, and Tamara Palmer. *Peoples of Alberta.* Saskatoon, SK: Western Producer Prairie Books, 1995.

Strathern, Gloria M. *Alberta Newspapers, 1880–1982: An Historical Directory.* Edmonton: University of Alberta Press, 1988.

ADDRESSES

Alberta Family Histories Society
712 16th Ave. N.W.
Calgary, AB T2M 0J8

Alberta Genealogical Society
116-10440 108th Avenue
Edmonton, AB T5H 3Z9

Alberta Vital Statistics
Registry Connect
PO Box 386
Edmonton, AB T5J 2J6

Anglican Diocese of Calgary
560-1207 11th Avenue S.W.
Calgary, AB T3C OM5

Catholic Archdiocese of Edmonton
Chancery Office
8421 101st Avenue
Edmonton, AB T6A 0L1

Hudson's Bay Company Archives,
130-200 Vaughan Street
Winnipeg, MB R3C 1T5

Catholic Diocese of Calgary
Pastoral Centre
120 17th Avenue S.W.
Calgary, AB T2S 2T2

Glenbow Museum and Archives
130 9th Avenue S.E.
Calgary, AB T2G 0P3
Library and Archives Canada
395 Wellington Street
Ottawa, ON K1A 0N4

Lutheran Historical Institute
7100 Ada Boulevard
Edmonton, AB T5E 4R4

Mennonite Historical Society of Alberta
2946 - 32 Street N.E.
Calgary, AB T1Y 6J7

Provincial Archives of Alberta
8555 Roper Road
Edmonton, AB T6E 5W1

Figure 17-1. British Columbia

BRITISH COLUMBIA

Captain James Cook claimed the northern Pacific coast for Britain in 1778, and the first post for trading with Aboriginals was established ten years later. In the early 1800s, rival trading companies established about twenty forts throughout the region, which by that time was claimed by both Britain and the United States. The two countries signed a joint occupancy agreement in 1818. In 1846, the Oregon Treaty established the international boundary along the forty-ninth parallel on the mainland, with Vancouver Island and several smaller islands that extend south of the forty-ninth going to Canada as well.

In 1849 the colony of Vancouver Island was created, with Victoria, which had been established as a fur-trading post six years earlier, as its capital. Another colony, called British Columbia, was created on the mainland in 1858, with New Westminster as its capital. Financial pressures forced the merger of the two colonies in 1866. In 1869 Victoria was declared the capital of the new colony, which bore the name British Columbia. It became a province of Canada in 1871. A rail link to Ontario, a condition of Confederation, was completed in 1885.

British Columbia's abundance of natural resources has prompted several waves of immigration, including the coal miners who went to Vancouver Island in the middle of the nineteenth century and the gold miners who went to the Cariboo and then the Yukon a few years later. On Vancouver Island, Victoria boomed as it became the key source of supplies for miners heading off in search of their fortune.

The completion of the Canadian Pacific Railway in 1885 brought dramatic changes. The railway made it possible for immigrants to get to British Columbia with little difficulty and for the resources of the province to be taken out. It influenced the growth of the province in other ways, too: Vancouver grew to be the largest and most important city.

Natural resources, including lumber, coal, and fisheries, drew most of the early settlers. Today, British Columbia has about 4 million people, with three-quarters of them clustered in a relatively small area in the province's southwestern corner. British Columbia's temperate climate has also made it a destination of choice for many people from other areas of Canada. This is a good place to look when family connections disappear from other provinces to the east.

FINDING LOCALITIES

Most genealogical records are filed on a province-wide basis. There are counties, but they can be ignored (a good thing because the names are confusing). The county of Yale, for example, includes the most populated areas in the British Columbia Interior but bears the name of one the smallest communities. The counties *are* relevant if you are dealing with certain judicial records.

Two websites, BC Geographical Place Names and Canadian Geographical Names, will help you find places. Several printed guides are available, including federal and provincial gazetteers. Most of the populated places are listed in *British Columbia Place Names* (Akrigg, 1988).

Historic place-names are found in directories published early in the twentieth century. Check the online list of places on the federal government's website, as well as the list of post offices in the Library and Archives Canada (LAC) website.

Many place-names in British Columbia are based on Aboriginal names. These include Nanaimo, Kamloops, and Cowichan. Many others, such as Vancouver and Quadra Island, are from early explorers or settlers.

CENSUS

The first federal census to include British Columbia was taken in 1881, ten years after the province joined Confederation. That census was indexed and is on the FamilySearch website. Indexes to the 1881 census for Vancouver Island are on the BC GenWeb site and the viHistory site. An index to the Yale District, which included much of the BC Interior, is on the Living Landscapes website.

Indexes to the 1901 and 1911 censuses, linked to images on the LAC website, are available on Ancestry and at Automated Genealogy. An index to the 1901 census is also online, hosted by the British Columbia Genealogical Society. An index to the 1901 census for Victoria, including references to civil registration documents and obituaries, is on the BC GenWeb.

There are partial indexes online for the 1891 census. One for Vancouver Island is at viHistory, and another for the Yale District, covering much of the southern Interior, is on the Living Landscapes website.

Local censuses also exist. A transcript of the 1871 census of Victoria is on BC GenWeb. A special census of Victoria, taken in 1891 after city officials disagreed with the federal numbers, is on microfilm at the British Columbia Archives and LAC.

CIVIL REGISTRATION

The British Columbia Archives website has an online index to birth, death, and marriage records. The finding aid includes records since 1872, the start of civil registration, as well as some earlier baptisms and marriages taken from church records. You can search deaths up to twenty years ago, marriages to seventy-five years ago, and births up to 1903. A change in regulations means that no new birth entries will be made available until 2025, when those for 1904 will be posted.

The indexes provide the date and place of the event as well as a registration number. There are also two microfilm numbers—one using the archives numbering system and one using the film numbers of the Family History Library (FHL).

Not all events were recorded. People of Chinese descent were not included until 1897, and, except for 1897 and 1898, Aboriginal vital events were not registered until 1917. Even then, Aboriginal births, deaths, and marriages were kept in a separate series of records until 1956.

Copies of registrations more recent than those available through BC Archives can be obtained from the Vital Statistics Agency in Victoria. Application forms are available on the agency's website. The agency will perform searches for documents for a fee of fifty dollars. Along with records of births, marriages, and deaths, it can provide information on changes of name.

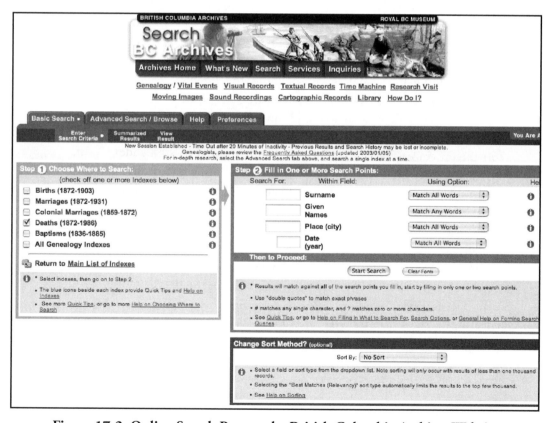

Figure 17-2. Online Search Page at the British Columbia Archives Website
<http://search.bcarchives.gov.bc.ca/sn-F4E3EB/gbsearch/Deaths>

Comprehensive divorce indexes from 1901 through 1983 are available at the British Columbia Archives. These indexes, which provide the date and location of the divorce, are available on microfilm. Access to the actual case files is restricted.

CHURCH RECORDS

Historically, the Anglican Church had more members than any other religion in Canada, followed by the United Church (formed in 1925 from Presbyterian and Methodist congregations) and the Roman Catholic Church. All three churches have major records repositories in British Columbia.

A few church records are available at the BC Archives, but you are more likely to find records by contacting the archive for the appropriate denomination. The Anglican Church has archives in Vancouver, Victoria, Prince Rupert, and Kelowna; a guide to resources online and links to archives in its network is on the Internet. The United Church and Roman Catholic Church have archives in Vancouver.

The BC Archives website includes two important indexes of church records. One covers marriages from 1859 to 1872, and the other covers baptisms starting in 1836. Baptisms from less than 120 years ago are not included because of privacy concerns. These indexes complement the records available through civil registration.

A few records and parish histories are in the FHL. Also check local churches directly, as they will know where records have been deposited.

CEMETERY RECORDS

Records for many cemeteries throughout the province have been transcribed by genealogical societies. Some have appeared in print, most issued by the British Columbia Genealogical Society, and some are available on the Internet.

The online British Columbia Cemetery Finding Aid is an index of 344,000 burials in the province. The finding aid can identify burial locations, link family members together, and include people who died outside the province, so it should be used along with the death index on the British Columbia Archives website.

Major burials databases are online for Vancouver (Mountain View), Victoria (Ross Bay), Kelowna, Vernon, Prince George, Kamloops, Abbotsford, Langley, and several smaller communities. Some of these are included in the cemetery finding aid. An index to 51,000 cemetery records from 1850 through 1986, compiled by the British Columbia Genealogical Society, is on microfilm at the FHL.

The rate of cremation in British Columbia has risen to about 80 percent of all deaths, the highest in Canada. That means you are less likely to find a burial marker for recent deaths, and cremation markers usually have much less information.

WILLS AND PROBATE RECORDS

Many British Columbia wills are readily available. Check the BC Archives website first. It has several searchable lists of probate files in local courts, including Chilliwack,

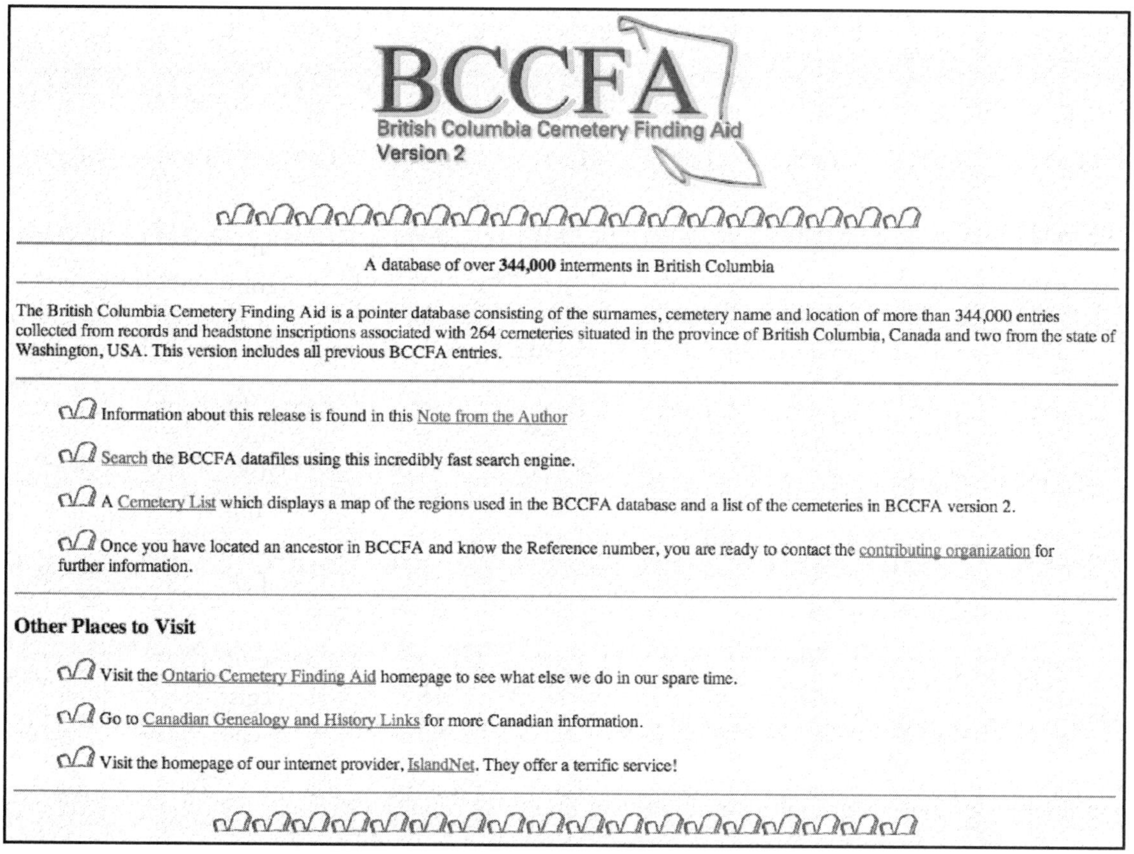

Figure 17-3. The British Columbia Cemetery Finding Aid Website
<http://www.islandnet.com/bccfa/homepage.html>

1916–1981; Courtenay, 1949–1986; Cranbrook, 1950–1985; Kamloops, 1946–1984; Kelowna, 1923–1981; Nelson, 1895–1989; New Westminster, 1881–1949; Penticton, 1925–1981; Prince George, 1921–1983; Rossland, 1934–1985; Vancouver, 1893–1949; and Vernon, 1901–1988. The wills themselves, as well as lists from other courts, are on microfilm at the archives in Victoria.

The FHL in Salt Lake City has an extensive collection of BC probate records, including all wills probated between 1861 and 1939. The FHL collection also includes probate files from Cumberland, 1901–1925; Cranbrook, 1905–1925; Fernie, 1905–1925; Fort Steele, 1901–1905; Grand Forks, 1904–1925; Kamloops, 1881–1932; Nanaimo, 1881–1928; Nelson, 1895–1926; New Westminster, 1881–1927; Prince Rupert, 1910–1927; Revelstoke, 1890–1949; Vancouver, 1893–1925; Vernon, 1892–1938; Victoria, 1859–1924; and West Kootenay, 1891–1926.

The BC Archives has other indexes and wills that are available only on microfilm. It also has succession duty records from 1934 to 1981. This collection, on microfilm, is the only centralized index of probate records before 1980.

The Abbotsford Genealogical Society has compiled two will indexes, one for residents and one for nonresidents. These indexes, including wills from the 1860s to about 1940, are on the society's website.

LAND RECORDS

The BC Archives website has a searchable list of homestead records from 1885 through 1949. A database of Crown land grants up to 1930 on the website of the Ministry of Sustainable Resource Management refers to file and microfilm numbers at the BC Archives as well as the FHL in Salt Lake City.

Both the BC Archives and the FHL have microfilmed copies of Crown land grants from 1851 to 1874, land grants with indexes from 1869 to 1930, and indexed Crown land preemption registers from 1860 to 1971.

Some provincial grants up to 1930 are also included in the Western Land Grants database on the LAC website. This series includes only those people who were successful in doing the work required to obtain title to their land.

The federal land survey in BC included the railway belt, a forty-mile-wide strip of land that followed the course of the Canadian Pacific Railway main line. Other surveying was carried out in the northeast corner of British Columbia near Dawson Creek. Like those of the other western provinces, the system was based on meridians and townships.

Land along much of the railway belt was too mountainous to be farmed. If you find a BC land description that ends with W6, referring to the sixth meridian, it will probably be for agricultural land in the northeast or in the Chilliwack area of the Fraser Valley.

West of Chilliwack, the basis for the subdivision of farms was the coast meridian, with townships noted as being east or west of it. Many rural roads in the lower Fraser Valley are on the allowances set out in the old survey, and Coast Meridian Road in Coquitlam ensures that the work will not be forgotten.

Modern land sale information is available from the land titles offices in New Westminster, Kamloops, and Victoria. An index of current landowners is available at those offices.

NEWSPAPERS

The oldest newspaper in British Columbia is the *Victoria Times Colonist*, a successor to the *British Colonist*, founded in 1858. Other daily newspapers include the *Sun* and the *Province* in Vancouver, the *Daily Free Press* (later *Daily News*) in Nanaimo, the *Sentinel* in Kamloops (which ceased publication in 1987), and the *Daily Courier* in Kelowna.

Along with the daily newspapers in the larger communities, weekly or biweekly newspapers have been published in towns and villages throughout the province since the late 1800s. The largest collection of newspapers on microfilm is at the BC Archives in Victoria. An extensive list of holdings is on the archives website.

The book *British Columbia Vital Statistics from Newspapers, 1858–1872* (Porter, 1994) is the best source of early birth, marriage, and death information extracted from newspapers. The BC GenWeb site has genealogical extracts from newspapers in Vancouver, New Westminster, and Victoria from 1861 to 1875. Both of these collections predate the start of formal civil registration in the province.

OTHER WAYS TO FIND PEOPLE

British Columbia has probably had more directories printed per capita than any other province, and they cover many communities, large and small. They were published from the 1860s through to 2000. Most are available on microfilm, the result of an extensive reproduction project organized by the University of British Columbia.

The 1868 directory of the province is on the BC GenWeb site, and an index to the 1871 directory is available in print form. The Our Roots website has several BC directories from the 1800s, covering cities such as Vancouver, Victoria, and New Westminster. BC directories are also found on Ancestry and the LAC website.

Federal voters lists are available from 1935 through 1979. Recent provincial voters lists are restricted because of privacy legislation, but the ones that have been released are available through the BC Archives. Provincial lists from 1875 and 1898 have been transcribed and are available on the BC GenWeb site. Municipal voters lists starting in the 1800s are also available for cities such as Vancouver and Victoria at local archives.

SPECIAL SOURCES

The British Columbia Archives has an excellent website with much information on early families. Beyond the vital statistics databases, check the textual records index for surnames or place-names.

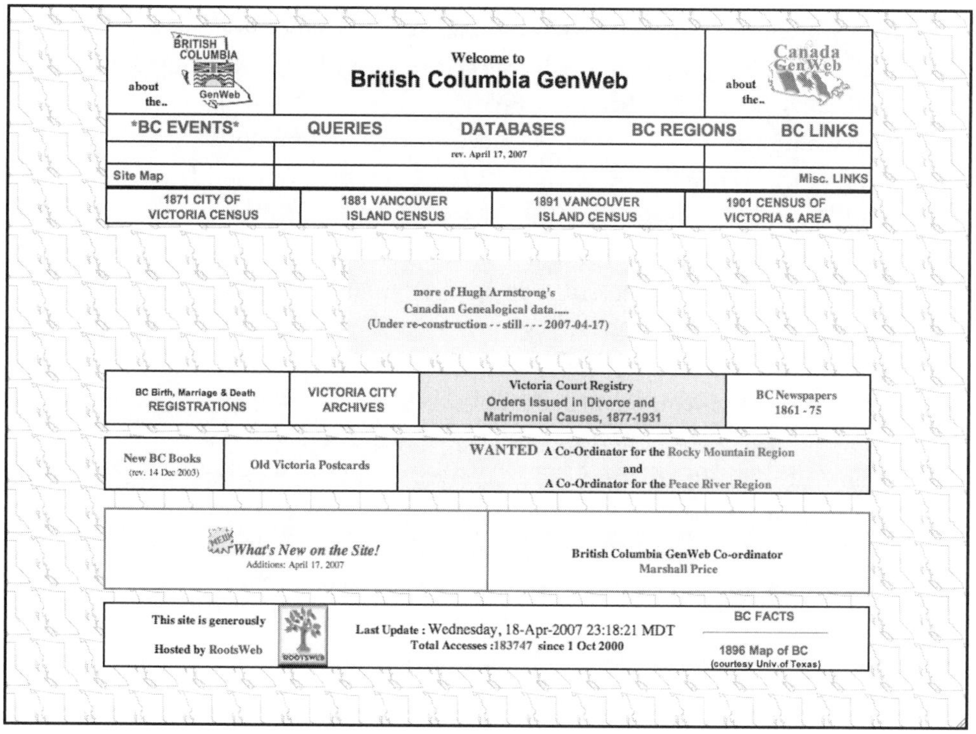

Figure 17-4. The BC GenWeb Site
<http://www.rootsweb.com/~canbc/>

The website has a comprehensive collection of photographs of people and places. Descriptions of more than 132,000 images are on the site, and many of the descriptions include small scans of the photos. The BC Archives has 63,000 maps, atlases, and architectural drawings. The website includes a descriptive index, although only a few images are available there.

The viHistory website brings together transcripts of census records, directories, documents, and maps from Vancouver Island. It's possible to build a clear image of the communities because of the depth of information included. Victoria's Victoria, on the University of Victoria website, includes a database of the *Colonist* newspaper covering 1858 through 1919.

The Vancouver Public Library's website has a section devoted to Chinese Canadian genealogy, with extensive background information and biographies. For the Interior, the Living Landscapes website provides a good start to records specific to that area.

WEBSITES

Abbotsford Genealogical Society: <www.abbygs.ca>

Ancestry: <www.ancestry.ca>

Anglican Church Archives Network for BC: <aabc.bc.ca/aabc/anglican.html>

Archives Association of British Columbia: <aabc.bc.ca/aabc>

British Columbia Archives: <www.bcarchives.gov.bc.ca>

British Columbia Cemetery Finding Aid: <www.islandnet.com/bccfa>

British Columbia Genealogical Society: <www.bcgs.ca>

British Columbia GenWeb: <www.rootsweb.com/~canbc>

British Columbia Geographical Names, Integrated Land Management Bureau: <ilmbwww.gov.bc.ca/bcnames>

British Columbia Vital Statistics Agency: <www.vs.gov.bc.ca>

City of Vancouver Archives: <www.city.vancouver.bc.ca/ctyclerk/archives>

City of Victoria Archives: <www.city.victoria.bc.ca/archives>

Crown Grant Search, 1869–1930: <srmapps.gov.bc.ca/apps/rd/crowngrantsearchrequest.do>

Geographical Names of Canada: <geonames.nrcan.gc.ca>

Jewish Genealogical Institute of British Columbia: <www.geocities.com/Heartland/Hills/4441>

Living Landscapes (BC Interior): <www.livinglandscapes.bc.ca>

Roman Catholic Archdiocese of Vancouver Archives: <www.rcav.org/Archives/index.htm>

United Church of Canada British Columbia Conference Archives: <www.united-church.ca/archives/bc/home.shtm>

Vernon and District Family History Society: <www.vdfhs.com>

Victoria Genealogical Society: <www.victoriags.org>

viHistory: <www.vihistory.ca>

VPL: Chinese-Canadian Genealogy: <www.vpl.ca/ccg>

BIBLIOGRAPHY

A Guide to the Archives of the Ecclesiastical Province of British Columbia and Yukon. Toronto: Anglican Church of Canada, 1993.

Akrigg, G. P. V., and Helen B. Akrigg. *British Columbia Place Names.* Victoria: Sono Nis Press, 1988.

Argent, Judith. *Planning a Genealogical Trip to the Vancouver Area.* Surrey, BC: Surrey Public Library, 2005.

Claydon, Peter S. N., and Valerie A. Melanson. *Vancouver Voters, 1886.* Vancouver: British Columbia Genealogical Society, 1994.

Genealogical Resources for British Columbians. Victoria: British Columbia Vital Statistics Agency, 1997.

Hayes, Derek. *Historical Atlas of British Columbia and the Pacific Northwest.* Delta, BC: Cavendish, 1999.

Main, Lorne W. *Index to the 1881 Canadian Census of British Columbia.* Vancouver: L. W. Main, 1981.

Obee, Dave. *British Columbia 1871: A List of Residents Based on the Work of Edward Mallandaine.* Victoria: Dave Obee, 2005.

Porter, Brian J. *British Columbia Vital Statistics from Newspapers, 1858–1872: Including, in an Appendix, Vital Statistics from Diaries, 1852–1857.* Richmond, BC: Brian J. Porter and the British Columbia Genealogical Society, 1994.

ADDRESSES

British Columbia Archives
675 Belleville Street
Victoria BC V8W 9W2

British Columbia Genealogical Society
PO Box 88054
Lansdowne Mall
Richmond, BC V6X 3T6

City of Vancouver Archives
1150 Chestnut Street
Vancouver, BC V6J 3J9

City of Victoria Archives
8 Centennial Square
Victoria, BC V8W 1P6
Mailing Address:
1 Centennial Square
Victoria, B.C. V8W 1P6

Hudson's Bay Company Archives
130-200 Vaughan Street
Winnipeg, MB R3C 1T5

Roman Catholic Archdiocese of Vancouver Archives
150 Robson Street
Vancouver, BC V6B 2A7

United Church of Canada British Columbia Conference Archives
6000 Iona Drive
Vancouver, BC V6T 1L4

University of British Columbia Library
1961 East Mall
Vancouver, BC V6T 1Z1

University of Victoria
3800 Finnerty Road
Victoria, BC V8P 5C2
Library Mailing Address:
University of Victoria
PO Box 1700 STN CSC
Victoria BC V8W 2Y2

Victoria Genealogical Society
PO Box 43021
Victoria North Post Office
Victoria, BC V8X 3G2

Vital Statistics Agency
PO Box 9657
Stn Prov Govt
Victoria, BC V8W 9P3

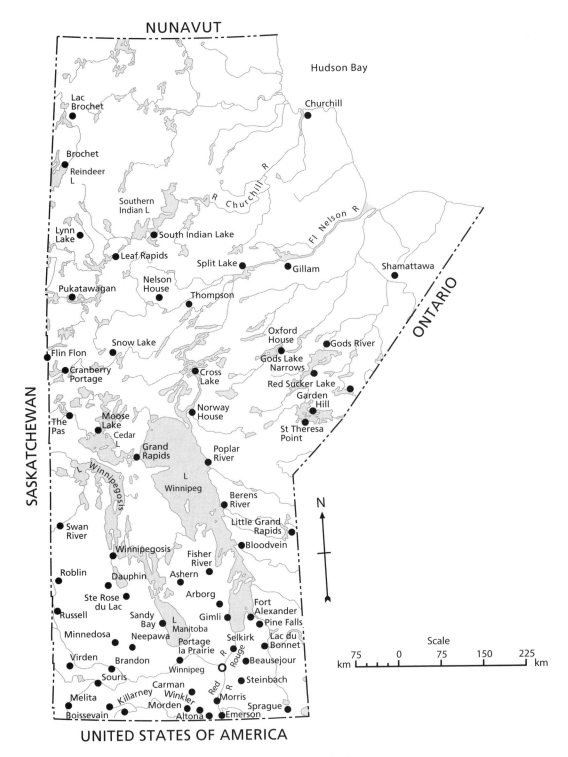

Figure 18-1. Manitoba

MANITOBA

The history of Manitoba is tied to that of the Hudson's Bay Company, which in 1670 was granted the rights to all of the lands draining into the bay by Charles II, king of England. This grant, which included the present-day province of Manitoba, disregarded the Assiniboine, Cree, and Ojibwa people who had been living on the land for generations.

Fur-trading posts were established by the Hudson's Bay Company and the rival North West Company. In 1812 the Earl of Selkirk established the Red River settlement, which eventually led to violent confrontations between the settlers and the Hudson's Bay Company on one side and the North West Company on the other. The merger of the two companies in 1821 ended the hostilities.

In 1869 the Canadian government bought the Hudson's Bay Company land, a move that led to confrontations with the Métis, people of mixed Aboriginal and white ancestry living in the region. A major concern was the system of land grants. The traditional French seigneurial system, with long lots extending away from rivers, had been in use, but the Canadian government wanted to introduce the system of square townships.

In 1870, after Manitoba was organized as a province, many of the Métis moved farther west, and settlers—at first mainly from Ontario—started moving in. During the 1880s, Manitoba's population doubled. Its area grew as well. Originally little more than the area surrounding the Red River settlement, the province was enlarged to the west and north in 1881 and to the north in 1912.

Access to Manitoba was a key factor in drawing new people, and the completion of a rail line to the United States in 1878 and the Canadian Pacific Railway seven years later set the land rush into high gear.

After that, the Canadian government advertised in Europe for immigrants to settle the Prairies, and large numbers arrived, including many from France and Belgium.

People from Iceland settled around Gimli, north of Winnipeg. Mennonites arrived to farm south and southeast of Winnipeg. Ukrainians took land near the fringes of settlement, in areas such as Ethelbert. Today, Ukrainians represent the largest contingent from continental Europe in Manitoba.

Manitoba's capital city has been a major transportation hub for more than a century. Most people who arrived in Western Canada from Europe went through Winnipeg, and the major colonization organizations had offices there.

FINDING LOCALITIES

Use modern maps, the Canadian Geographical Names website, and contemporary directories to track down most localities.

Another important resource is *Geographical Names of Manitoba*, published by the provincial government (2000). It lists all of the populated places in the province. To follow the expansion of settled areas, consult the *Historical Atlas of Manitoba* (Manitoba Historical Society, 1970). It includes maps showing communities, railroads, and farm areas.

CENSUS

Federal censuses were taken in 1881, 1891, 1901, 1906, and 1911. All have been indexed, with the 1891 indexes the only ones not available on the Internet. The 1901, 1906, and 1911 census images are on the Library and Archives Canada (LAC) website. Indexes to all three are at Ancestry, with links to the images. At Automated Genealogy there are indexes to the 1901, 1906, and 1911 returns, also linked to LAC images. The 1881 and 1891 returns must be viewed on microfilm.

A dozen censuses were taken in the Red River settlement and the adjacent Assiniboine District before Manitoba became a province. Most of these early counts, done by the Hudson's Bay Company, named only white or Métis heads of household. The total number of settlers was small; in 1849, for example, only 5,391 people were counted. The census of 1870, taken by the federal Department of Agriculture at the time that Manitoba was becoming a province, showed 25,228 people.

These censuses are available on microfilm from LAC, the Family History Library (FHL), the Hudson's Bay Company Archives, and the Archives of Manitoba, in Winnipeg.

CIVIL REGISTRATION

Registration of births, deaths, and marriages began in 1882. There are finding aids on the website of the provincial Vital Statistics department. The database contains early registrations, including deaths from more than seventy years ago, marriages from more than eighty years ago, and births from more than one hundred years ago.

Names appear as they were registered. Spelling was not consistent, so if you don't find what you are looking for, try variations.

Early registrations are available without restriction. More recent registrations are available only to people who qualify for access. For genealogical purposes, the registrations are available to the individuals themselves or close relatives. More information is on the Vital Statistics website.

Divorce in Manitoba was referred to the Canadian Parliament until 1919. At that time the province set up its own courts. Indexes to divorces in most courts are available on microfilm at the Archives of Manitoba in Winnipeg.

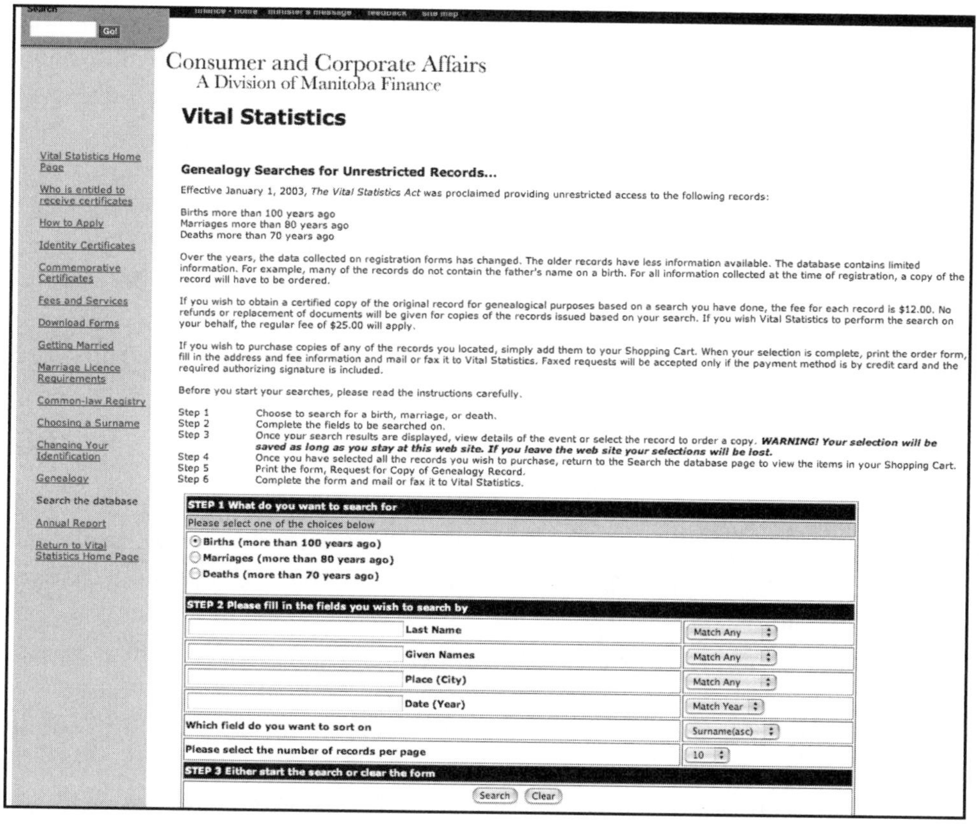

Figure 18-2. Search Page at the Manitoba Vital Statistics Department
<http://web2.gov.mb.ca/cca/vital/Query.php>

CHURCH RECORDS

Most of the major denominations have archives in Winnipeg. United Church records are in the Rare Book Room at the University of Winnipeg, and Anglican records are at the office of the Diocese of Rupert's Land.

The Roman Catholic Church is represented in Manitoba by the Archdiocese of Winnipeg and the Archdiocese of Saint Boniface, both based in Winnipeg; the Archdiocese of Keewatin-The Pas, in The Pas; and the Archdiocese of Churchill-Hudson's Bay, based in Churchill. Société Historique de St-Boniface has copies of Roman Catholic registers as well as Oblate church records for Western Canada.

Most Lutheran records are held in local churches, and the central district archive is in Regina, Saskatchewan. Most Jewish records are still held in local synagogues. Manitoba has also had a large Mennonite community, with archives in Winnipeg.

A limited number of parish registers can be found at the Archives of Manitoba. Others will be found at LAC in Ottawa and in the FHL in Salt Lake City.

CEMETERY RECORDS

The Manitoba Genealogical Society has an extensive collection of records from more than 1,400 cemeteries. Transcribed information is in a card index in the society's library. The society also sells transcripts of its cemetery projects, and a list can be found at the website.

Databases of burials at three Winnipeg cemeteries—Brookside, Transcona, and St. Vital—are on the Internet. Others on the Web include cemeteries in Brandon and Portage la Prairie. Transcripts of other cemeteries are available; check the Manitoba GenWeb site for an up-to-date list.

The Canadian GenWeb Project Cemetery Project has a list of cemeteries with location and availability of transcripts. The site also has some photographs and transcripts.

WILLS AND PROBATE RECORDS

An index to probate applications in the Manitoba Surrogate Court is available at the provincial archives. It includes 230,000 references up to 1981, and the wills themselves are available from the provincial archives.

Searching the films is a two-step process: first, check for the person's reference number in the main index; then look for the person by number in the master list. Information includes date of death and names of informants, who are usually relatives.

Along with the provincial index, each district has its own index. These are also on microfilm at the Archives of Manitoba, with another copy at the FHL in Salt Lake City. Since they are sorted by district, you should know where your family lived before searching.

The FHL collection includes estate files from 1871 to 1930 as well as indexes from 1884 to 1930 for the Eastern Judicial District; 1884 to 1937 for the Central Judicial District; from 1884 to 1970 for the Western Judicial District; from 1902 to 1948 for the Southern Judicial District; 1908 to 1962 for the St. Boniface Judicial District; and 1817 to 1950 for the Dauphin Judicial District.

LAND RECORDS

An index to patent holders for homestead files produced by the province's Crown Lands Branch is at the Archives of Manitoba. The files themselves are on microfilm and include people who did not obtain grants to their land. It's possible to order the

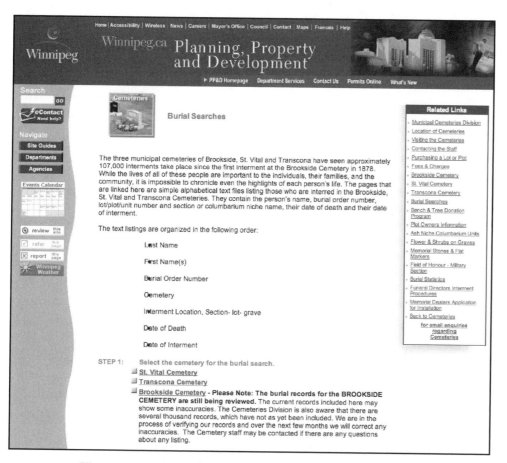

Figure 18-3. City of Winnipeg Online Burial Search Aid
<http://www.winnipeg.ca/ppd/cemetery_search.stm>

files directly from the archives or even buy the entire films. The films are organized by location, which makes it possible to research your ancestors and those who lived nearby. Crown land grants in Manitoba are on the LAC website.

You can usually tell at a glance if a homestead was in Manitoba. All meridian numbers in the province are based on the principal meridian, which is just west of Winnipeg. If a land description says the meridian is E1 or EPM, it's in Manitoba, east of the principal meridian. If the land is west of the principal meridian, noted as W1 or WPM, it's in Manitoba as long as the range number is no higher than 29.

Staff members at land titles offices will, for a fee, trace ownership of a parcel of land back to the original owner. These searches are based on the legal land description, and staff can help you find that. Land titles offices are in Brandon, Neepawa, Dauphin, Portage la Prairie, Morden, and Winnipeg.

NEWSPAPERS

The first newspapers in Manitoba were published in 1859. For many years, the *Winnipeg Free Press* (which has also used names such as *Manitoba Free Press* and

Morning Free Press) was the dominant newspaper on the Prairies. It continues to be the key newspaper in Manitoba. The largest collection of old Manitoba newspapers, as well as rural newspapers from throughout the province, is at the Legislative Library of Manitoba in Winnipeg.

Old issues of the *Free Press* are readily available on microfilm at many university libraries in Canada; it is found in more libraries than any other newspaper from Western Canada. The newspaper is part of the historic newspapers collection at both Ancestry.ca and NewspaperArchive.com. Issues available date from 1874 to 1923, but not all have been scanned, and you will find gaps.

The Manitoba Genealogical Society has also published five indexes of nineteenth-century marriage and death notices in Manitoba newspapers.

OTHER WAYS TO FIND PEOPLE

The first directory covering Manitoba was published in Winnipeg in 1876, with new ones produced for the city of Winnipeg almost every year until 1993. The early ones contained the most prominent people, but the coverage was expanded in the early twentieth century to include virtually every adult. These directories provide legal addresses.

Province-wide directories, which included the most prominent people in smaller communities throughout Manitoba, were published until 1908. There were also directories for Brandon starting in 1913, Portage la Prairie from 1954, and Dauphin from 1969.

Thirteen directories published between 1881 and 1901 included alphabetical lists of farmers, including the name of the nearest post office as well as the section, township, and range of their property.

Peel's Prairie Provinces contains many early references to Manitoba communities and residents, including directories, early local histories, and government publications prepared to encourage further settlement.

Federal voters lists are available from 1935 through 1979. The Legislative Library has provincial voters lists, subject to access restrictions. Municipal voters lists might also be found; check with local libraries and archives to determine availability.

SPECIAL SOURCES

Government records, including court and land documents, as well as private holdings such as church registers, are in the Archives of Manitoba in Winnipeg. An online search aid is available, which is helpful for planning a research trip.

The Hudson's Bay Company Archives, the official repository for the records of the company that once owned most of Western Canada, is part of the Archives of Manitoba. These records deal with everything from key events in the company's history to personnel files to land sales to logs of the company's ships. If your ancestor worked for the Bay, there is a good chance you will find a reference here. A detailed search aid is on the Internet, and two published guides are available.

The Manitoba Legislative Library, in the same building as the archives, has a superb collection of newspapers on microfilm, as well as local histories, directories on microfilm, scrapbooks, and newspaper clipping files.

Two websites, Peel's Prairie Provinces and Our Roots, provide access to digitized pages from local histories and other publications. Search by town name or by surname.

WEBSITES

Ancestry: <www.ancestry.ca>
Anglican Diocese of Rupert's Land: <www.rupertsland.ca>
Archives of Manitoba: <www.gov.mb.ca/chc/archives/>
Canada GenWeb Cemetery Project: <continue.to/cgwcem>
A Genealogical Guide to the Archives of Manitoba:
    <www.gov.mb.ca/chc/archives/genealogy/gen_text/>
Guide to Probate Records: <www.daveobee.com/columns/manitoba.htm>
Hudson's Bay Company Archives: <www.gov.mb.ca/chc/archives/hbca>
Manitoba Genealogical Society: <www.mbgenealogy.com>
Manitoba GenWeb: <www.rootsweb.com/~canmb/index.htm>
Manitoba Land Titles: <www.gov.mb.ca/tpr/landtitles.html>
Our Roots: <www.ourroots.ca>
Peel's Prairie Provinces: <peel.library.ualberta.ca>
Roman Catholic Archdiocese of Winnipeg: <www.archwinnipeg.ca>
Société Historique de St-Boniface: <www.shsb.mb.ca>
United Church of Canada, Conference of Manitoba and Northwestern Ontario
    Archives: <www.united-church.ca/archives/mnwo/home.shtm>
Vital Statistics search page: <web2.gov.mb.ca/cca/vital/Query.php>

BIBLIOGRAPHY

Briggs, Elizabeth, and Ann Morton. *Biographical Resources at the Hudson's Bay Company Archives.* Vol. 1. Winnipeg: Westgarth Publisher, 1996.

———. *Biographical Resources at the Hudson's Bay Company Archives.* Vol. 2. Winnipeg: Westgarth Publisher, 2003.

Gazetteer of Canada: Manitoba. Ottawa: Canadian Permanent Committee on Geographical Names, 1968.

Hanowski, Laura. *Finding Your Ancestors in Manitoba.* Toronto: Heritage Productions, 2005.

Loveridge, D. M. *A Historical Directory of Manitoba Newspapers, 1859–1978.* Winnipeg: University of Manitoba Press, 1981.

Manitoba Conservation. *Geographical Names of Manitoba.* Winnipeg: Manitoba Conservation, 2000.

Manitoba Historical Society. *Historical Atlas of Manitoba.* Winnipeg: Manitoba Historical Society, 1970.

Main, Lorne W. *Index to 1881 Canadian Census of Manitoba with Extensions & East Rupert's Land.* Vancouver: L.W. Main, 1984.

Morin, Gail, comp. *1870 Manitoba Census.* Pawtucket, RI: Quintin Publications, 2003.

Morton, William Lewis. *Manitoba: A History.* Toronto: University of Toronto, 1961.

Stokes, Kathleen Rooke, ed. *An Index of Marriage and Death Notices from Manitoba Newspapers; Volume One, 1859–1881.* Winnipeg: Manitoba Genealogical Society, 1986.

————. *An Index of Births, Marriage and Death Notices from Manitoba Newspapers, 1882–1887.* 5 vols. Winnipeg: Manitoba Genealogical Society, 1986.

ADDRESSES

Anglican Diocese of Brandon
341 13th Street
Brandon, MB R7A 4P8

Anglican Diocese of Rupert's Land
935 Nesbitt Bay
Winnipeg, MB R3T 1W6

Archives of Manitoba and the Hudson's Bay Company Archives
130-200 Vaughan Street
Winnipeg, MB R3C 1T5

Glenbow Museum and Archives
130 9th Ave. S.E.
Calgary, AB T2G 0P3

Jewish Historical Society of Western Canada
C 116-123 Doncaster
Winnipeg, MB R3N 2B2

Library and Archives Canada
395 Wellington Street
Ottawa, ON K1A 0N3

Lutheran Church Central District Archives
1927 Grant Drive
Regina, SK S4S 4V6

Manitoba Genealogical Society Inc.
Unit E - 1045 St James Street
Winnipeg, MB R3H 1B1

Manitoba Legislative Library
100-200 Vaughan Street
Winnipeg, MB R3C 1T5

Mennonite Brethren Canadian Conference Archives
169 Riverton Avenue
Winnipeg, MB R2L 0N1

Mennonite Heritage Centre Archives
600 Shaftesbury Boulevard
Winnipeg, MB R3P 0M4

Roman Catholic Archdiocese of Churchill-Hudson's Bay
PO Box 10
Churchill, MB R0B 0E0

Roman Catholic Archdiocese of Keewatin-The Pas
108 1st Street West
PO Box 270
The Pas, MB R9A 1K4

Roman Catholic Archdiocese of Saint Boniface
151 Avenue de la Cathédrale
Saint-Boniface, MB R2H 0H6

Roman Catholic Archdiocese of Winnipeg
Catholic Centre
1495 Pembina Highway
Winnipeg, MB R3T 2C6

Société historique de St-Boniface
340 Provencher Boulevard
Saint-Boniface, MB R2H 0G7

United Church of Canada
Conference of Manitoba and Northwestern Ontario Archives
University of Winnipeg
515 Portage Avenue
Winnipeg, MB R3B 2E9

Vital Statistics Agency
254 Portage Avenue
Winnipeg, MB R3C 0B6

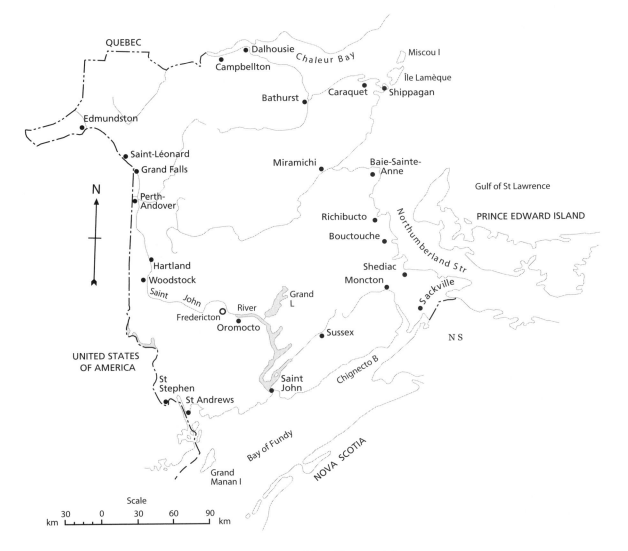

Figure 19-1. New Brunswick

NEW BRUNSWICK

New Brunswick went by other names before 1784. The first settlers in the region were French, and the whole area that is now modern Nova Scotia and southern and eastern New Brunswick was known as Acadia. In 1713 Acadia was ceded to Britain, and the British called it Nova Scotia.

At that time the population was small, and settlements were along the coast. British rule did not alter the lives of the Acadians for over thirty years. However, they were in the center of territorial conflicts between France and Britain. Eventually, their situation changed.

The deportation of the Acadian people began in 1755, just before another war broke out. New Englanders were encouraged to move north and take up the land. Peace between France and Britain in 1763 allowed the Acadians to return, but they could not resettle in the same areas. On the eve of the American Revolution the population of the region remained small, a mix of Acadians and New England Planters.

In 1783–84 the sudden influx of 14,000 Loyalists caused dramatic change. The area was given its own administration in 1784, becoming the colony of New Brunswick. Most Loyalists settled in the valleys of the St. Croix and Saint John rivers.

By the early 1800s New Brunswick was showing signs of prosperity. Cheap land brought increased immigration from the British Isles. The Irish famine brought another wave of new settlers between 1847 and 1851. Their arrival coincided with a decline in the economy, but negotiation of a trade agreement with the United States improved things.

Whether or not to become part of Canada was hotly debated in the colony. Failure to renew the American trade deal favored the pro-Confederation side, and New Brunswick joined in 1867. Unfortunately, economic reality did not match the promised benefits. The increasing industrial might of central Canada and the onset of the world recession in the 1870s initiated a period of decline. New Brunswick did not regain the prosperity or position of influence it enjoyed at the time of Confederation.

In 1871 people of Irish origin were the largest group, followed by the English, Scots, and French. The French segment of the population rose from 16 percent to 32 percent between 1871 and 1931. Today it remains at roughly 30 percent, and New Brunswick is the only officially bilingual province of Canada.

FINDING LOCALITIES

When New Brunswick was created in 1784 it had eight counties. As the population grew and settlement spread, the original eight were divided and new ones established until the total number reached fifteen. Counties are the main geographical unit for the arrangement of records.

Counties are subdivided into civil parishes. Not all the parishes were created at once, and some were carved from existing parishes. Some civil parishes straddle a county line.

Detailed guides to the fifteen counties are at the website of the Public Archives of New Brunswick. Each guide includes a county map, date of creation, and details of boundary changes. Expect to find evidence of county and parish boundary changes as you search New Brunswick records.

For pinpointing New Brunswick place-names, start online with the Canadian Geographic Names Database. Another resource, *An Atlas of the Maritime Provinces of the Dominion of Canada* (published in 1878), contains a map of every county, is on microfilm in the Family History Library (FHL), and has recently been reprinted (2005).

CENSUS RETURNS

New Brunswick was enumerated in all the Canadian censuses now open to the public, 1871 to 1911; copies are widely available. Ancestry and Automated Genealogy have indexes for the returns of 1901 and 1911, and these are linked to the record images at the Library and Archives Canada (LAC) website. A detailed index for the 1881 census of Canada is at FamilySearch, but images must be viewed on microfilm.

The 1851 and 1861 returns were taken on 1 November 1851 and 15 August 1861. In New Brunswick both censuses named everyone in the household. People were asked in 1851 to state the date of arrival and in 1861 to indicate religious affiliation. Images of the 1851 colonial census are online at LAC. Ancestry.ca has indexed the returns with links to these images.

New Brunswick GenWeb offers a guide, the Central Access Project. Censuses of the French regime, British colonial period, and after Confederation are included. There are links to online lists and indexes, with a preference for free websites.

Some censuses have published indexes, and some can be purchased at the website of the Associates of the Provincial Archives of New Brunswick.

Figure 19-2. New Brunswick Census 1851

New Brunswick Carleton County, subdistrict 10, page 26, film # C994. The information across the page is name, sex (in 2 columns), relationship to head of household, age, race, rank or occupation, how long in the colony, sick or infirm. The appearance and details of census pages vary by county and by district.

Available at Ancestry.ca

CIVIL REGISTRATION

Government civil registration began in 1888, but the records are not described as being complete until 1920. Historical records have been transferred to the archives. The transfer is made when birth records are more than ninety-five years old and when marriages and deaths are over fifty. For information about records within those restrictions, contact the Vital Statistics Office.

The Provincial Archives of New Brunswick also holds collections of other vital events, collected centrally and by counties, some of which go back to the early 1800s. Microfilm copies of many of the county vital records, particularly marriages, are in the FHL.

At the archives website you can search an index to over 750,000 vital records. Several series went into creating the index; however, not all vital records are included. This is a list of what makes up the online index.

- Index to Late Registration of Births, 1810–1911
- Index to Late Registration of Births: County Series, 1869–1901
- Index to County Birth Registers, 1800–1902
- Index to Provincial Registrations of Births, 1898–1910

- Index to New Brunswick Marriages, 1847–1955
- Index to County Death Registers, 1885–1921
- Provincial Returns of Deaths, 1815–1919
- Index to Death Certificates, 1920–1956

At the search page there are links to a detailed description of the whole index and shorter descriptions of the items listed here. You should read this information, and if your research focuses on one county, read the county guide. That way you will be aware of records either not included or missing.

Birth entries in the index may include the name of the child, date and place of birth, and full names of the parents. Some death entries indicate the birthplace and birth date of the deceased. Marriage entries have no information about parents. All have references to enable ordering or viewing on microfilm, which must be done to be sure you have every detail of the original.

The civil authorities of New Brunswick kept information about marriage bonds, which were required when couples married by license. An index to all those named in the records—grooms, brides, and cosigners of the bonds—is among the archives databases. The range of years is 1810 to 1932. The existence of a bond is not proof that a marriage took place. The bonds can be viewed on microfilm at the archives, at the FHL, and through Family History Centers.

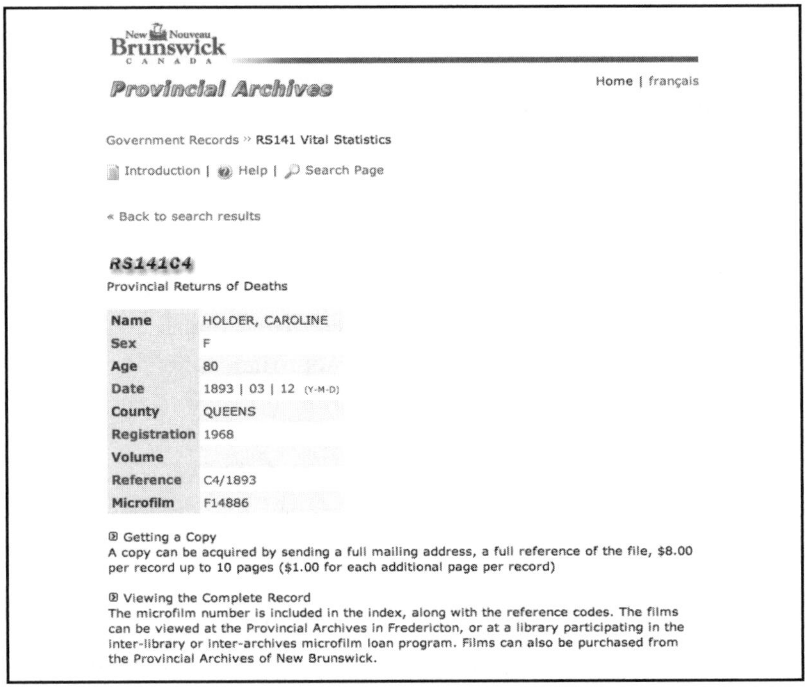

Figure 19-3. New Brunswick Online Vital Records Index

Results page for a death, New Brunswick Vital Statistics, RS 141, Reference C4/1893, Film F1 4886.

<http://archives.gnb.ca/APPS/GovRecs/VISSE/141C4.aspx?L=EN&Key=11471>

CHURCH REGISTERS

The largest collection of church registers is at the Provincial Archives of New Brunswick. Many registers of several denominations have been microfilmed, but the collection is unevenly distributed. The major denominations are Church of England (Anglican), Methodist, Presbyterian (including Free Church), Baptist, Roman Catholic, and United (formed 1925). Names of the churches and the range of years for register entries are listed in each of the county genealogy guides at the archives website. Access to some Catholic registers is restricted, and written permission must be obtained from the priest before they can be consulted.

The FHL has microfilm copies of many registers, and you should check the Family History Library Catalog (FHLC) for what is available. Very little is within the International Genealogical Index.

The creation of the United Church of Canada in 1925 amalgamated Methodist, Presbyterian, and other Protestant congregations. Keep this in mind when searching for church records because the records of two churches may actually come together under a third name. The archives for the Maritime Conference are in Sackville, and they hold records of roughly three hundred congregations, but few date before 1850, and less than one-third are registers of baptism, marriage, and burial.

When copies are not available on microfilm you will have to check with church archives, diocesan offices, and individual churches. Make sure you have researched what churches were in the area and what is held by the archives and the FHL first.

Here is an example of how Protestant records could be combined after the establishment of the United Church of Canada. This example is a title description from the FHLC.

Microfilm of original records in possession of St. Paul's Church, Sussex, New Brunswick. Contains Chalmers Presbyterian Church records of baptisms, marriages and burials, 1857–1926, with a roll of pastors, 1842–1917, and elders, 1879–1926; contains Wesley Methodist Church records of baptisms, 1861–1926, marriages, 1860–1926, and burials, 1913–1926; and contains St. Paul's United Church baptisms, marriages, and burials, 1926–1970. (Family History Library Catalog, Church Records, Sussex, St. Paul)

CEMETERY RECORDS

The index to cemetery records is another important database at the website of the Provincial Archives of New Brunswick. It contains over 220,000 entries from nearly one thousand cemeteries. It is possible to search one county at a time and within a particular cemetery.

The cemeteries are for several religious denominations—Anglican, Baptist, United, Catholic, and Presbyterian—as well as family plots and town cemeteries. There may be few cemeteries in a given county; read the database details before you search. Other transcriptions and related information are described in the online county guides.

Also online at the archives is an Index to Saint John Burial Permits, 1889–1919, in a separate database.

New Brunswick GenWeb is another source of online cemetery transcriptions. You may also want to look at publications of local societies and listings within the FHLC.

County Name	Number of Cemeteries	Total Entries
Albert	1	23
Carleton	129	26,166
Charlotte	109	19,294
Gloucester	70	34,601
Kent	55	16,083
Kings	119	16,599
Madawaska	3	2,611
Northumberland	8	2,312
Queens	145	13,872
Restigouche	7	6,411
Saint John	23	6,108
Sunbury	53	10,185
Victoria	12	2,090
Westmorland	66	13,104
York	147	48,333

Summary of Record Totals in Cemetery Index at the Provincial Archives of New Brunswick Website
Check for details like this before you search an index so you understand the extent of your search.

WILLS AND PROBATE

Probate court files are held by the provincial archives for the years 1850 to 1984. They include wills, petitions, affidavits, letters of administration, inventories, bonds, and miscellaneous items. Microfilms of these files are not held by the FHL.

The online county guides list all relevant microfilm numbers for the court files of each county, with dates covered by each film. The work of the probate court was recorded in Probate Act Books, which contain only the basic court documents. Film numbers for these are also listed in the county guides.

An alphabetical name index was prepared for each of the fifteen counties. You can consult the indexes at the provincial archives or use microfilm copies in the FHL or Family History Centers. There are a small number of probate indexes in the county sections of the GenWeb site.

Early New Brunswick Probate Records, 1785–1835 (Hale, 1989), contains abstracts of all probate records for the first fifty years of the colony, and these summaries include place of residence, occupation, relationships, and other genealogically useful facts.

LAND RECORDS

Land records are important from the time of the first Loyalist settlers and are available into the twentieth century. There are two main types of records, petitions and grants, and three online finding aids to help you access them.

New colonists wanting land presented a petition to the authorities giving reasons and often including family information. The date range for the original series of land petitions is 1783 to 1918, and they include the petitions of those who failed to obtain a grant. There is an index at the Provincial Archives of New Brunswick website.

When you find an entry, follow through to the original records at the archives, or use microfilm copies available through the FHL and Family History Centers.

At the Nova Scotia Archives and Records Management website there is an index to land petitions in the colony of Nova Scotia from 1769 to 1799. A small number are from what became New Brunswick. There are names here that are not in other petition and land grant lists, so include this site in any search of early land records.

Later land petitions are in a collection labeled the Current Series because the collection is still being added to. These petitions are not indexed online, nor are the records as informative as the others. Petitions from 1830 to 1966 are in the provincial archives, and an index is available.

The second type of land records, land grants, date from 1784 to 1997. An index is available at the provincial archives website. Grants are less informative than petitions, giving only names and land descriptions. Microfilm copies of grants are in the archives and the FHL.

The University of New Brunswick has a slightly different land grant database at the Harriet Irving Library website. This one covers forty years, 1763 to 1803, twenty years either side of the arrival of Loyalists and the creation of the colony. In the first twenty years, the grants were made by the colony of Nova Scotia. In the last twenty years, this database overlaps with the one at the provincial archives. Where there is overlap you will find identical entries.

Each county had a land registry office, and some of their records are in the Provincial Archives of New Brunswick. In addition, some documents were filmed by the New Brunswick Museum. The FHL has microfilm copies of these selected county land records for five counties: Charlotte, Northumberland, Restigouche, Sunbury, and York.

NEWSPAPERS

The first papers, the *Royal St. John's Gazette* and *Nova Scotia Intelligencer*, appeared in 1783, and in 1803 the *Fredericton Telegraph* began publication. There were papers for political and religious views and for communities. An Acadian newspaper, *Le moniteur acadien,* started in Shediac in 1867.

The provincial archives website has a database of information for nearly seven hundred New Brunswick newspapers. For every title it gives the place of publication, name, how regularly the paper appeared, details concerning missing issues, and the locations of original and microfilm copies.

Also at the archives site is the Database of Vital Statistics from New Brunswick Newspapers, covering 1784 to the end of 1896. It indexes nearly 300,000 entries with 641,000 names from seventy-five newspapers. Entries include the date, newspaper, and place.

OTHER WAYS TO FIND PEOPLE

There have been literally hundreds of directories for the whole of the province, towns, or counties. Also, New Brunswick was included in regional directories. At the Our Roots website you can find *McAlpine's Maritime Provinces Directory, 1870–71*.

The provincial archives presents two of Hutchinson's directories online, those for 1865–66 and 1867–68, combined in one database. Lovell's two-volume *Canadian Directory* for 1871 included New Brunswick, and names from it are also in a database at the provincial archives website. All have been microfilmed. A few directories are available through Family History Centers for years between 1867 and 1903.

From the New Brunswick GenWeb main page you can access a link to a transcript of the *New Brunswick Telephone Company Limited Official Telephone Directory, Eastern Division, July 1912*.

SPECIAL SOURCES

Other online resources at the Provincial Archives of New Brunswick website include lists of teachers and a finding aid to thousands of family histories. Particularly significant is the list of Irish famine immigrants, which contains more than 23,000 separate references to Irish immigrants between 1845 and 1852.

Loyalists, being such a significant group in New Brunswick, have attracted extra attention. In addition to church and land records, there are consolidated lists (see bibliography), records of regiments, and, online at the provincial archives, lists of veterans in poor circumstances who were granted government assistance. Legislation was passed in 1839 for the "Relief of Old Soldiers of the Revolutionary War and Their Widows." There are records of applications and payments from the office of the Provincial Secretary and local councils in five counties. You can search the database by personal name or county and view document images.

The Ward Chipman Papers at LAC include muster rolls of some Loyalist regiments that settled in New Brunswick. There is an online database that can be searched using personal names.

The University of New Brunswick has a significant collection of Loyalist material, which also includes the Winslow Papers. There is a finding aid to the Loyalist collection, and the Winslow Papers are fully digitized. (See chapter on Loyalists.)

WEBSITES

Ancestry: <www.ancestry.ca>

Anglican Diocese of Fredericton: <http://anglican.nb.ca/synod/>

Archives, Convention of Atlantic Baptist Churches, Acadia University, Esther Clark Wright Archives: <http://library.acadiau.ca/archives/>

Associates of the Public Archives of New Brunswick/Publications: <http://archives.gnb.ca/Associates/Associates.aspx?L=EN>

Automated Genealogy: <www.automatedgenealogy.com>

Canadian Geographic Names Database: <http://geonames.nrcan.gc.ca/index_e.php>

Catholic Diocese of Saint John New Brunswick:

FamilySearch: <www.familysearch.org>

GenWeb New Brunswick: <www.rootsweb.com/~cannb/>

New Brunswick Genealogical Society: <www.nbgs.ca>

New Brunswick Genealogy Articles: <www.rubycusack.com/glindex.html>

New Brunswick Newspaper Directory: <http://archives.gnb.ca/APPS/NewspaperDirectory/?L=EN>

Nova Scotia Archives and Records Management: <www.gov.ns.ca/nsarm/>

Public Archives of New Brunswick: <http://archives.gnb.ca/Archives/>

United Church Regional Archives: <www.united-church.ca/archives/maritime/home.shtm>

University of New Brunswick Land Grant Database: <www.lib.unb.ca/gddm/data/panb/panbweb.html>

University of New Brunswick Loyalist Collection: <http://www.lib.unb.ca/collections/loyalist/>

BIBLIOGRAPHY

Dubeau, Sharon. *New Brunswick Loyalists, a Bicentennial Tribute.* Agincourt, ON: Generation Press, 1983.

Geyh, Patricia Keeney, et al. *French-Canadian Sources: A Guide for Genealogists.* Orem, UT: Ancestry, 2002.

Hale, R. Wallace. *Early New Brunswick Probate Records, 1785–1835.* Bowie, MD: Heritage Books, 1989.

Historical Atlas of the Maritime Provinces 1878 / with an introduction by Joan Dawson. Halifax: Nimbus Pub., 2005. (a new edition of Roe's *Atlas of the Maritime Provinces of the Dominion of Canada*)

Hutchinson's New Brunswick Directory for 1865–66, Containing Alphabetical Directories of Each Place in the Province, with a Post Office Directory and an Appendix Containing Much Useful Information. Saint John, NB: T. Hutchinson, 1866.

Hutchinson's New Brunswick Directory, for 1867–1868. Montreal: J. Lovell, 1867.

Lovell's Canadian Dominion Directory for 1871: Containing Names of Professional and Business Men, and Other Inhabitants, in the Cities, Towns and Villages, throughout the Provinces of Ontario, Quebec, Nova Scotia, New Brunswick, Newfoundland, and Prince Edward Island, … Corrected to January 1871. Montreal: J. Lovell, 1871.

McAlpine's Maritime Provinces Directory for 1870–71. Halifax: David McAlpine, 1871.

Toner, Peter M. *An Index to Irish Immigrants in the New Brunswick Census of 1851.* Frederiction, NB: Provincial Archives of New Brunswick, 1991.

Roe, Frederick B. *Atlas of the Maritime Provinces of the Dominion of Canada.* St. John, N.B.; Halifax, N.S.: Roe Bros., 1879.

Wright, Esther Clark. *The Loyalists of New Brunswick.* Fredericton, NB: 1955. (includes an alphabetical list of men aged eighteen and over, giving former residence, service, place of settlement)

ADDRESSES

Archives, Libraries, Vital Statistics, etc.
Anglican Diocese of Fredericton
115 Church Street
Fredericton, NB E3B 4C3

Department of Supply and Services
Provincial Archives
Bonar Law - Bennet Building
PO Box 6000
Fredericton, NB E3B 5H1

Harriet Irving Library
University of New Brunswick
5 Macaulay Lane
PO Box 7500
Fredericton, NB E3B 5H5

Library and Archives Canada
395 Wellington Street
Ottawa, ON K1A 0N3

Maritime Baptist Archives
Vaughan Library
Acadia University
Wolfville, NS B0P 1X0

New Brunswick Genealogical Society
PO Box 3235, Station B
Fredericton, NB E3A 5G9

Roman Catholic Church
Diocese of Saint John
One Bayard Drive
Saint John, NB E2L 3L5

United Church Maritime Conference Archives
32 York Street
Sackville, NB E4L 4R4

Vital Statistics Office
Service New Brunswick
Suite 203 (second floor)
435 King Street
Fredericton, NB
E3B 1E5

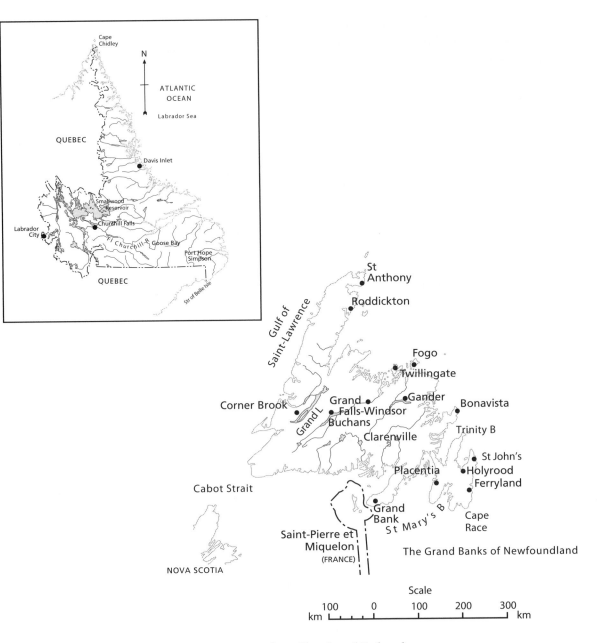

Figure 20-1. Newfoundland and Labrador

NEWFOUNDLAND AND LABRADOR

Newfoundland was a British colony until it joined Canada in 1949. Labrador was briefly part of the colony of Quebec but was reannexed to Newfoundland in 1809. The Labrador boundary dispute, resolved in 1927, confirmed it as part of Newfoundland.

Settlement in Newfoundland happened slowly because Europeans came for the seasonal fishery and because the British discouraged settlement. Late colonization and less than sixty years as a province of Canada have influenced record keeping in Newfoundland, and there are some striking differences from other parts of the country.

In 1634 the English issued the Western Charter, which declared each harbor would be under the authority of the captain of the first ship to arrive in the spring. From 1727 to 1817 the commander of the naval group arriving for the season was also the governor and the commander in chief. Newfoundland got a resident governor in 1817, a house of assembly in 1832, and responsible government in 1855.

Despite the discouragement of permanent settlement, people wintered over, and year-round residents gradually grew in number. Those from England came from southern counties such as Hampshire, Dorset, Devon, and Somerset. In the 1700s and again after 1815, Irish settlers came; generally they were from Wexford, Waterford, Tipperary, and Kilkenny.

Newfoundland was not out of reach of the wars between Britain and France in the eighteenth century. Some areas changed hands back and forth by conflict or treaty. Ultimately, France lost all settlements except the islands of St. Pierre and Miquelon and exclusive use of the French Shore in the fishing season. From 1783 to 1904 this area stretched from Notre Dame Bay around the Great Northern Peninsula and all the way down the west coast. In 1904 the French gave up any rights to the French Shore.

The fishery was of greatest importance to the colony's economy; other industries were mining and lumber. A network of railways crossed the island at the end of the 1800s. There were times of serious depression and hardship, notably in the 1830s and 1840s and during the Great Depression a hundred years later. Local government was suspended during both periods, and Newfoundland was administered from London.

FINDING LOCALITIES

The Newfoundland Heritage website has a gazetteer and a selection of maps, and at the Grand Banks website are two databases: Newfoundland and Labrador Community Names and Newfoundland and Labrador Community Name Changes. In print you can refer to the *Atlas of Newfoundland and Labrador* (1991) and the *Atlas of the Maritime Provinces of the Dominion of Canada* (1878, 2005).

The Natural Resources Canada website offers a selection of Newfoundland maps. For other place-name information, check within each of the regional sections of the Newfoundland GenWeb site and at Our Roots for *Lovell's Directory for the Province of Newfoundland, 1870*. Many small villages are named, and all places have at least a brief description.

CENSUS RETURNS

Newfoundland census records began early and have odd dates that bear little relation to dates elsewhere in eastern Canada. The records are open to public research to the middle of the twentieth century.

Years of official Newfoundland census returns were 1836, 1845, 1869, 1884, 1901, 1911, 1921, 1935, and 1945. Newfoundland and Labrador are included in Canadian national censuses after 1949, the year they became part of Confederation. This creates a special situation, and all pre-1949 enumerations are available. Unfortunately, only small parts of the 1911 and 1921 returns survive, but 1935 and 1945 are complete. Surviving returns, which are at The Rooms Provincial Archives, can be obtained on microfilm loan. Library and Archives Canada holds copies for 1921, 1935, and 1945. There are many indexes at the GenWeb and Grand Banks websites.

The earliest English list of inhabitants was made in 1675. Some early lists are nominal, but many name only heads of households. Before the authorities were reconciled to permanent settlement, they kept track of people in order to discourage this from happening. Check at the Grand Banks and GenWeb sites, where you will find transcripts of early returns.

The Family History Library (FHL) holds Newfoundland census returns from all periods. The entries in the Family History Library Catalog (FHLC) can be used as a checklist of Newfoundland censuses. In print, a list appears in the *Genealogist's Handbook for Atlantic Canada Research* (Punch, 1997).

CIVIL REGISTRATION

You can start searching online with the Grand Banks and GenWeb sites if you know where and when your Newfoundland ancestors were living. Both websites have vital statistics data arranged by district; some districts have more data than others.

In 1891 the colonial government required all church ministers to report vital events, signaling the start of civil records. Some years of the first decades of civil records have been microfilmed and can be consulted at The Rooms and through Family History Centers. Official copies can be obtained from the Vital Statistics Division.

Births—filmed, 1891–1899
Marriages—filmed, 1891–1922
Deaths—filmed, 1891–1949

There are indexes to these reported vital events, some not fully alphabetical and some created by the Genealogical Society of Utah. They are also on microfilm.

The government acquired another collection of vital records from churches, predominantly births and marriages, made before 1892. The earliest among them is from 1753, and the most recent is 1893. The Vital Statistics Division set up the project more than fifty years ago to preserve early records. Churches were asked to supply the data, and there was a little financial compensation for doing the work; even so, not all complied. A list of those churches, the Community Index, with dates of records, can be accessed at The Rooms website. These records are on microfilm and are also available through Family History Centers. The films have an index to place-names, and personal names are partially indexed.

Another archives collection of vital record information is titled All Newfoundland Births, 1840 to 1915. The title is somewhat confusing; it means from across all Newfoundland rather than an inclusive list of all births. Among this group are transcripts, retrospective entries, extracts, and sworn affidavits. Some of the data can be found nowhere else, and some of it duplicates information in other vital records collections. There is an index at The Rooms, and both records and indexes are available on microfilm in the FHL and through Family History Centers.

More modern vital records must be applied for via post or in person. Forms to apply for copies of birth, marriage, and death records, along with instructions, are available at the website of the Vital Statistics Division of the Newfoundland government.

CHURCH REGISTERS

The provincial archives holds a substantial collection of church registers. This is mainly a microfilm collection with some transcripts and photocopies. Some other resources, such as confirmations and minutes of parish meetings, are also available. Agreements were reached with the churches; they decided what could be filmed and retain their original registers.

The earliest Anglican ministers came with one of the missionary services, such as the Society for the Propagation of the Gospel. The provincial archives holds microfilm

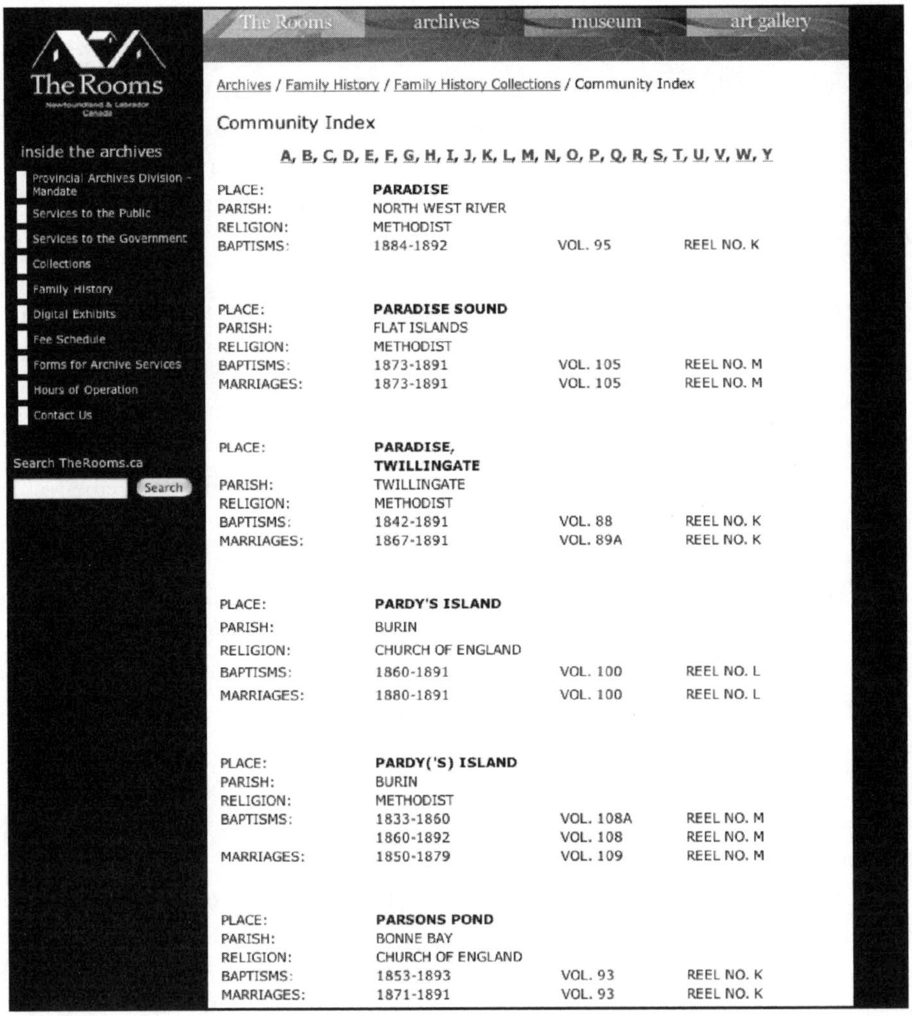
The Rooms
Newfoundland & Labrador Canada

The Rooms | archives | museum | art gallery

inside the archives
- Provincial Archives Division - Mandate
- Services to the Public
- Services to the Government
- Collections
- Family History
- Digital Exhibits
- Fee Schedule
- Forms for Archive Services
- Hours of Operation
- Contact Us

Search TheRooms.ca
Search

Archives / Family History / Family History Collections / Community Index

Community Index

A, B, C, D, E, F, G, H, I, J, K, L, M, N, O, P, Q, R, S, T, U, V, W, Y

PLACE:	**PARADISE**		
PARISH:	NORTH WEST RIVER		
RELIGION:	METHODIST		
BAPTISMS:	1884-1892	VOL. 95	REEL NO. K
PLACE:	**PARADISE SOUND**		
PARISH:	FLAT ISLANDS		
RELIGION:	METHODIST		
BAPTISMS:	1873-1891	VOL. 105	REEL NO. M
MARRIAGES:	1873-1891	VOL. 105	REEL NO. M
PLACE:	**PARADISE, TWILLINGATE**		
PARISH:	TWILLINGATE		
RELIGION:	METHODIST		
BAPTISMS:	1842-1891	VOL. 88	REEL NO. K
MARRIAGES:	1867-1891	VOL. 89A	REEL NO. K
PLACE:	**PARDY'S ISLAND**		
PARISH:	BURIN		
RELIGION:	CHURCH OF ENGLAND		
BAPTISMS:	1860-1891	VOL. 100	REEL NO. L
MARRIAGES:	1880-1891	VOL. 100	REEL NO. L
PLACE:	**PARDY('S) ISLAND**		
PARISH:	BURIN		
RELIGION:	METHODIST		
BAPTISMS:	1833-1860	VOL. 108A	REEL NO. M
	1860-1892	VOL. 108	REEL NO. M
MARRIAGES:	1850-1879	VOL. 109	REEL NO. M
PLACE:	**PARSONS POND**		
PARISH:	BONNE BAY		
RELIGION:	CHURCH OF ENGLAND		
BAPTISMS:	1853-1893	VOL. 93	REEL NO. K
MARRIAGES:	1871-1891	VOL. 93	REEL NO. K

Figure 20-2. The Community Index
<http://www.therooms.ca/archives/ci_P.asp>

copies of the reports of the ministers. The Church of England was the only church permitted in Newfoundland, until the first Methodist services were held in 1765. Congregational ministers came in the 1780s and Presbyterian in 1842; these two Protestant groups merged in 1938. Newfoundland and Labrador Methodist churches joined the United Church of Canada when it was formed in 1925.

The provincial archives website provides a list of any indexes available for individual churches arranged by denomination. The finding aid listings are for these denominations:

- Church of England / Anglican
- Congregational
- Methodist / United Church
- Moravian
- Presbyterian

- Roman Catholic
- Salvation Army

You can refer to a checklist of registers in the archives collection at the Grand Banks website. It is arranged by denomination and gives place-name, event type, range of years, and reference. Church register indexes are under development by the archives.

The Family History Society of Newfoundland and Labrador has indexed about two dozen church registers. Searches can be carried out at their research center or by applying for a paid search; costs are reasonable and details are at the website. For some records you must contact local churches or regional archives, where they exist. Check the websites and addresses at the end of this chapter.

To discover all surviving church records, look for registers available on film; check the two collections of the Vital Statistics Division that contain pre-1892 data; check for transcripts using the GenWeb, Grand Banks, and society websites; and check church resources.

CEMETERY RECORDS

The Family History Society of Newfoundland and Labrador has done a tremendous amount of work transcribing headstones; presently, one thousand have been transcribed, and most have been added to their database. The transcriptions and the index are at the society resource center. Online you can check a list of the two hundred communities represented and find details about requesting a search.

The Rooms has some miscellaneous inscriptions and provides a list within the Parish Finding Aids at their website. Grand Banks has extensive transcriptions, complete for some parishes, and at the GenWeb site you find a similar situation. There is a wide variation in data available; for some districts there is nothing at all, and for others there are several dozen transcriptions.

There is also a private project, stonepics.com, to take pictures of all gravestones in all cemeteries in the province. The work moved along at a great pace up until 2005, and there are pictures for more than 1,700 cemeteries available for purchase.

WILLS AND PROBATE

Probate records begin in the early 1800s. Online transcripts are numerous and therefore should be the first thing you investigate. This province is probably unique for the proportion of transcribed wills available online; you should start research at the GenWeb and Grand Banks websites.

Since 1832, probate has been the responsibility of the Supreme Court. For those working in St. John's, copies of records can be obtained from the court office. The probate record collection at The Rooms, both indexes and estate files, dates from 1825 to 1900.

In addition, records are available on microfilm through Family History Centers. The FHL holds probate files covering a period from the early 1800s to 1930. The earlier records are from particular probate districts—Central, Northern, Bonavista, and Trinity—and there is a Supreme Court collection, 1824 to 1930. The documents include wills, administrations, transfers of property, and even a few marriage records. It is a good idea to read all the details in relevant film notes. For later years the types of records are estate files, will books, and act books.

The FHL also holds microfilm copies of Supreme Court indexes in two series, 1830–1975 and 1976–September 1996. Names are arranged by first letter of the last name and then chronologically.

LAND RECORDS

There are two types of records, Crown land grants and deeds. One details the initial grant of land from the Crown, and the other is concerned with the later conveyance or transfer of land.

Crown grants could be in the form of a grant or a lease. Records begin in the early 1800s, and they have been indexed first by region and then chronologically. Records of Registry of Crown Land Grants, 1830–1930, are available at the provincial archives. These records are not complete.

Deeds were filed by year, and within each year there is an alphabetical index for buyers and sellers. There are some wills within the Registry of Deeds, a few from as early as 1744.

For deeds, the search is similar to probate. Begin with the GenWeb and Grand Banks websites, where some transcriptions can be found, and then check the FHLC. Microfilm copies of Registry of Deeds records from 1825 to 1931 are in the FHL, along with indexes up to 1938. Filmed records from the Crown Lands Office go up to 1930. There are name indexes to about 1940 and geographical indexes to 1990.

There is a different sort of "land" record for costal plots of land known as "fishing rooms." Those who arrived for the seasonal fishery would take possession of some foreshore for drying and curing fish. As more and more ships came, space became short, and the timber required for building sheds and racks was in short supply, so people wanted to retain their "room" from year to year. Registers of owners of fishing rooms can be found at the GenWeb and Grand Banks websites.

NEWSPAPERS

Memorial University of Newfoundland maintains an online Historical Directory of Newfoundland Newspapers; there were about one hundred. In addition, the university sells a CD-ROM of more than 40,000 vital records from newspapers, *Births, Deaths & Marriages in Newfoundland Newspapers, 1810–1890.*

From the GenWeb home page there are direct links to newspaper transcripts at many of the district sites: Notre Dame Bay, Conception Bay North, and St. John's are three of them. These contain vital records, ship lists, and a variety of news items.

The archives holds extracts of births, marriages, and deaths, 1850–1900, taken from newspapers of the Conception Bay area; a collection of death announcements in

Figure 20-3. Newfoundland Fishing Room at Cape Rogue Harbour
More about the history of the fishery can be found in History of Newfoundland from the English, Colonial and Foreign Records *(Prowse, 1895) online at Ancestry.*
From Prowse, pg. 258

the *Daily News*, 1913–1963; and the data gathered by Gertrude Crosbie. She collected birth, death, and marriage records in Newfoundland newspapers. These were also published and are listed in the bibliography at the end of this chapter.

OTHER WAYS TO FIND PEOPLE

Because of the gaps in the census, you need directories and voters lists. *Lovell's Directory* has already been mentioned for its geographical detail, and it is useful for the names it lists as well. The range of dates for voters lists available at the archives is 1832 to the 1980s.

You should check the appropriate district or topic sections at the GenWeb and Grand Banks websites, as they contain transcripts from several directories.

SPECIAL SOURCES

The resources at the Maritime History Archive of Memorial University of Newfoundland are extensive. From their holdings they have compiled *Ships and Seafarers of Atlantic Canada,* which is a fully searchable CD containing data on the vessels, captains, and crews of Great Britain and Atlantic Canada, 1787–1936. The staff will search several items in a series of indexed records for a fee. This includes the Keith Matthews Name Files, made up of records from 1500 to 1830 about people involved in fishing, trade, and settlement. Another resource is the Index to Newfoundland Captains, 1820–1889.

WEBSITES

Ancestry: <www.ancestry.ca>

Anglican Church of Canada (links to diocesan websites): <www.anglican.ca/about/diocese.htm#cnfld>

Cemetery transcriptions photographs: <www.stonepics.com>

Family History Society of Newfoundland and Labrador:

GenWeb Nefoundland and Labrador: <www.rootsweb.com/~cannf/index.html>

Grand Banks: <http://ngb.chebucto.org/>

Historical Directory of Newfoundland and Labrador Newspapers: <www.library.mun.ca/qeii/newspapers/index.php>

Memorial University Maritime History Archive: <www.mun.ca/mha/index.php>

Memorial University Religion, Society & Culture site: <www.ucs.mun.ca/~hrollman/>

Newfoundland Heritage (history, maps, gazetteer): <www.heritage.nf.ca/introduction.html>

Newfoundland and Labrador Vital Statistics Division: <http://www.gs.gov.nl.ca/gs/vs/>

Roman Catholic Archdiocese of St. John's, Archives: <www.stjohnsarchdiocese.nf.ca>

The Rooms Provincial Archives of Newfoundland and Labrador: <www.therooms.ca/archives/>

United Church Regional Archives: <www.newlabconf.com/ArchivesConf.htm>

BIBLIOGRAPHY

Crosbie, Gertrude. *Births, Deaths and Marriages in Newfoundland Newspapers 1825–1850.* St. John's, NF: Maritime History Archive, 1986. (There is a second volume up to 1867.)

Historical Atlas of the Maritime Provinces 1878 / with an introduction by Joan Dawson. Halifax: Nimbus Pub., 2005. (a new edition of Roe's *Atlas of the Maritime Provinces of the Dominion of Canada*)

Lovell's Directory for the Province of Newfoundland. Montreal: Lovell, 1870.

McCarthy, Mike. *The Irish in Newfoundland, 1600–1900.* St. John's, NF: Creative Book Pub, 1999.

McManus, Gary E., and Clifford H. Wood. *Atlas of Newfoundland and Labrador.* St. John's, NF: Breakwater, 1991.

Prowse, D. W., ed. *History of Newfoundland from the English, Colonial and Foreign Records.* London: Macmillan, 1895. (available online at Ancestry)

———, ed. *A History of the Churches in Newfoundland.* London: Macmillan, 1895. (available online at Ancestry)

Punch, Terence M., with G. F. Sanborne. *Genealogist's Handbook for Atlantic Canada Research.* 2nd ed. Boston: New England Historic Genealogical Society, 1997.

Roe, Frederick B. *Atlas of the Maritime Provinces of the Dominion of Canada*. St. John, NB: Halifax, NS: Roe Bros., 1879.

Seary, E. R., and S. M. P. Lynch. *Family Names of Newfoundland*. Montreal: McGill-Queen's University Press, 1998.

ADDRESSES

Family History Society of Newfoundland and Labrador
657 Topsail Road
Waterford Valley Plaza
St. John's, NL A1E 2E3

Maritime History Archive
Memorial University of Newfoundland
Henrietta Harvey Mathematics Building
St. John's, NL A1C 5S7

Newfoundland and Labrador Conference Archives
United Church of Canada
320 Elizabeth Avenue
St. John's, NL A1B 1T9

Probate Office
Supreme Court of Newfoundland
Courthouse Building
Duckworth Street
St. John's, NL A1C 5M3

Roman Catholic Archdiocese of St. John's, Archives
200 Military Road
PO Box 37
St. John's, NL A1C 5H5

The Rooms Provincial Archives
9 Bonaventure Avenue
PO Box 1800, Station C
St. John's, NL A1C 5P9

Vital Statistics Division
Department of Government Services and Lands
Government Services Centre
5 Mews Place
PO Box 8700
St. John's, NL A1B 4J6

Figure 21-1. Nova Scotia

NOVA SCOTIA

The abundance of fish in coastal waters brought Europeans to Nova Scotia in the 1500s. In 1605 at Port Royal (now Annapolis Royal), a small group of French settlers stayed through the winter. French settlements increased and the colony was called Acadia. It was in the midst of lands contested by the British and French and changed hands many times. In 1713 what is now peninsular Nova Scotia became a British possession, and the French settlers claimed political neutrality.

The nearly continual conflict between France and England made the Acadian settlements unacceptable to Governor Lawrence of Nova Scotia. Starting in 1755 he ordered the settlers' expulsion. Eight years later, when the French surrendered all interest in Canada, the Acadians were permitted to return.

In the meantime Protestant settlement had been encouraged, and by 1775 the Planters from New England made up about two-thirds of Nova Scotia's population. There were also some returned Acadians, mostly in southwestern Nova Scotia, and Foreign Protestants (most of them recruited in Germany and Switzerland) at Lunenburg. The colony at this time included Cape Breton and what became New Brunswick.

As the American Revolution drew to a close in 1783–84, about 35,000 Loyalists arrived in Nova Scotia. The colony was not ready for them, conditions were harsh, and a new name began to circulate—Nova Scarcity. By the 1790s, many Loyalists had moved on into Upper and Lower Canada. Others were in areas recently split off as separate colonies: New Brunswick (1784), Cape Breton (1785), and Prince Edward Island (1763).

It took a long time to establish any basis for economic prosperity, but conditions gradually improved. By the middle of the 1800s, the population was swelled by in-migration from the British Isles. The colony became stronger and was granted responsible government. Major industries were agriculture, fishing, mining, timber, and shipbuilding.

Shipbuilding expanded rapidly during and after the Napoleonic Wars with France, 1792–1815. The timber trade to Britain created an unprecedented demand for bulk cargo carriers. So many ships were constructed in New Brunswick that roughly half of all British registered shipping was recorded as being built in British North America. Prosperity helped take Nova Scotia into Confederation in 1867 and gave it considerable influence in Canada's early years.

There were, however, difficult times ahead for the province through the later decades of the nineteenth century and well into the twentieth. The capital city, Halifax, was on the front line in the First and the Second World Wars and has become an important regional center today.

FINDING LOCALITIES

Two resources on the Internet can help you find places and boundaries. These are *Place-Names and Places of Nova Scotia* (1967) and Lovell's *Canadian Dominion Directory* (1871). The first can be found at the Nova Scotia Archives and Records Management (NSARM) website and the latter within the directories collection at Library and Archives Canada (LAC).

Place-Names and Places of Nova Scotia has over 2,400 entries. Lovell's descriptions are brief but include valuable geographic data. Between the two you may discover exact locations, names of early settlers, churches, and local occupations. Both publications are accessible on microfilm in Family History Centers.

The NSARM website has two other geographical aids, a map showing the boundary lines of the eighteen counties with a table underneath listing principal town, date formed, and whether original or created from another county. Also, T. C. Haliburton's detailed *New Map of Nova Scotia* (1829), digitized with a magnification feature.

There is a finding aid to present-day place-names, with links to maps, within the Nova Scotia government website.

CENSUS RETURNS

Nova Scotia was part of the first census of Canada in 1871, and there are federal records from that year through to the most recently available, 1911. Like other British colonies, it was enumerated in 1851 and 1861, but in Nova Scotia these are head-of-household lists. Very little of the 1851 census survives. There were eight censuses taken in Nova Scotia between 1800 and 1871 (see the box on page 166 for details about surviving returns).

Online you can find indexes for the 1851, 1901, and 1911 returns (all three are available at Ancestry, 1901 and 1911 at Automated Genealogy). These are linked to record images at LAC. A detailed index for the 1881 census is at FamilySearch, but images must be viewed on microfilm.

If your research takes you back before 1800, there are early listings for Acadia and Île Royale (Cape Breton). British colonial officials also carried out censuses between 1749 and 1799. Many have been printed either privately or in reports of provincial or

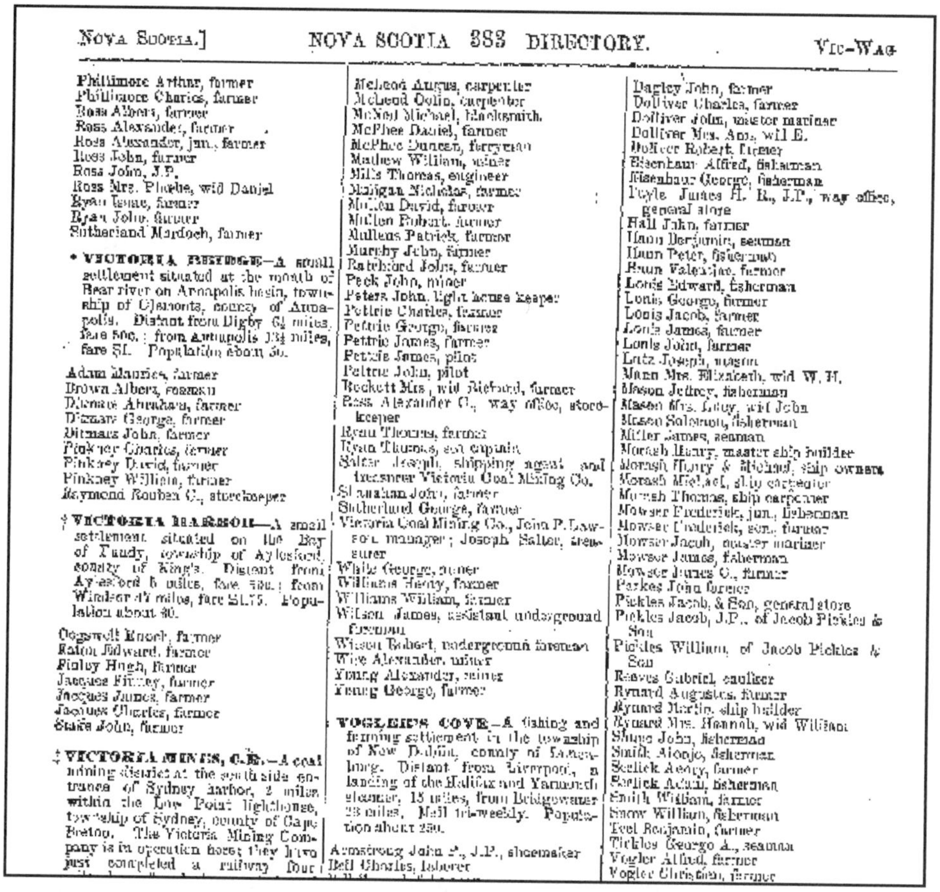
NOVA SCOTIA.] NOVA SCOTIA 383 DIRECTORY. VIC-WAG

Phillimore Arthur, farmer
Phillimore Charles, farmer
Ross Albert, farmer
Ross Alexander, farmer
Ross Alexander, jun., farmer
Ross John, farmer
Ross John, J.P.
Ross Mrs. Phoebe, wid Daniel
Ryan Isaac, farmer
Ryan John, farmer
Sutherland Murdoch, farmer

* **VICTORIA BRIDGE**—A small settlement situated at the mouth of Bear river on Annapolis basin, township of Clements, county of Annapolis. Distant from Digby 6½ miles, fare 50c.; from Annapolis 13½ miles, fare $1. Population about 50.

Adam Maurice, farmer
Brown Albert, farmer
Ditmars Abraham, farmer
Ditmars George, farmer
Ditmars John, farmer
Pinkney Charles, farmer
Pinkney David, farmer
Pinkney William, farmer
Raymond Reuben C., storekeeper

† **VICTORIA HARBOR**—A small settlement situated on the Bay of Fundy, township of Aylesford, county of King's. Distant from Aylesford 6 miles, fare 50c.; from Windsor 47 miles, fare $1.75. Population about 80.

Cogswell Enoch, farmer
Eaton Edward, farmer
Finley Hugh, farmer
Jacques Finney, farmer
Jacques James, farmer
Jacques Charles, farmer
Stairs John, farmer

‡ **VICTORIA MINES, C.B.**—A coal mining district at the south side entrance of Sydney harbor, 2 miles within the Low Point lighthouse, township of Sydney, county of Cape Breton. The Victoria Mining Company is in operation here; they have just completed a railway four

Mcleod Angus, carpenter
Mcleod Colin, carpenter
McNeil Michael, blacksmith
McPhee Daniel, farmer
McPhee Duncan, ferryman
Mathew William, miner
Mills Thomas, engineer
Mulligan Nicholas, farmer
Mullen David, farmer
Mullen Robert, farmer
Mullens Patrick, farmer
Murphy John, farmer
Ratchford John, farmer
Peck John, miner
Peters John, light house keeper
Pettrie Charles, farmer
Pettrie George, farmer
Pettrie James, farmer
Pettrie James, pilot
Peltrie John, pilot
Reckett Mrs., wid Richard, farmer
Ross Alexander G., way office, storekeeper
Ryan Thomas, farmer
Ryan Thomas, sea captain
Salter Joseph, shipping agent and treasurer Victoria Coal Mining Co.
Shanahan John, farmer
Sutherland George, farmer
Victoria Coal Mining Co., John P. Lawson manager; Joseph Salter, treasurer
White George, miner
Williams Henry, farmer
Williams William, farmer
Wilson James, assistant underground foreman
Wilson Robert, underground foreman
Wise Alexander, miner
Young Alexander, miner
Young George, farmer

VOGLER'S COVE—A fishing and farming settlement in the township of New Dublin, county of Lunenburg. Distant from Liverpool, a landing of the Halifax and Yarmouth steamer, 15 miles, from Bridgewater 23 miles. Mail tri-weekly. Population about 250.

Armstrong John P., J.P., shoemaker
Bell Charles, laborer

Dagley John, farmer
Dolliver Charles, farmer
Dolliver John, master mariner
Dolliver Mrs. Ann, wid E.
Dolliver Robert, farmer
Eisenhaur Alfred, fisherman
Eisenhaur George, fisherman
Foyle James H. R., J.P., way office, general store
Hall John, farmer
Hann Benjamin, seaman
Hann Peter, fisherman
Hann Valentine, farmer
Louis Edward, fisherman
Louis George, farmer
Louis Jacob, farmer
Louis James, farmer
Louis John, farmer
Lutz Joseph, mason
Mann Mrs. Elizabeth, wid W. H.
Mason Jeffrey, fisherman
Mason Mrs. Lucy, wid John
Mason Solomon, fisherman
Miller James, seaman
Morash Henry, master ship builder
Morash Henry & Michael, ship owners
Morash Michael, ship carpenter
Morash Thomas, ship carpenter
Mowser Frederick, jun., fisherman
Mowser Frederick, sen., farmer
Mowser Jacob, master mariner
Mowser James, fisherman
Mowser James C., farmer
Parkes John, farmer
Pickles Jacob, & Son, general store
Pickles Jacob, J.P., of Jacob Pickles & Son
Pickles William, of Jacob Pickles & Son
Reeves Gabriel, caulker
Rynard Augustus, farmer
Rynard Martin, ship builder
Rynard Mrs. Hannah, wid William
Shupe John, fisherman
Smith Alonzo, fisherman
Seelick Henry, farmer
Seelick Adam, fisherman
Smith William, farmer
Snow William, fisherman
Teel Benjamin, farmer
Tickles George A., seaman
Vogler Alfred, farmer
Vogler Christian, farmer

Figure 21-2. A Page of Lovell's Province of Nova Scotia Directory, 1871

The Vogler's Cove entry reads: "A fishing and farming settlement in the township of New Dublin, county of Lunenburg. Distance from Liverpool, a landing of the Halifax and Yarmouth steamer, 15 miles, from Bridgewater, 23 miles. Mail tri-weekly. Population about 250."

<http://www.collectionscanada.ca/canadiandirectories/>

national archives, and from these, online transcripts have been made. *French-Canadian Sources: A Guide for Genealogists* (Geyh et al., 2002) contains detailed lists of surviving censuses. Some are online; GenWeb and the search tool AVITUS, available at the Canadian Genealogy Centre website, can help you find them.

The Genealogical Association of Nova Scotia has published several volumes of census indexes. Microfilm and print copies of any early returns in the Family History Library (FHL) are listed in the Family History Library Catalog (FHLC).

CIVIL REGISTRATION

Modern records are held by the Vital Statistics Division within the Department of Service Nova Scotia and Municipal Relations. Records defined as modern are births in the last hundred years, marriages in the past seventy-five, and deaths in the past fifty. All other records have been transferred to Nova Scotia Archives and Records Management (NSARM).

Government registration of vital events has two starting dates, 1 October 1908 and an earlier series that ran for fourteen years from 1864. The first few years were patchy, followed by a decade of better records, and eventually all birth and death entries ceased at the end of 1877.

Surviving birth and death records, 1864 to 1876, are available at NSARM, have been filmed, and can be used at the FHL or Family History Centers. Consolidated indexes exist for births and deaths and have been filmed.

TITLE: SUMMARY OF PRE-CONFEDERATION CENSUSES IN NOVA SCOTIA

1671–1753: Acadian censuses (see chapter 15)

1752: Halifax and vicinity

1770–1787: Miscellaneous returns for areas outside of Halifax

1809: Cheticamp and Margaree

1811: Cape Breton

1817: Counties of Antigonish, Guysborough, Hants, Pictou

1818: Cape Breton

1827: Cumberland and Halifax counties; townships of Annapolis, Antigonish, Argyll, Barrington, Clare, Clements, Liverpool, Shelburne, Wilmot, Yarmouth; districts of Bras d'Or and Louisbourg

1838: All of Nova Scotia except Cumberland County

1851: Counties of Halifax, Kings, and Pictou

1861: All of Nova Scotia

Note: These returns list heads of households only and an age/sex breakdown for other members of the household; the occupation of the head is included in most, and 1818 gives origin and time in Cape Breton.

Marriage records did not stop in 1877 but continued into the twentieth century. These and their indexes also have been filmed. The cutoff date for each county between old and new series of marriage records falls anywhere from 1906 to 1917, and the indexes were created in separate county sections.

Nova Scotia Archives and Records Management recently completed online consolidated indexes, linked to digitized images, for post-1864 vital records of births, marriages, and deaths. The years available for online searching are births from 1864 to 1877, marriages from 1864 to 1930, and deaths from 1864 to 1877 and October 1980 to 1955. NSARM worked in cooperation with the Record Access program of the LDS Church to complete the project. Indexes and images are accessible via a distinct website, novascotiagenealogy.com, and will later become available at FamilySearch.

Also online are death records for the city of Halifax. There is a searchable database for the years 1890 to 1908 via the regular NSARM website; the entries are linked to images.

In addition to civil vital records, the archives collection includes marriage bonds beginning in 1763 and licenses that start in 1849. The bonds are incomplete; years available are 1763 to 1864. The licenses run from 1849 to 1918. There is an index to the marriage bonds at the archives website, soon to be complete to 1871. NSARM has an index to the licenses. The bonds and licenses have been filmed for the FHL.

Civil divorce has always been possible in Nova Scotia. There is an index to names, 1759 to 1960, with the archival reference and year, within the databases at the NSARM website. The case files may include marriage records and documents related to the court proceedings.

CHURCH REGISTERS

The registers of many Protestant churches in Nova Scotia were filmed by NSARM over a quarter century from the 1960s to the 1980s. Date coverage for most registers falls between 1780 and 1914, which was just after the start of civil registration. Some early Acadian Catholic records were also filmed, and the registers of one church, St. Jean-Baptiste at Annapolis Royal, 1702 to 1755, can be searched at the NSARM website. While many records have not survived or been filmed, NSARM's Parish Records Collection offers the largest centralized resource for this kind of research in Nova Scotia.

Most records of Anglican churches, including baptisms, marriages, burials, and confirmations up to approximately 1950, have been filmed and are available at NSARM in Halifax. Some additional filmed records for Cape Breton can be searched at the Beaton Institute in Sydney. Copies from a few parishes around the province are in the FHL.

The United Church of Canada was established in 1925 by the amalgamation of Methodist and Congregational churches plus most Presbyterian congregations. Sometimes a new church name was created when congregations joined together. The archives for the Maritime Conference are in Sackville, New Brunswick. It holds records of nearly three hundred congregations, but less than a third of these are registers. Few of them date before 1850. In most instances, if the registers have been microfilmed, they are available at NSARM.

Records of some Catholic churches, mostly for parishes within the Archdiocese of Halifax, are available on microfilm at the FHL or at NSARM. Check the FHLC, and then check with the offices of one of the three dioceses: Halifax, Antigonish, or Yarmouth. The archives of the Convention of Atlantic Baptist Churches are at the Vaughn Library of Acadia University within the Esther Clark Wright Archives. These records, however, contain few registers.

Some help is available on the Internet. At Nova Scotia GenWeb there are indexes within several county sections for a limited number of churches. The years covered may be one or two, or many more, and a variety of denominations are represented. NSARM plans to have online in 2007 a searchable database with descriptions of individual holdings in the Parish Records Collection. To find information about holdings in other archives in Nova Scotia, use Archway, the online guide to archival records. Finally, if your ancestors came from the western part of the province, check for township books, which are discussed in the final section of this chapter.

CEMETERY RECORDS

Transcriptions in cemeteries began a long time ago, and NSARM has a collection covering the 1700s to the 1900s; the largest numbers are for the counties of Annapolis, Colchester, Halifax, Kings, Lunenburg, Pictou, and Queens. The records have been filmed and can be accessed using Family History Centers.

If you are working online, start at GenWeb. The Canada Cemetery Project page is useful because of its lists of cemeteries and their locations. There is information for all areas except Cape Breton, but only a few cemetery names link to databases. Look also at the pages for individual counties in the Nova Scotia section of GenWeb.

You can use a search engine as well. A search should help you find municipal, church, or private cemeteries. The Catholic Cemeteries Commission, which manages three cemeteries in Halifax, has a website with a searchable database.

The Genealogical Association of Nova Scotia published an index to the records of the Halifax Funeral Home beginning in 1939. The index can be accessed at the association website or by using the Halifax GenWeb page.

PROBATE

Probate was the responsibility of the county courts. Today there are eleven courts, but that number has fluctuated, and two counties, Guysborough and Shelburne, had two districts for a while. The earliest probate record is for Halifax in 1749.

The FHL has filmed probate records (most of the films go up to the 1960s). Copies of the films are in NSARM and can also be accessed at the FHL and through Family History Centers. Be sure to check the FHLC as part of your search.

Some probate records are indexed, but don't count on this. Some others have abstracts either for a particular area or for one surname. When not indexed, the records may be in rough chronological order. Lunenburg has an online index to all wills for nearly two hundred years that is accessible via GenWeb.

LAND RECORDS

Grants from the Crown to individuals are one type of land record; subsequent transfers of land are recorded in deeds. Grants were administered centrally from Halifax, while a system of county-based registries developed around the province to manage deeds and conveyances. There are extensive records, including the petitions of people requesting land, the transactions for sales, wills that mention land, mortgages, and maps. Petitions are informative because they include reasons given for requesting a land grant, which can include family details.

The LDS Church, working with NSARM, has filmed grants and deeds for various years, some into the middle of the 1900s. These microfilmed records are available at the provincial archives, the FHL, and through Family History Centers.

Land record resources are appearing on the Internet. There is an online index to land grant petitions for mainland Nova Scotia, 1769 to 1799, and for Cape Breton,

1787 to 1843, at the NSARM website. This index can be searched by personal name and on a geographic basis.

The Crown Lands Department is responsible for maintaining a database of all land grants from the 1700s to the present. The information is graphically displayed on a set of 138 index map sheets, copies of which can be obtained through the Department

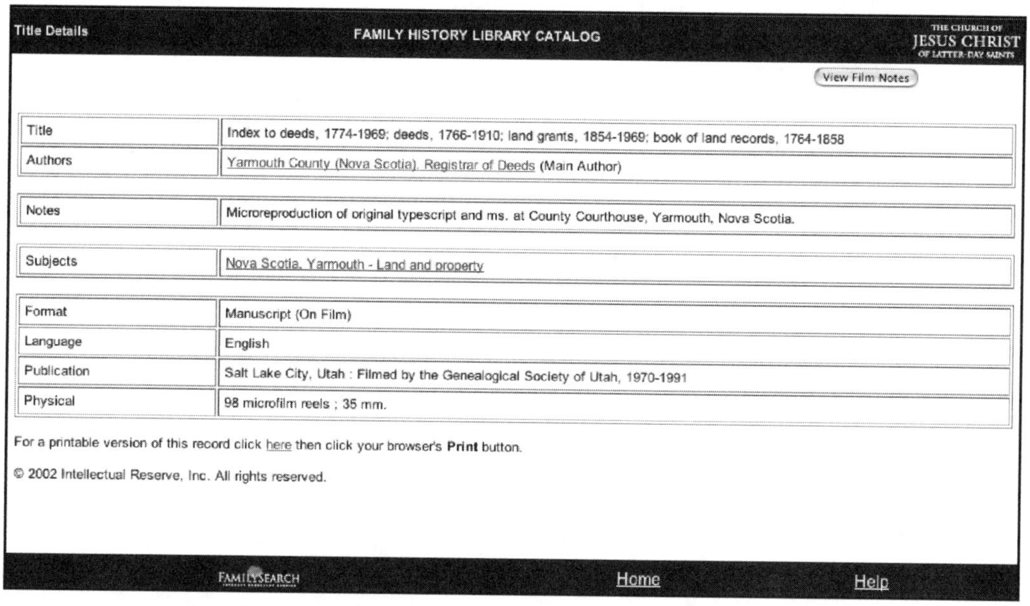

Title Details	FAMILY HISTORY LIBRARY CATALOG	THE CHURCH OF JESUS CHRIST OF LATTER-DAY SAINTS

(View Film Notes)

Title	Index to deeds, 1774-1969; deeds, 1766-1910; land grants, 1854-1969; book of land records, 1764-1858
Authors	Yarmouth County (Nova Scotia). Registrar of Deeds (Main Author)
Notes	Microreproduction of original typescript and ms. at County Courthouse, Yarmouth, Nova Scotia.
Subjects	Nova Scotia, Yarmouth - Land and property
Format	Manuscript (On Film)
Language	English
Publication	Salt Lake City, Utah : Filmed by the Genealogical Society of Utah, 1970-1991
Physical	98 microfilm reels ; 35 mm.

For a printable version of this record click here then click your browser's **Print** button.

© 2002 Intellectual Reserve, Inc. All rights reserved.

FAMILYSEARCH   Home   Help

Figure 21-3. FHLC Entry for Yarmouth County Land Records
The details for this Yarmouth County entry indicate why anyone without access to Halifax should check the Family History Library Catalog for copies of land records.
<www.familysearch.org>

of Natural Resources Library. Copies of individual land grants are also available at the office of the Provincial Crown Lands Record Centre.

To find evidence of land grants or deeds, first look for any online resources, beginning at the websites of NSARM and GenWeb. Then turn to the FHLC to check for indexes and records accessible in Family History Centers; most counties are represented. Online indexes are not yet as extensive as those on microfilm, but that will change.

Land papers held by NSARM were used to prepare the lists found within *Loyalists and Land Settlement in Nova Scotia* (M. Gilroy, 1937). The book remains a useful finding aid to Loyalist settlement.

NEWSPAPERS

The Halifax Gazette was Canada's first newspaper, starting publication in 1752. By the late 1800s there were a variety of newspapers around the province, mostly in Halifax and the vicinity, although Yarmouth and Pictou counties and Cape Breton also had several papers.

NSARM holds the province's largest collection of historical newspapers. Most have been microfilmed, and many are also held by Library and Archives Canada. There is also a guide to newspapers and their survival, *Nova Scotia Newspapers: A Directory and Union List, 1752–1988* (1990).

Many church organizations published newspapers: for example, the *Weslayan* (Methodist), the *Colonial Churchman* (Anglican), the *Christian Messenger* (Baptist), and the *Presbyterian Witness*. Some included vital events, and these may have been extracted or indexed.

The Genealogical Association of Nova Scotia connects you to an online index to the *Colonial Patriot* for the period December 1827 to May 1834 and to published indexes to vital events available for purchase. You can also check county sections of Nova Scotia GenWeb. The LAC website has lists of newspapers they have available on microfilm and links to some newspaper indexes.

OTHER LISTS AND DIRECTORIES

The website Canadian Directories—Who Was Where features directories in the collection of LAC. The city of Halifax is particularly well represented, with thirty editions of city directories spanning the years 1869 to 1901, all fully searchable and with page images. This site also includes all-Nova Scotia directories for 1864–65, 1866–67, and 1871 and a business directory from the 1890s.

NSARM includes *McAlpine's 1908 Nova Scotia Directory* among its online sources. Search for the name of the town or village, and then read through the listings; an individual name search is not available.

As you explore GenWeb and the NSARM websites, you will find other lists of inhabitants, including lists of taxpayers, first settlers, and voters. You should look at two parts of the GenWeb site: the genealogy resources and the individual county pages.

Halifax Public Libraries have extensive resources, including directories and local and family histories. Roots to the Past, a section at their website, offers many guides to research; topics include Acadians, the Halifax Explosion, and African Heritage.

SPECIAL SOURCES

If your ancestors lived in the western part of the colony or province, you may find information in township books. These begin in 1760 with the arrival of the New England Planters and last for approximately sixty years, but some have references to events at the start of the 1700s and as recently as 1920. A township was 100,000 acres and was originally planned as a unit of local government.

The contents of township records are characterized by variety. You can find vital records in between land records and town accounts. Records are available at NSARM and through the FHL or Family History Centers; look in the catalog under the name of the place and vital records.

Military records, victualling lists, militia lists, and names of members of disbanded Loyalist regiments who received land may help you locate early Nova Scotia ancestors.

There are lists of many of these at Nova Scotia GenWeb, but you must get into the individual county sections to look for them. The records are held by NSARM.

The NSARM website is your access point to several special databases, and some have been mentioned in the chapters on Aboriginal records and the Acadians. You can look at the *Halifax Explosion Remembrance Book*, which features a database of the 1,953 casualties of the 1917 disaster. The poll tax records of 1791–1793 are another searchable database, with over ten thousand names of people who paid tax a few years after the arrival of the Loyalists. African Nova Scotians in the Age of Slavery and Abolition is an exhibit and online documentary resource with a searchable database containing the names of about five thousand African Americans who came to Nova Scotia in 1783 and 1815–16. In addition to these resources, there are online exhibits of Nova Scotia history, all of them with background useful for genealogists.

WEBSITES

Archives, Convention of Atlantic Baptist Churches, Acadia University, Esther Clark Wright Archives: <http://library.acadiau.ca/archives/>

Archives search aid, Archway: <www.councilofnsarchives.ca/archway/>

Canadian Genealogy Centre: <www.collectionscanada.ca/genealogy/>

Catholic Cemeteries Commission: <www.ccchalifax.com>

Collections Canada Directories (where to start a search and find a list): <www.collectionscanada.ca/canadiandirectories/index-e.html>

Diocese of Nova Scotia and PEI: <www.nspeidiocese.ca>

Genealogical Association of Nova Scotia: <www.chebucto.ns.ca/recreation/GANS/>

Halifax Public Libraries Roots to the Past (history and genealogy resources): <www.halifaxpubliclibraries.ca/roots/links.html>

Library and Archives Canada Newspaper Resources List: <www.collectionscanada.ca/8/16/index-e.html>

Nova Scotia Archives and Records Management: <www.gov.ns.ca/nsarm/map/>

Nova Scotia Genealogy Network Association: <http://nsgna.ednet.ns.ca/index.html>

Nova Scotia GenWeb Project: <http://www.rootsweb.com/~canns/index.html>

Nova Scotia Geographical Names:

Nova Scotia Vital Statistics Division: <www.gov.ns.ca/snsmr/vstat/history.asp>

United Church, Maritime Conference Archives: <www.marconf.ca/archives.htm>

BIBLIOGRAPHY

Conrad, Margaret, ed. *They Planted Well: New England Planters in Maritime Canada*. Fredericton, NB: Acadiensis Press, 1988. (now online at <http://atlanticportal.hil.unb.ca:8000/publications/planters/01/>)

Ewing, Calum, D. Trask, and P. Collins. *Nova Scotia Museum Graveyard Inventory Guide and Data*. Halifax: History Section Nova Scotia Museum, 1990.

Gilroy, Marion, with D. C. Harvey. *Loyalists and Land Settlement in Nova Scotia.* Halifax: Public Archives of Nova Scotia, 1937. (reprinted many times)

Geyh, Patricia Keeney, et al. *French-Canadian Sources: A Guide for Genealogists.* Orem, UT: Ancestry, 2002.

Hamilton, William B. *Place Names of Atlantic Canada.* Toronto: University of Toronto Press, 1996.

Historical Atlas of the Maritime Provinces, 1878 / with an introduction by Joan Dawson. Halifax: Nimbus Pub., 2005. (a new edition of Roe's *Atlas of the Maritime Provinces of the Dominion of Canada*)

Lovell's Province of Nova Scotia Directory for 1871: Containing Names of Professional and Business Men, and Other Inhabitants, in the Cities, Towns and Villages throughout the Province ... Corrected to January, 1871. Montreal: John Lovell, 1871.

Nova Scotia Newspapers: A Directory and Union List, 1752–1988. Halifax: Dalhousie University, School of Library and Informational Studies, 1990.

Peterson, Jean. *The Loyalist Guide: Nova Scotian Loyalists and Their Documents.* Halifax: Public Archives of Nova Scotia, 1983.

Punch, Terence M. *Genealogical Research in Nova Scotia.* Halifax: Nimbus, 1998.

Roe, Frederick B. *Atlas of the Maritime Provinces of the Dominion of Canada.* St. John, NB: Halifax, N.S.: Roe Bros., 1879.

Smith, Leonard H. *Nova Scotia Immigrants to 1867.* 2 vols. Baltimore: Genealogical Publishing Co., 1992–1994.

Whyte, Donald. *Dictionary of Scottish Emigrants to Canada Before Confederation.* Vols. 1–4. Toronto: Ontario Genealogical Society, 1986–2005.

Wright, Esther Clark. *Planters and Pioneers.* Hantsport, NS: Lancelot Press, 1978.

ADDRESSES

Beaton Institute
Cape Breton University
PO Box 5300
Sydney, NS B1P 6G4

Centre d'etudes acadiennes
Universite de Moncton
Moncton, NB E1A 3E9

Diocese of Nova Scotia and Prince Edward Island Diocesan Archives
Anglican Diocesan Centre
5732 College Street
Halifax, NS B3H 1X3

Halifax Public Libraries
Spring Garden Road Memorial Public Library
5381 Spring Garden Road
Halifax, NS B3J 1E9

The Legislative Library
Province House
1726 Hollis Street
Halifax, NS B3J 2Y3

Maritime Baptist Archives
Vaughan Memorial Library
Acadia University
50 Acadia Street
PO Box 4
Wolfville, NS B4P 2RP

Nova Scotia Archives and Record Management
6016 University Avenue
Halifax, NS B3H 1W4

Provincial Crown Lands Information Management Office
Founders Square
1701 Hollis Street
Halifax, NS B3J 3M8

Roman Catholic Church in Nova Scotia
(for Cumberland, Colchester, Hants, Halifax, Lunenburg, and Queens counties)
PO Box 1527
Halifax, NS B3J 2Y3

(for Yarmouth, Shelburne, Digby, Annapolis, and Kings counties)
43 Albert St.
Yarmouth, NS B5A 3N1

(for Antigonish, all of Cape Breton, Guysborough, and Pictou counties)
PO Box 1060
Antigonish, NS B2G 2L7

Service Nova Scotia and Municipal Relations
Vital Statistics Office
Joseph Howe Building
1690 Hollis Street
PO Box 157
Halifax, NS B3J 3J9

United Church of Canada
Maritime Conference Archives
32 York Street
Sackville, NB E4L 4R4

Figure 22-1. Ontario

ONTARIO

Ontario, the most populous province in Canada, came into being as a result of the American Revolution. Loyalists, people who supported the British Crown, moved north in 1783, first to Nova Scotia and Quebec, and then to the best agricultural land, which was in the western part of Quebec, the area that is now Ontario.

In 1791, Quebec was divided into Upper Canada (today's Ontario) and Lower Canada (today's Quebec). The move was deemed necessary by the authorities because of the large influx of English-speaking settlers in the western part of the colony. The settlement by the Loyalists, followed by the British victory in the War of 1812, helped create a pro-British, conservative culture that survived in Ontario into the 1900s.

Ontario's population grew rapidly to 77,000 people in 1812 and to 430,000 by 1840. Many new inhabitants came from the British Isles, including former soldiers who had served with the British forces in the American Revolution or the War of 1812. There were immigrants from continental Europe and others from the United States who were not Loyalists or ex-soldiers. At the end of the War of 1812, slightly more than half the residents of Upper Canada were non-Loyalist Americans.

In 1841, after the union of Upper Canada and Lower Canada, Upper Canada became known as Canada West. It kept that name until 1867, when it joined the new country of Canada as the province of Ontario. (For simplicity's sake, we will refer to the area as Ontario in this chapter, regardless of the time frame.)

By Confederation, Ontario was on its way to becoming the economic powerhouse of British North America. It had the population, and the railways and canals provided an efficient transportation system. Growth and opportunity attracted immigrants, the majority coming from England, Ireland, Scotland, and Wales.

While many people were leaving Ontario in the last quarter of the nineteenth century, many others were arriving from across the Atlantic. Some were attracted west by the government's glowing pictures of homesteads and opportunity there, and many others went south across the border into the United States. Their place was taken by new arrivals from the British Isles and the European continent.

Ontario's boundaries were expanded three times after Confederation. The province grew to the west and north in 1874 after the Canadian government bought Rupert's Land from the Hudson's Bay Company. In 1889, Ontario was given the Kenora area, which had also been claimed by Manitoba. The province's final expansion came in 1912, when the boundary with Manitoba was set all the way north to Hudson Bay.

This new territory did not shift the population; most people chose to live in the extreme south, and this remains the same today. The northern part of the province, occupying part of the Canadian Shield, is rich in minerals and has a harsh climate. Canada's largest city, Toronto, and the nation's capital, Ottawa, are both in Ontario.

FINDING LOCALITIES

Ontario established the county as the basic unit for most municipal and judicial matters in 1849, replacing a system of districts that had been in place, with modifications, for sixty years. Boundaries of both districts and counties went through several changes.

Grey County, for example, was formed in 1850, taking land from Waterloo and Simcoe counties. You might also find records for residents of Grey under the Western District (1788–1798), the Home District (1798–1837), or the Simcoe or Wellington districts (both 1837–1850).

Maps showing districts and counties are in the book *Genealogy in Ontario: Searching the Records* (Merriman, 2002). They are also included in the Hugh Armstrong collection on the CanGenealogy website, along with lists of townships and the counties or districts to which they belong.

Don't be confused by references to counties before 1849 or districts after that year. The first counties were created in 1792 as electoral districts only, and they did not become significant to genealogists until the 1840s. Districts still exist in the sparsely populated northern region of Ontario.

Modern maps, the Canadian Geographical Names website, and Ontario Locator, a website with information on almost 10,000 Ontario place-names, will help you find locations in the province.

The best printed reference to Ontario communities is *Places in Ontario* (Mika, 1977–83). A reprint of an 1867 map of the province, by Jonathan Sheppard Books, is helpful, showing many small locations. Several gazetteers, almanacs, directories, and atlases have been published since the first one appeared in 1799. You can find some of them using the full-text books at Our Roots and online catalogues of reference libraries.

CENSUS

Several Ontario censuses and indexes are available on the Internet. Ancestry has indexes to the returns from 1851, 1871, 1901, and 1911, with links to images of the census pages on the Library and Archives Canada (LAC) website. An index to 1871 is on the

LAC site, and additional indexes to the 1901 and 1911 censuses are at Automated Genealogy. The FamilySearch website has a detailed index to the 1881 census.

The first census returns for Ontario date from 1783, and scattered returns from before 1842 exist for several areas. These were local enumerations, not province-wide. The most important of the early censuses, taken in 1842, recorded heads of households and statistics about others in the house. There were also censuses in 1848 and 1850, but returns survive for only three of the nineteen districts.

The 1851 census, taken in January 1852, is also incomplete. No returns survive for the largest city, Toronto. That is a great misfortune because this was the first census to include all members of each family. The surviving returns have been indexed by Ancestry, and search results are linked to digital images on the LAC website.

From 1851, censuses were taken every ten years until 1951 and every five years after that. These returns provide information on all household members—name, age, gender, country of birth, religion, ethnic origin, occupation, marital status, and education.

Along with being available on the Internet, an 1871 census index, done by heads of household, was published on a county-by-county basis by the Ontario Genealogical Society.

Census returns can be consulted on microfilm using interlibrary loan and the facilities at Family History Centers or LAC.

CIVIL REGISTRATION

The registration of births, deaths, and marriages in Ontario started on 1 July 1869, although county marriage registers covering 1858–1869 are also available. The Ancestry database includes marriages from civil registrations as well as the earlier county registers.

Birth registrations usually include the name, gender, father's name, mother's maiden name, and father's rank or occupation. Marriage registrations include name, age, place of residence and birth, marital status, occupation, father's name, mother's maiden name, and religious denomination for each person. Death registrations have the person's name, age, sex, religious affiliation, rank or profession, birthplace, cause of death, and, after 1907, the place of burial and the name of the parents. The county or district is shown on all registration documents.

Indexes and registrations are made public after ninety-five years for births, eighty years for marriages, and seventy years for deaths. These records are on microfilm at the Archives of Ontario and the Family History Library (FHL). Images and indexes are also on the Ancestry website.

Registrations not yet turned over to the archives are available from the Office of the Registrar General. Application forms are on the Internet. Indexes to these registrations are not open to the public.

Ontario Marriage Registrations is an online database of marriage record transcripts. The sources used were civil registrations, 1869–1924, and county marriage records, 1858–1869.

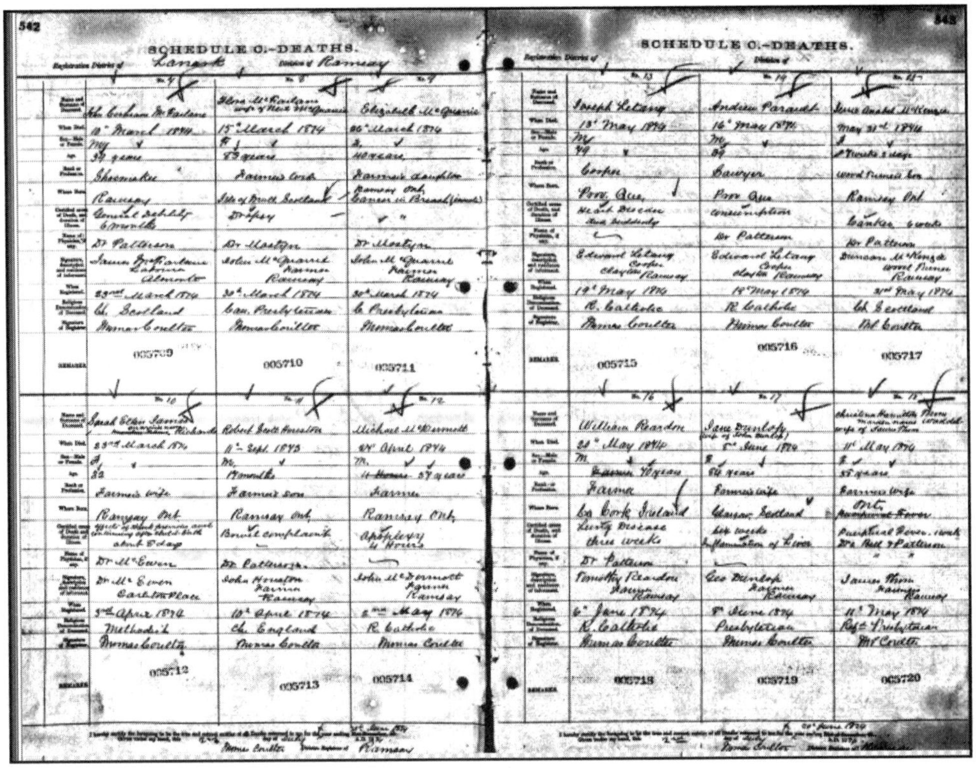

Figure 22-2. Civil Registration: Ontario Death Record
Available at Ancestry.ca

District clerks of the peace registered marriages from 1831 to 1858, before counties assumed the task of compiling the registers. The transcripts from registrations are sorted by year; the others are sorted by county or district. The records are held by the Archives of Ontario. County and district marriage registers are on microfilm in the FHL.

The civil authorities also recorded marriage bonds. On the Web at LAC is an index to the Upper Canada marriage bonds for 1803 to 1865.

Divorces in Ontario were granted by acts of the federal parliament until 1930. Divorce certificates after 1930 are available from the court where the divorce case was heard.

CHURCH RECORDS

Historically, the most important church in Ontario has been the Church of England, now known as the Anglican Church of Canada. The largest denomination, however, has been the United Church, formed by the merger in 1925 of the Methodist, Presbyterian, and Congregationalist churches.

More than 100,000 Wesleyan Methodist baptisms from 1825 through 1910 have been transcribed, indexed, and made available on the Internet. The work was based on microfilm at the Victoria University Library in Toronto; the films are also in the FHL.

The Victoria University Library is the main archives of the United Church of Canada and holds significant Methodist collections. Ontario also has large numbers of Anglicans, Roman Catholics, Baptists, Lutherans, and Jews. Most of the denominations have archives. Websites are listed at the end of this chapter. There are scattered records of some of these churches in the FHL. The Archives of Ontario and LAC hold small, nonduplicated collections of Ontario church records.

A database of Roman Catholic marriages is at Ancestry. It covers six counties between 1827 and 1870: Peel, York, Ontario, Simcoe, Lincoln, and Welland. The index includes name, year of marriage, county of marriage, and source information and is derived from records at the Archives of Ontario. Ancestry also has records from the Institut Généalogique Drouin, including French Catholic records from Ontario from 1747 through 1967.

Use the Internet to look for more resources, checking GenWeb, Cyndi's List, and the Olive Tree Genealogy website. The Olive Tree site summarizes the marriage

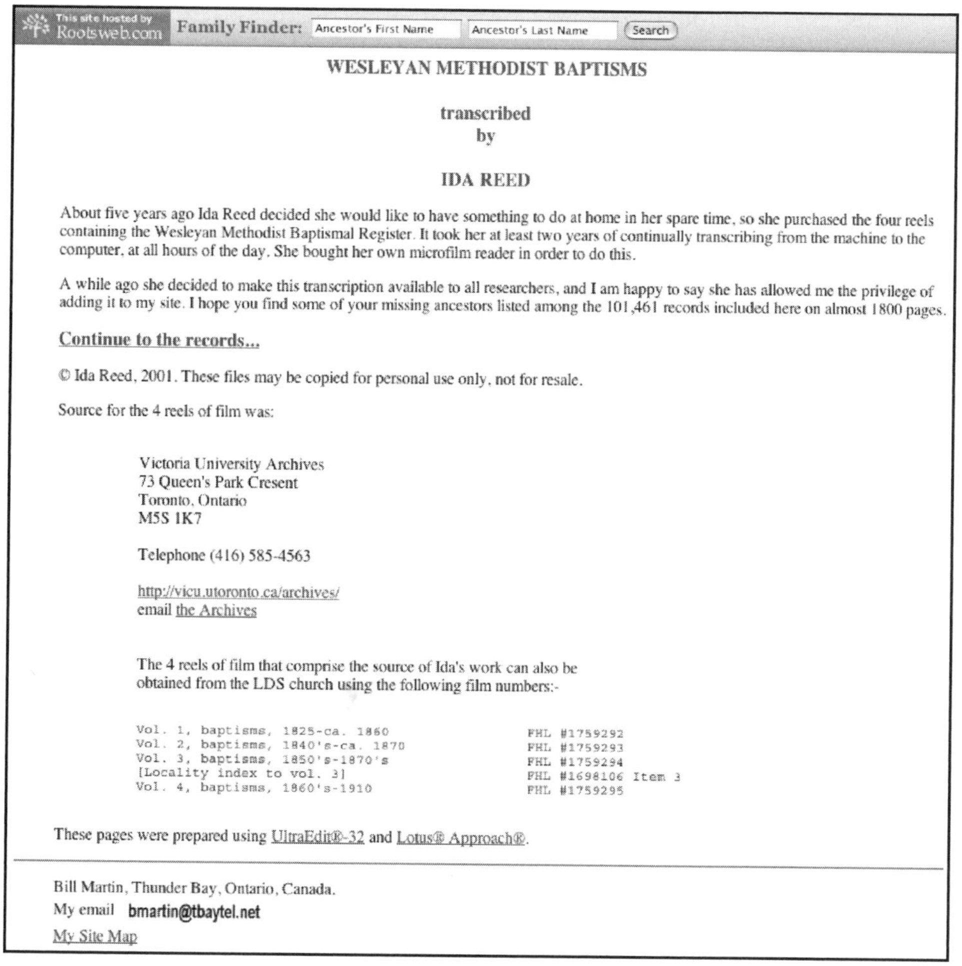

This site hosted by Rootsweb.com   **Family Finder:** Ancestor's First Name | Ancestor's Last Name | (Search)

WESLEYAN METHODIST BAPTISMS

transcribed
by

IDA REED

About five years ago Ida Reed decided she would like to have something to do at home in her spare time, so she purchased the four reels containing the Wesleyan Methodist Baptismal Register. It took her at least two years of continually transcribing from the machine to the computer, at all hours of the day. She bought her own microfilm reader in order to do this.

A while ago she decided to make this transcription available to all researchers, and I am happy to say she has allowed me the privilege of adding it to my site. I hope you find some of your missing ancestors listed among the 101,461 records included here on almost 1800 pages.

Continue to the records...

© Ida Reed, 2001. These files may be copied for personal use only, not for resale.

Source for the 4 reels of film was:

> Victoria University Archives
> 73 Queen's Park Cresent
> Toronto, Ontario
> M5S 1K7
>
> Telephone (416) 585-4563
>
> http://vicu.utoronto.ca/archives/
> email the Archives

The 4 reels of film that comprise the source of Ida's work can also be obtained from the LDS church using the following film numbers:-

```
Vol. 1, baptisms, 1825-ca. 1860        FHL #1759292
Vol. 2, baptisms, 1840's-ca. 1870      FHL #1759293
Vol. 3, baptisms, 1850's-1870's        FHL #1759294
[Locality index to vol. 3]             FHL #1698106 Item 3
Vol. 4, baptisms, 1860's-1910          FHL #1759295
```

These pages were prepared using UltraEdit®-32 and Lotus® Approach®.

Bill Martin, Thunder Bay, Ontario, Canada.
My email **bmartin@tbaytel.net**
My Site Map

Figure 22-3. An Online Link to Wesleyan Methodist Baptismal Records Transcribed by Ida Reed

<http://freepages.genealogy.rootsweb.com/~wjmartin/wesleyan.htm>

regulations; before 1793, only Church of England and Catholic clergy could perform marriages. This was gradually expanded to include all clergy by 1831.

Some branches of the Ontario Genealogical Society are publishing books listing the churches within their areas, what records are available (if any), and where they can be found. Some county GenWebs in Ontario have lists of churches in their coverage areas.

CEMETERY RECORDS

Branches of the Ontario Genealogical Society have recorded and published cemetery records from all corners of the province. If you are unsure where your people lived and died, a couple of databases might help you pin them down.

The Ontario Cemetery Finding Aid (OCFA) includes references to more than 2 million burials in 3,800 cemeteries. The aid does not include dates of death. For that information, consult the cemetery transcriptions upon which the OCFA is based.

A similar aid is the Ontario Cemetery Ancestor Index on the website of the Ontario Genealogical Society. It includes references to more than 1 million burials. With the information you glean from the finding aid and the index, contact the local branch of the society to purchase the published transcript or obtain other information.

Other Ontario burial information is available through the Ontario Cemeteries Resources website, which provides contact information for people willing to do lookups or provide transcriptions. Local GenWeb pages might also provide links to transcriptions of interest.

Several websites feature cemetery records. Examples include the Northeastern Ontario Gravemarker Gallery, with about 115,000 markers; Cemeteries in the County of Oxford, with more than one hundred burial places; Cemeteries of Stormont and Dundas Counties; and Thunder Bay District and Rural Cemeteries, with lists from more than thirty cemeteries.

WILLS AND PROBATE RECORDS

Wills that were filed with the Court of Probate and the Surrogate Courts between 1793 and 1963 are available. You'll need to know whether to look before or after 1859. Before 1859, wills for large estates were probated by the province-wide Court of Probate, while local Surrogate Courts looked after smaller estates. The Surrogate Courts have had complete responsibility for estate actions since that year. Surname indexes from each court level for estate files before 1859 are on the Archives of Ontario website.

The FHL in Salt Lake City has microfilmed copies of the probate registers from 1793 to 1858 and the estate files from 1793 to 1859.

The Archives of Ontario website also has a guide to help you find wills from after 1859. If you know the county or district in which the estate was handled, a table listing locations will point you to the right jurisdiction. That will help you find the indexes available on microfilm.

If you don't know which courthouse handled the estate, check the "application to probate" books at the archives. They list every estate file from 1859 through 1982 and identify the courthouse. These lists are lengthy, so if your name is common, they will take a lot of time to peruse.

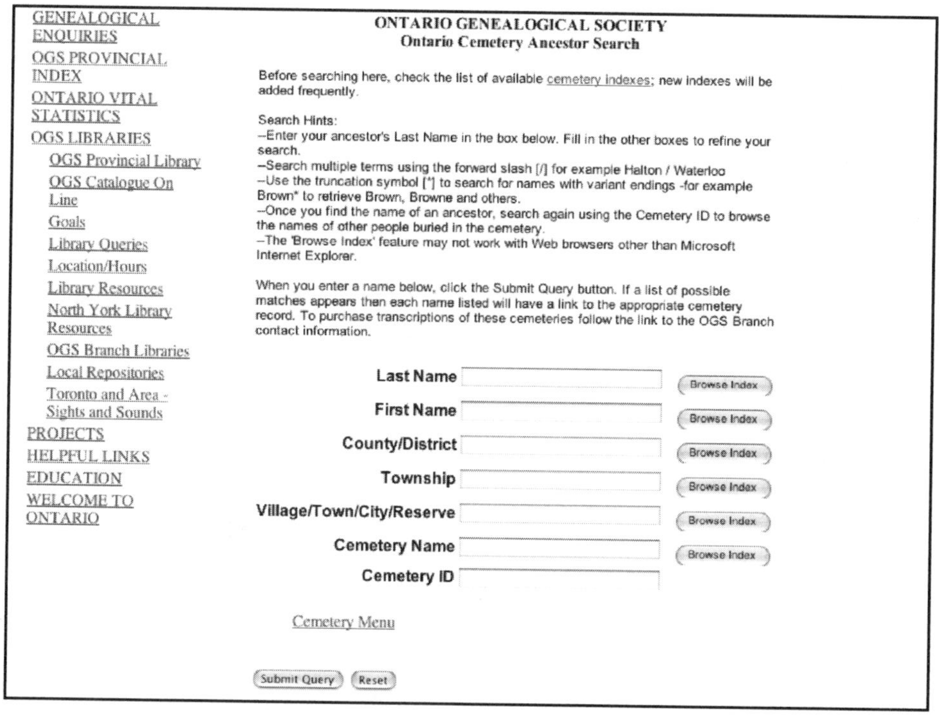
GENEALOGICAL ENQUIRIES
OGS PROVINCIAL INDEX
ONTARIO VITAL STATISTICS
OGS LIBRARIES
OGS Provincial Library
OGS Catalogue On Line
Goals
Library Queries
Location/Hours
Library Resources
North York Library Resources
OGS Branch Libraries
Local Repositories
Toronto and Area - Sights and Sounds
PROJECTS
HELPFUL LINKS
EDUCATION
WELCOME TO ONTARIO

ONTARIO GENEALOGICAL SOCIETY
Ontario Cemetery Ancestor Search

Before searching here, check the list of available cemetery indexes; new indexes will be added frequently.

Search Hints:
--Enter your ancestor's Last Name in the box below. Fill in the other boxes to refine your search.
--Search multiple terms using the forward slash [/] for example Halton / Waterloo
--Use the truncation symbol [*] to search for names with variant endings -for example Brown* to retrieve Brown, Browne and others.
--Once you find the name of an ancestor, search again using the Cemetery ID to browse the names of other people buried in the cemetery.
--The 'Browse Index' feature may not work with Web browsers other than Microsoft Internet Explorer.

When you enter a name below, click the Submit Query button. If a list of possible matches appears then each name listed will have a link to the appropriate cemetery record. To purchase transcriptions of these cemeteries follow the link to the OGS Branch contact information.

Last Name — Browse Index
First Name — Browse Index
County/District — Browse Index
Township — Browse Index
Village/Town/City/Reserve — Browse Index
Cemetery Name — Browse Index
Cemetery ID

Cemetery Menu

Submit Query Reset

Figure 22-4. Cemetery Search Web Page from the Ontario Genealogical Society
<http://ogs.andornot.com/OldFiles/CemeteryIndex.htm>

The twenty-seven volumes of the *Surrogate Court Index of Ontario, Canada, 1859–1900,* may help you track down the location of the probate records for some of your ancestors.

Once you have obtained a reference to a will, consult it on microfilm at any library that has interlibrary loan or, if it has not yet been microfilmed, in its original paper format at the Archives of Ontario. All estate files after 1963 remain with the original courthouses.

LAND RECORDS

Ontario's districts and counties have been subdivided into townships, which were usually rectangular unless geography, such as a lake or a river, made that impossible. Townships were divided into bands of land 1.25 miles wide called concessions. These can run in any direction necessary to provide access to a lake or a river.

Concessions were labeled with a number, usually a Roman numeral, or a letter. They were further subdivided into numbered lots, which were originally two hundred acres in size, but most have been subdivided further over the years.

The British Crown began to issue grants of land in Ontario in 1791, primarily to attract settlers to Canada. To obtain land, settlers had to complete formal written applications. These petitions, dating from 1764 to 1867, are on microfilm.

To find a land record, you'll need to know where your ancestor lived. Use census records, directories, or the Ontario Land Records Index, a microfiche set available at the Archives of Ontario, the FHL, and many local libraries. The index includes only original nominees or grantees and draws from Crown land records, the settlement projects organized by the Canada Company or by Peter Robinson in the 1820s, and land-related documents in other collections. The index can be searched by the name of the settler or the location.

Available records include the following:

- The Upper Canada Land Petitions Series at LAC, with petitions and grants from 1791 to 1867. The petitions include the name of the petitioner, the date of the petition, and military regiment, if applicable. There might be information on the petitioner's family, as well as an indication as to whether he was a soldier or a United Empire Loyalist. The collection is available on microfilm from the Archives of Ontario, LAC, or the FHL. A more recent and also more complete index for land grants is a series of nine volumes compiled by the Ontario Genealogical Society, *Index to the Upper Canada Land Books* (2001–2005).

- Land patents, which declared that a settler had completed the terms of settlement and was given ownership of the property. They are indexed by township (1793 to 1852), by district (1793 to 1825), and by surname (1826 to 1912). Patents from before 1850 are at the Archives of Ontario, and patents from after 1850 are at the provincial Ministry of Natural Resources.

- Township papers, which reflect activity and claims on a property before the Crown patent officially transferred title to an individual. Available at the Archives of Ontario, they are arranged by location and might include letters written by settlers, certificates of settlement duties, and more. Sometimes, however, there is nothing at all.

- Land registry office documents, also known as instruments. These were created when land was transferred from one person to another. The documents have been microfilmed and are available only by contacting the local registry offices. The Archives of Ontario and the FHL have microfilms of the nineteenth-century county and township copybooks. Original copybooks and other historic registry office material have been dispersed to local archives.

Alphabetical indexes to deeds, filed under both grantor and grantee, are available for some townships after 1865. Also, the Abstract Index of Deeds, a chronological history of a property, was created in 1865. If you have a property description, you can follow all transactions connected with it in the index, which is found in local registry offices and at the Archives of Ontario.

The Archives of Ontario collection includes land records from as late as 1955. The FHL has copies of most of the microfilmed records from the archives. The FHL collection includes records of the heir and devisee commissions, which were created by the government to settle disputes or resolve unclear rights over who was entitled to claim a parcel of land.

A series of historical atlases covers almost every county in Ontario. They show the lot and concession numbers of each township as well as the names of property owners at the time the atlas was compiled in the late 1800s. These atlases are available online through the Canadian County Atlas Digital Project.

NEWSPAPERS

There were newspapers in York and Niagara in the 1790s. Several important newspapers were launched in Ontario in the early years of the nineteenth century. They include the *Kingston Gazette* in 1810; the *Bytown Packet*, now the *Ottawa Citizen*, in 1844; and the *Toronto Globe* in 1844.

Thousands of issues of Ontario newspapers are on the Internet. Back issues of the *Toronto Star* from 1895 to 2002 can be viewed online for a fee. The *Globe and Mail* and its predecessor, the *Globe*, are included in an online database available through many local libraries.

The Archives of Ontario has newspapers from most Ontario cities and towns from 1793 to about 1930 and a collection of newspapers from multicultural communities from 1930 to 1987. A list is on the Archives of Ontario website. The Toronto Reference Library has more recent newspapers from the largest cities, as well as a more comprehensive collection of newspapers from Toronto.

The best guide is *Inventory of Ontario Newspapers, 1793–1986* (Gilchrist, 1987). It lists where existing copies may be found on microfilm or paper.

Several books listing death and marriage notices in newspapers have been published for the years before civil registration began. Ten of these books, for Methodist churches, have been compiled by Donald A. McKenzie. References to about half a million Ontario obituaries are on the Ontario Obits website.

OTHER WAYS TO FIND PEOPLE

Directories listing businesspeople and other residents have been published in Ontario for decades. Most directories cover urban areas, although a variety of county directories were published in Ontario from 1870 through 1910.

Many early Ontario directories have been scanned and placed online. The Toronto Reference Library has nineteenth-century directories from that city. The Canadian Directories collection on the LAC website features Ottawa directories from 1861 through 1901. Directories from other communities are also on the LAC website.

Some early directories are available on microfilm and microfiche. The Archives of Ontario has an extensive collection that is available for loan across the province, and local archives and libraries are likely to have the early directories for their areas.

Federal voters lists are available from 1935 through 1979. Check with local libraries and archives for local lists.

The Ontario Genealogical Society Provincial Index, on the society's website, is a hypertext library with more than 2.8 million names. The information included was drawn from many different resources, including censuses; birth, marriage, and death registers; references in books; land records; ship lists; military records; and more. Every entry points to the original source.

SPECIAL SOURCES

Bill Martin of Thunder Bay has compiled an impressive collection of resources on his personal website. His work includes transcripts of directories and gazetteers, church records, land records, census extracts, and more. The Wesleyan Methodist baptism transcription, mentioned in the church records section, is part of Martin's site.

The website of the Archives of Ontario includes guides to the major record groups of interest to genealogists. Use these guides to gain a better understanding of the availability and value of the records. Most of the microfilmed records in the archives are available through interlibrary loan.

Loyalist sources are many; begin by consulting a guide devoted to this subject in Ontario, *United Empire Loyalists: A Guide to Tracing Loyalist Ancestors in Upper Canada* (Merriman, 2006). Loyalist names appear in several published lists, in early land records, and in records of compensation paid by the British government. You can find more information on Loyalists in chapter 16. There are sixteen branches of the United Empire Loyalists' Association of Canada in Ontario, and the association website gives locations and websites.

There are hundreds of histories of cities, towns, and villages and many family histories as well. Check the Our Roots website, which has digitized copies of about two hundred local histories, and library catalogs using the search capabilities of AMICUS at LAC.

Several websites will provide names, other information, and clues for people doing research in Toronto. The Ontario Genealogical Society's Toronto branch has a superb website. Another one to look at is Ontario Roots.

WEBSITES

Anglican Church of Canada: <www.anglican.ca/about/departments/General-Secretary/archives/archives-list.htm>
Archives of Ontario: <www.archives.gov.on.ca>
Bill Martin's Web page: <my.tbaytel.net/bmartin>
Canadian County Atlas Digital Project: <digital.library.mcgill.ca/countyatlas>
CanGenealogy: <www.cangenealogy.com>
Cemeteries in the County of Oxford, Ontario: <freepages.genealogy.rootsweb.com/~dcoop>
Cemeteries of Stormont and Dundas Counties: <freepages.genealogy.rootsweb.com/~sbresearch/cemeteries.html>
Mennonite Archives of Ontario: <grebel.uwaterloo.ca/mao>

Northern Ontario Canada Gravemarker Gallery:
    <freepages.genealogy.rootsweb.com/~murrayp>
Olive Tree Genealogy: <www.olivetreegenealogy.com>
Ontario Cemeteries Resources: <www.wightman.ca/~dkaufman>
Ontario Cemetery Ancestor Search:
    <ogs.andornot.com/OldFiles/CemeteryIndex.htm>
Ontario Cemetery Finding Aid: <www.islandnet.com/ocfa>
Ontario Genealogical Society: <www.ogs.on.ca>
Ontario Genealogical Society, Toronto Branch:
    <www.torontofamilyhistory.org>
Ontario GenWeb: <www.rootsweb.com/~canon>
Ontario Locator: <www.geneofun.on.ca/ontariolocator>
Ontario Marriage Registrations: <homepages.rootsweb.com/~maryc/thisisit.htm>
Ontario Obits: <www.ontarioobits.com>
Ontario Roots: <www.ontarioroots.com>
Presbyterian Church Archives: <www.presbycan.ca/archives/geneal.html>
RegistrarGeneralofOntario:<www.cbs.gov.on.ca/mcbs/english/births&marriages.
    htm>
Société franco-ontarienne d'histoire et de généalogie: <www.sfohg.com>
Thunder Bay District Cemeteries: <freepages.genealogy.rootsweb.com/~jmitchell/
    cemeteries.html>
Toronto Public Library (including Toronto Reference Library):
    <www.torontopubliclibrary.ca>
United Church of Canada Archives: <unitedchurcharchives.vicu.utoronto.ca>
United Empire Loyalists' Association of Canada: <www.uelac.org>
Wesleyan Methodist Baptisms, 1825–1910: <freepages.genealogy.rootsweb.com/
    ~wjmartin/wesleyan.htm>

BIBLIOGRAPHY

Britnell, W. E., and Elizabeth Hancocks. *County Marriage Registers of Ontario, Canada, 1858–1869*. Agincourt, ON: Generation Press, 1979–. (series)

Elliot, Noel Montgomery. *The Central Canadians, 1600–1900: An Alphabetized Directory of the People, Places and Vital Dates*. Toronto: Genealogical Research Library, 1995.

Gazetteer of Canada: Southern Ontario. Ottawa: Canadian Permanent Committee on Geographical Names, 1968.

Gibson, June, Elizabeth Hancocks, and Shannon Hancocks. *Surrogate Court Index of Ontario, Canada, 1859–1900*. 27 vols. Agincourt, ON: Generation Press, 1988.

Gilchrist, J. Brian. *Inventory of Ontario Newspapers, 1793–1986*. Toronto: Micromedia, 1987.

Jonasson, Eric. *Canadian Veterans of the War of 1812*. Winnipeg: Wheatfield Press, 1981.

Lovell's Gazetteer of British North America, 1873. Milton, ON: Global Heritage Press, 1999.

Loyalist Lineages of Canada, 1783–1983. 2 vols. Agincourt, ON: Generation Press and Toronto: Toronto Branch, United Empire Loyalists' Association, 1984–1991.

Main, Lorne W. *Index to 1881 Canadian Census of North West Territories & Algoma, Ontario.* Vancouver: L.W. Main, 1984.

Merriman, Brenda Dougall. *Genealogy in Ontario: Searching the Records.* 3rd ed. Toronto: Ontario Genealogical Society, 2002.

Merriman, Brenda Dougall. *United Empire Loyalists, A Guide to Tracing Loyalist Ancestors in Upper Canada.* Toronto: Global Heritage Press, 2006.

Mika, Nick, and Helma Mika. *Places in Ontario.* 3 vols. Belleville, ON: Mika Publishing, 1977, 1981, 1983.

Stratford-Devai, Fawne, and Ruth Burkholder. *Ontario Land Registry Office Records: A Guide.* Campbellville, ON: Global Heritage Press, 2003.

Taylor, Ryan. *Books You Need to Do Genealogy in Ontario.* Fort Wayne, IN: Round Tower Books, 2000.

ADDRESSES

Anglican Church—Diocese of Toronto
and the Ecclesiastical Province of Ontario
135 Adelaide Street East
Toronto, ON M5C 1L8

Archives of Ontario
77 Grenville Street
Toronto, ON M5S 1B3

Archives of the Roman Catholic Archdiocese of Toronto
1155 Yonge Street
Toronto, ON M4T1W2

Canadian Baptist Archives
McMaster Divinity College
1280 Main St W, Room 152
Hamilton, ON L8S 4K1

Jewish Archives
4600 Bathurst Street
Willowdale, ON M2R 3V2

Library and Archives Canada
395 Wellington Street
Ottawa, ON K1A 0N3

Lutheran Church Archives
Wilfrid Laurier University
75 University Avenue West
Waterloo, ON N2L 3C5

Mennonite Archives of Ontario
Conrad Grebel University College
140 Westmount Road N.
Waterloo, ON N2L 3G6

Office of the Registrar General
PO Box 4600
189 Red River Road
Thunder Bay, ON P7B 6L8

Ontario Genealogical Society
40 Orchard View Boulevard, Ste. 102
Toronto, ON M4R 1B9

The Presbyterian Church in Canada
50 Wynford Drive
Toronto, ON M3C 1J7

United Church of Canada Archives
73 Queen's Park Crescent East
Toronto, ON M5S 1K7

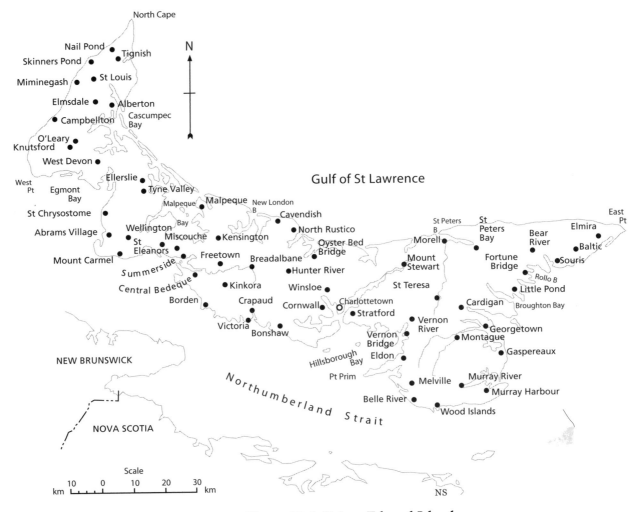

Figure 23-1. Prince Edward Island

PRINCE EDWARD ISLAND

Many who know little of Canada have heard of Prince Edward Island. It is the home of Anne of Green Gables, a delightful character made famous by the novels of Lucy Maud Montgomery. This small island is also known for potatoes. It ships seed potatoes around the world, produces a third of Canada's potato crop, and provides the potatoes used by many fast food restaurants.

Prince Edward Island is the smallest province in Canada, both in size and population. The 2001 census reported 138,000 inhabitants; more than two dozen Canadian cities are larger. The island belonged first to France (Île Saint-Jean) and was settled by Acadians, but it was captured by Britain in 1758, and the Acadians were expelled. Prince Edward Island was a British colony from 1763 to 1873, when it joined Canada.

The peace treaty with France in 1763 confirmed British possession. Land was not opened to settlers; instead, a semifeudal form of tenure was introduced. This discouraged settlement and made land a hot political issue for one hundred years. Many who did come to Prince Edward Island were from Scotland and the west of England.

Agriculture has always been a major part of the economy, but mixed farming predominated before potatoes became the most important crop. The Island had a significant ship-building industry in the middle of the 1800s. Islanders have also worked in fishing and seaweed harvesting.

Failure to resolve the land issue kept Prince Edward Island out of Confederation in 1867. Six years later a combination of financial problems, a railway, and the promise of a solution to the land problem led to a change of view. One outstanding issue, a fixed link to the mainland, was finally resolved in 1997 with the completion of the Confederation Bridge.

Geographical Names of Prince Edward Island Index O-R

Prince Edward Island

O

Oak Valley P.O. in **Pembroke** 8 mi NE of **Murray River** (1912-14) - Lot 63

Oak River flows N into **Gulf of St. Lawrence** at **Cable Head East** (*Ore River, Oar River, Sore River*) - Lot 42

Oar River flows N into **Gulf of St. Lawrence** at **Cable Head East** (*Oak River, Ore River, Sore River*) - Lot 42

O'Brien Road School District at **O'Brien Road** 4 mi NW of **Alberton** c1892 - Lot 4

O'Brien Road 'community' 4 mi NW of **Alberton** (*Wells O'Brien*) -Lot 4

O'Briens Road 5 mi S of **Morell** (*Windon*) - Lot 40

Observation Cove adjacent to **Hillsborough Bay** S of **Charlottetown** (**Holland Cove**, *Anse au Sanglier*) - Lot 65

Ocean View / Surrey 11 mi SW of **Montague** - Lot 58

Ocean View P.O. at **Ocean View / Surrey** 11 mi SW of **Montague** (1906-65) - Lot 58

Ocean View School District at **Ocean View** 11 mi SW of **Montague** 1898 - Lot 58

Ocean View School District at **Surrey / Ocean View** 11 mi SW of **Montague** 1898 (*Surrey School District* 1857-1898) - Lot 58

O'Connells Pond (**Glenfinnan Lake**, *Glenfinnan Pond, Oval Lake*) - Lots 35/36

Officers Pond on **Winter River** (*Suffolk Pond, Johnstons Pond*) - Lot 34

O'Halloran Road 8 mi SW of **Alberton** (**Bloomfield**) - Lot 5

O'Keefe Lake at **Avondale** (**O'Keefes Lake**, *Keef's Lake, Keefe's Lake, Keefes Lake*) - Lot 49

O'Keefes Lake at **Avondale** (*Keefe's Lake, Keef's Lake, O'Keefe Lake, Keefes Lake*) - Lot 49

Old Battery Point site of **Fort Edward Battery** at **Victoria Park** extends into **Charlottetown Harbour** (*Battery Point*) - **Charlottetown Royalty**

Old Ferry Spit at mouth of **Boughton River** (*Solander Point, Morrissons Point*) - Lot 55

Figure 23-2. A Cross-Index to Geographical Names of Prince Edward Island by Alan Rayburn, for Canadian Permanent Committee on Geographical Names and Published by Surveys and Mapping Branch, Dept. of Energy, Mines and Resources, Ottawa. 1973

A note on the title page of this list explains that names in bold are modern names and names in italics are former names. The cross-referencing index is a help to using the book, which contains a great deal of information.

<http://www.islandregister.com/placenames/opqr.html>

Confederation may have solved some things, but it did not bring prosperity. The population of the island peaked in 1891 and then went into a decline that lasted nearly fifty years. Those who left in this period were attracted first to the New England states and later to central Canada. Today the Island's population grows slowly, and the economy centers on potatoes, tourism, and the fishery.

FINDING LOCALITIES

The principal unit of organization for Prince Edward Island records is the county; there have always been three: King's, Queen's, and Prince. Changes in place-names have occurred, and a number of French and Mi'kmaq names remain.

The Island Register website has three geographic aids to locating places:

- A cross-index to names past and present
- A table putting lot numbers beside community names
- Names used by Acadian settlers and those of Mi'kmaq origin

In addition, the provincial government website offers an online place finder. More than a gazetteer, it includes useful facts and links and a choice of maps for two, four, and six kilometers around a selected spot.

On microfilm from Family History Centers or in a recently reprinted edition, you can consult the *Atlas of the Maritime Provinces of the Dominion of Canada* (1878, 2005).

CENSUS RETURNS

The first every-name census return was taken in 1841; some of it survives. There was a census of the city of Charlottetown in 1848 that is also available. For later censuses, you can consult partial returns for 1861 and then regular, fairly complete returns from 1881 to 1911. There was no 1871 census. Most of these returns have online indexes, and some have images.

The Public Archives and Record Office (PARO) website offers lots of background information and a series of shaded maps that show all of the island's sixty-seven township lots and what material survives for each. This site also has its own indexes to the 1841, 1881, 1891, and 1901 census returns.

Prince Edward Island joined Confederation in 1873 and is included in all the online formats for census material for 1881, 1901, and 1911. These are the indexes at Ancestry and Automated Genealogy, linked to the images at Library and Archives Canada (LAC). The detailed 1881 index at FamilySearch includes the island.

All census returns can be viewed on microfilm. You can use interlibrary loan or Family History Centers to obtain them.

Online at the Island Register is a tabular summary of facts about all censuses from the first list of Acadia, prepared in 1728, up to 1911. Lists of names in seven of the ten censuses taken before 1841 can also be accessed at this website.

CIVIL REGISTRATION

Government vital statistics date from 1906. Any records prior to that date come from church registers or marriage license records. The Office of Vital Statistics created a card catalog to earlier church baptism records for the years 1886 to 1906. This is held by PARO, and the information in it has been incorporated into the PEI Baptismal Index at the archives website.

Earliest information in the baptismal index dates from the 1770s in Charlottetown, but for most areas of the province, entries begin sometime after 1800. Search results appear in a table; not all entries have a full fourteen lines of facts.

At PARO you will find other resources: a finding aid to deaths and burials taken from church records and newspapers; marriage register books for 1832–1923;

BAPTISMAL INDEX INFORMATION

Child's Full Name
Birth Date
Place of Birth
Baptismal Date
Place of Baptism
Officiating Clergy
Father's Name
Mother's Name
Church Name
Church Location
Record Book Number
Record Book Page
Entry Number
Notes

marriage licenses, 1787–1919; and marriage bonds, 1849–1902. The marriage register books should provide names, places of residence, date of marriage, and the names of witnesses and the minister. The licenses and bonds were filmed and indexed separately and contain similar information.

Some of this material is in the Family History Library (FHL), including marriage records and indexes, 1832 to 1888, and copies of the archives' index to deaths prior to 1906.

Copies of civil registrations of births, deaths, and marriages from 1906 can be obtained from Vital Statistics Services. Some restrictions apply, particularly with respect to who may obtain birth and marriage certificates. Details are at the website, accessible from Info PEI.

CHURCH REGISTERS

The finding aids developed by Vital Statistics and PARO and described above incorporate a lot of church data and should be consulted first. Another finding aid is the Master Name Index described later in the chapter. It contains any indexed church register information. The Island Register website has several lists of church records.

You can find many registers of Prince Edward Island churches on microfilm at the provincial archives. Denominations at one time or another have included Church of Scotland (Presbyterian), Free Church of Scotland, Roman Catholic, Church of England (Anglican), Methodist, and United (formed 1925). United Church registers may include entries from before the amalgamation.

Microfilm copies of church registers can be consulted using the FHL or Family History Centers. Some registers from the Acadian period are on film, as are many others from Anglican, Catholic, United Church, Presbyterian, Methodist, and Congregational churches. Search the Family History Library Catalog (FHLC) by place-name.

The United Church archives are in Sackville, New Brunswick, and the Anglican archives are in Halifax. Copies of Catholic registers are in the archives of the Diocese of Charlottetown. There are few Catholic records from before 1829.

CEMETERY RECORDS

All island cemeteries have been transcribed, and a comprehensive index has been prepared by the Heritage Foundation. This index is in PARO, and the Cemetery Transcription Collection (1979) is on microfilm in the FHL. All entries, over 40,000, have been incorporated into the Master Name Index.

You can pinpoint the location of all known Prince Edward Island cemeteries using the location guide at the Island Register website. Set out in seven columns, the table includes the name of the cemetery, place, lot number, and the longitude and latitude. The Info PEI section of the provincial government website also includes a list of all cemeteries.

WILLS AND PROBATE

Probate records up to 1920 are held by PARO and more recent records by the Estates Division of the Prince Edward Island Law Courts. Probate records have been filmed and indexed. Most of the records are from after 1800.

The FHL has a large collection of materials held by the Supreme Court in Charlottetown. The records run from 1807 to 1958, the indexes from 1786 to 2000.

There is a recently published book to help you explore island resources in depth: *Early Prince Edward Island Probate Records—1786–1850* (Nicholson, 2005). It describes the records, probate process, and included summaries of records.

LAND RECORDS

Prince Edward Island land records are split between two locations: modern ones at the Office of the Registrar of Deeds in Charlottetown and those before 1900 in the Public Archives and Record Office. Land records began in 1769 and contain registers, conveyances, mortgage records, rent books, and leases. Up until 1973 there is an alphabetical index, and thereafter the arrangement is by county. Some of the leases may have been exchanged for deeds after the passage of land purchase legislation.

A related source is the ledger books, which were created after the first land act in 1853 to record purchases of land from the government. Under the legislation, the government bought the land from the owners so that it could, in turn, sell it to the people who held the leases.

In addition, there are maps and atlases of the island related to land, the lots, owners, and occupiers. An index to the *Illustrated Historical Atlas of the Province of Prince Edward Island* (Allen, 1880) is at Ancestry, and there is a partial index at the Island Register site. Maps can help you follow the transfer of land by inheritance; until 1939, land could be transferred by will without registration of the transaction.

Prince Edward Island land records have been filmed and can be viewed through Family History Centers. Online transcriptions of several dozen records, such as grants and leases, have been contributed by researchers to the Island Register. It is worth browsing to look for a lucky find and to see examples of the text or format of land documents.

NEWSPAPERS

Along with pamphlets and periodicals, there is a newspaper collection in the Robertson Library at the University of Prince Edward Island in Charlottetown. Prince Edward Island newspapers can also be found at PARO and at LAC.

Vital event announcements from newspapers have been incorporated into the Master Name Index. Some entries are more informative than others.

To complete your quest for newspaper copies, check the list of repository holdings at the GenWeb site and the FHLC.

Muster Rolls, Soldiers and Loyalists, Spring 1785 List

The following Muster Roll of Disbanded Officers, Discharged & Disbanded Soldiers with their respective families that are settled and preparing to settle in the Island of Saint John, is undated, but has the number "153" scrawled above the Names Column. This is believed to be the list of those from Rhode Island who arrived on the Island in the spring of 1785, brought to the Island by Daniel Grandin [who had first arrived on the Island in Sept. 1784 and drawn land in Pinette River - see 19 Sept 1784 list]. They had expected to settle upon lot 66, but, as Grandin could not fulfill the condition of his agreement with Gov. Patterson that he bring 1500 settlers and they settled on land in lots 56 and 58 instead.

Note: The following table is very wide. Use your scroll bars to scroll to see the entire table.

Description	Name	Men	Women	Child10+	Child-10	Where Land Granted	Acres	How Held	Age	To what time had drawn Provisions
17th Light Drag.	Geo Anderson	1				Pinette River Lot 58	500	Grant from His Majesty	34	24 Sept 1784
17th Light Drag.	Joseph Brown	1				d.o.	300	d.o.	39	not certified
17th Light Drag.	William Thompson	1	1			d.o.	300	d.o.	36	24 Sept 1784
17th Light Drag.	John Hopewith [..well?]	1				d.o.	300	d.o.	23	d.o.
22 Rgt.	Herbert Ryan	1				Lot 56	100	d.o.	23	d.o.
22 Rgt.	William Wallace	1				d.o.	100	d.o.	36	d.o.
B. Legion?	Pat'k Connolly	1				d.o.	100	d.o.	42	d.o.
B. Legion?	Aaron Westwood	1				d.o.	100	d.o.	27	not certified
B. Legion?	Rich'd Aylwood	1				d.o.	100	d.o.	29	d.o.
42nd	John McKenzie	1				d.o.	100	d.o.	25	d.o.
42nd	John McGregor	1				d.o.	100	d.o.	31	d.o.
42nd	Rob't McLeod	1				d.o.	100	d.o.	25	d.o.
64th	Matt Merridith	1				d.o.	100	d.o.	33	d.o.
64th	Joseph Carr	1				d.o.	100	d.o.	37	d.o.
64th	James Burke	1				d.o.	100	d.o.	24	d.o.
64th	Mich'l Neale	1				d.o.	100	d.o.	28	d.o.
64th	Morris Lysart	1				d.o.	100	d.o.	38	d.o.
7th	Isaac Colthorp	1				d.o.	100	d.o.	28	24 Sept 1784
7th	John Davis	1				d.o.	100	d.o.	43	24 Sept 1784
7th	John Griffin	1				d.o.	100	d.o.	43	not certified
54th	James Carver	1	1		1	d.o.	100	d.o.	38	d.o.
54th	Enoch Groom	1				d.o.	100	d.o.	52	d.o.
54th	Rich Kearsby	1				d.o.	100	d.o.	47	d.o.
76th	Murdoch McLeod	1				d.o.	100	d.o.	27	d.o.
80th	David Young	1				d.o.	100	d.o.	25	25 Sept 1784
64th	Jos Hepworth	1				d.o.	100	d.o.	34	not certified
?	John Brannan [Burnham]	1				d.o.	100	d.o.	37	d.o.

Figure 23-3. Muster Roll Soldiers and Loyalists Spring 1785 List
Within the Island Register website are several lists of disbanded soldiers and Loyalists on the Island of St. John, contributed by the Abegweit Branch of the United Empire Loyalists' Association of Canada.
<http://www.islandregister.com/spring1785.html>

OTHER WAYS TO FIND PEOPLE

Many Loyalists arrived on the Island in 1784 and 1785. There are lists of disbanded officers and soldiers and their families from three regiments—the King's Rangers, Saint John's Volunteers, and the Royal Nova Scotia Volunteers—as well as muster rolls and miscellaneous lists. Names and details, set out in tables, are accessible from the Island Register website.

Transcriptions of the Prince Edward Island entries from several directories are found at the Island Register website; look within the heading Censuses, Maps and Related Documents. Years available range from the 1860s to 1930s.

The Canadian National Library Catalog, AMICUS, can be used to identify books about settlement and Island families. Our Roots is worth checking for full-text books online because it has several Prince Edward Island titles.

SPECIAL SOURCES

Long before the Internet became a significant factor in genealogical research, genealogists and historians began creating an index to the people of Prince Edward Island. Volunteers extracted names from resources spanning more than two hundred years, from the 1700s to the 1900s: atlases, business papers, censuses, church records, cemetery records, undertakers' files, inquest records, land records, newspapers, personal papers, and school registers.

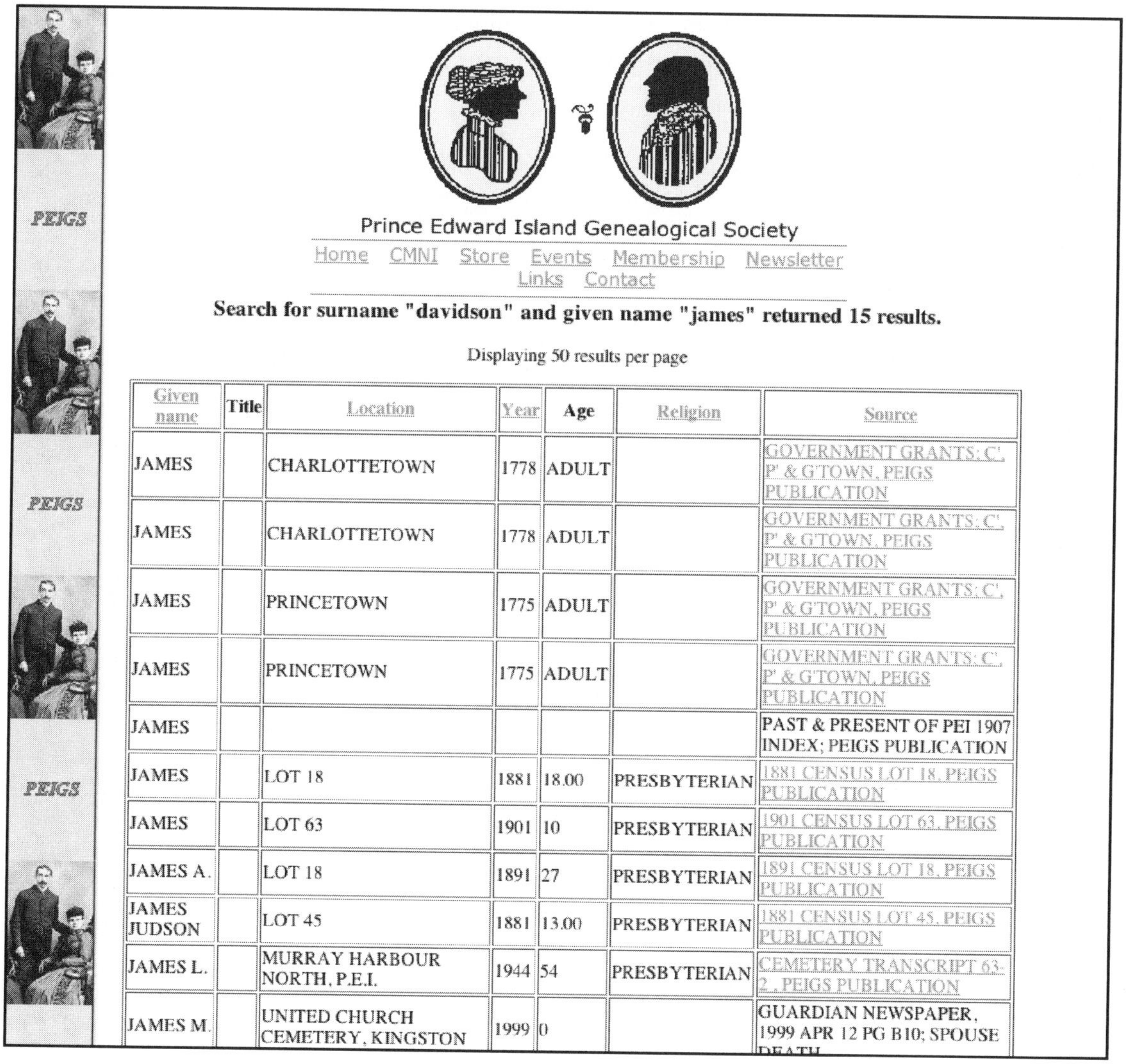

Prince Edward Island Genealogical Society
Home CMNI Store Events Membership Newsletter
Links Contact

Search for surname "davidson" and given name "james" returned 15 results.

Displaying 50 results per page

Given name	Title	Location	Year	Age	Religion	Source
JAMES		CHARLOTTETOWN	1778	ADULT		GOVERNMENT GRANTS: C', P' & G'TOWN, PEIGS PUBLICATION
JAMES		CHARLOTTETOWN	1778	ADULT		GOVERNMENT GRANTS: C', P' & G'TOWN, PEIGS PUBLICATION
JAMES		PRINCETOWN	1775	ADULT		GOVERNMENT GRANTS: C', P' & G'TOWN, PEIGS PUBLICATION
JAMES		PRINCETOWN	1775	ADULT		GOVERNMENT GRANTS: C', P' & G'TOWN, PEIGS PUBLICATION
JAMES						PAST & PRESENT OF PEI 1907 INDEX; PEIGS PUBLICATION
JAMES		LOT 18	1881	18.00	PRESBYTERIAN	1881 CENSUS LOT 18, PEIGS PUBLICATION
JAMES		LOT 63	1901	10	PRESBYTERIAN	1901 CENSUS LOT 63, PEIGS PUBLICATION
JAMES A.		LOT 18	1891	27	PRESBYTERIAN	1891 CENSUS LOT 18, PEIGS PUBLICATION
JAMES JUDSON		LOT 45	1881	13.00	PRESBYTERIAN	1881 CENSUS LOT 45, PEIGS PUBLICATION
JAMES L.		MURRAY HARBOUR NORTH, P.E.I.	1944	54	PRESBYTERIAN	CEMETERY TRANSCRIPT 63-2, PEIGS PUBLICATION
JAMES M.		UNITED CHURCH CEMETERY, KINGSTON	1999	0		GUARDIAN NEWSPAPER, 1999 APR 12 PG B10; SPOUSE DEATH

Figure 23-4. Computerized Master Name Index, Online Version
<http://www.peigs.ca/cmni.php?surname=davidson&givennamesearch=james&perpage=50&page=1&sort=givenname>

There have been three phases to the growth of the Master Name Index. They are called the Master Name Index, Phase II, and the Computerized Master Name Index (CMNI). Phase II was a continuation of the original; both were created on index cards and microfilmed. The Computerized Master Name Index is intended to eventually incorporate everything from all three parts of the project, but not all of the data in the first two phases has been converted. Updates are usually made twice a year.

If you search the CMNI you must remember that this is not yet a complete search of all data; both earlier phases need to be consulted as well. If you consult the microfilm copies of the card indexes, they do not include data recently added only to the CMNI. The Prince Edward Island Genealogical Society says no further additions will be made to the earlier phases held by the archives and available on microfilm at Family History Centers.

PEI Lineages is another source worth checking and is a feature at the Island Register. Contributors are uploading information on hundreds of Island families. Access is through an alphabetical list of surnames.

WEBSITES

Abegweit Branch United Empire Loyalist Association of Canada: <www.islandregister.com/uel.html>

Ancestry: <www.ancestry.ca>

Anglican Diocese of Nova Scotia and Prince Edward Island: <www.nspeidiocese.ca>

Canadian Genealogy Centre: <www.collectionscanada.ca/genealogy/>

GenWeb Prince Edward Island: <www.islandregister.com/pegenweb.html>

The Island Register: <www.islandregister.com/index.html>

Library and Archives Canada, AMICUS: <http://amicus.collectionscanada.ca/aaweb/aalogine.htm>

Library and Archives Canada Newspaper Lists: <www.collectionscanada.ca/8/16/index-e.html>

Prince Edward Island Computerized Master Name Index: <www.peigs.ca/cmni.php>

Prince Edward Island Genealogical Society:

Provincial Government, InfoPEI: <www.gov.pe.ca/infopei/>

Provincial Government, InfoPEI, PlaceFinder: <www.gov.pe.ca/placefinder/index.php3>

Public Archives and Records Office: <www.edu.pe.ca/paro/>

Roman Catholic Diocese of Charlottetown: <www.dioceseofcharlottetown.com>

United Church of Canada, Maritime Conference Archives: <www.united-church.ca/archives/maritime/home.shtm>

University of Prince Edward Island, Robertson Library, Genealogy Guide: <www.upei.ca/~library/html/genealogy.html>

BIBLIOGRAPHY

Allen, C. R. (cartography). *Illustrated Historical Atlas of the Province of Prince Edward Island.* Toronto: J. H. Meacham & Co., 1880.

Daley, Louis J. *A Roman Catholic Census of Charlottetown, 1878–1879.* Prepared for the Diocese of Charlottetown. Charlottetown, PE: 1993.

———. *A Roman Catholic Census of Charlottetown, 1886.* Prepared for the Diocese of Charlottetown. Charlottetown, PE: 1994.

Frederick's Prince Edward Island Directory and Book of Useful Information for 1889–90. Charlottetown, PE: Frederick Pub. Co, 1889. (available at Ancestry.ca)

Gallant, Peter, Nelda Murray, and Prince Edward Island Genealogical Society. *An index of English immigrants based on obituaries and death notices in Prince Edward Island newspapers, 1835-1910.* Charlottetown, PE: Prince Edward Island Genealogical Society, 1991. (also known as *From England to Prince Edward Island*)

———. *Scottish Immigrants to Prince Edward Island from Death and Obituary Notices in Prince Edward Island Newspapers, 1835–1910.* Charlottetown, PE: Prince Edward Island Genealogical Society, 1993. (also known as *From Scotland to Prince Edward Island*)

Gallant, Peter, and Prince Edward Island Genealogical Society. *An Index of Irish Immigrants Based on Obituaries and Death Notices in Prince Edward Island Newspapers, 1835–1910.* Charlottetown, PE: Prince Edward Island Genealogical Society, 1990. (also known as *From Ireland to Prince Edward Island*)

Historical Atlas of the Maritime Provinces, 1878 / with an introduction by Joan Dawson. Halifax: Nimbus Pub., 2005. (a new edition of Roe's *Atlas of the Maritime Provinces of the Dominion of Canada*)

Jones, Orlo, and Doris Haslam. *An Island Refuge: Loyalists and Disbanded Troops on the Island of Saint John.* Charlottetown, PE: Abegweit Branch of the United Empire Loyalist Association of Canada, 1983.

MacQueen, Malcolm A. *Skye Pioneers and The Island.* Winnipeg: Stovel Co., 1929. (also on CD-ROM by Scotpress)

———. *Hebridean Pioneers.* Winnipeg: M. MacQueen, 1957. (also on CD-ROM by Scotpress)

Nicholson, Linda Jean. *Early Prince Edward Island Probate Records, 1786–1850.* Charlottetown, PE: Transcontinental Prince Edward Island, 2005. (ordering information at the GenWeb site)

Roe, Frederick B. *Atlas of the Maritime Provinces of the Dominion of Canada.* St. John, NB: Halifax: Roe Bros., 1879.

ADDRESSES

Diocese of Nova Scotia and Prince Edward Island
Diocesan Archives
Anglican Diocesan Centre
5732 College Street
Halifax, NS B3H 1X3

Estates Division
Sir Louis Henry Davies Law Courts
42 Water Street
PO Box 2290
Charlottetown, PE C1A 8C1

Library and Archives Canada
395 Wellington Street
Ottawa, ON K1A 0N4

Office of the Registrar of Deeds
Box 2000
Charlottetown, PE C1A 7N8

The Prince Edward Island Genealogical Society, Inc.
PO Box 2744
Charlottetown, PE C1A 8C4

Prince Edward Island Public Archives and Record Office
Hon. George Coles Building
Richmond Street
PO Box 1000
Charlottetown, PE C1A 7M4

Robertson Library
University of Prince Edward Island
550 University Avenue
Charlottetown, PE C1A 4P3

Roman Catholic Diocese of Charlottetown
PO Box 907
Charlottetown, PE C1A 7L9

United Church of Canada, Maritime Conference Archives
32 York Street
Sackville, NB E4L 4R4

Office of Vital Statistics
Department of Health and Social Services
126 Douses Road
Montague, PE C0A 1R0

Figure 24-1. Quebec

QUEBEC

Jacques Cartier, a French explorer, arrived in what is now Quebec in 1534. The village of Quebec was founded in 1608, but growth was slow; twenty years later there were seventy-six residents. At the time of the first census in 1666 the colony numbered 3,418.

From 1686 to 1763 was a period of nearly constant struggle between France and Britain. New France was at a disadvantage in North America. The French government did not provide adequate support, and the American colonies had more than ten times the population. The peace treaty of 1763 ceded all French possessions east of the Great Lakes to Britain.

With the end of French sovereignty, most high-ranking people returned to France. The British authorities did not permit French Catholics to be part of the colony's administration; however, the French population was allowed to retain its religion, language, and legal system. The system of landholding, the seigneurial system, was also retained.

Twenty years later, in 1783–84, the end of the American Revolution led to an inflow of new English settlers, refugee Loyalists. Some settled southwest of Montreal, but most went to the western part of the colony. The authorities split Quebec in two, creating Upper and Lower Canada, which would become eventually the provinces of Ontario and Quebec.

In the 1840s an economic crisis precipitated the first emigration out of Quebec to the United States. About 1 million French-Canadians crossed the border from that time to the Great Depression of the 1930s, when the flow stopped; two-thirds of the emigrants stayed in New England. Other Quebecers moved west within Canada, particularly after 1880.

At the same time, immigrants were coming to Quebec. Many Catholic Irish came in the wake of the Irish famine from 1847 to 1851, and people arrived from continental Europe as well. There were significant numbers of Italians and Germans.

Quebec was a founding province of Canada in 1867. At that time 20 percent of the population lived in cities, but the shift to an industrialized, urban society was underway. In 1921, 52 percent of the population lived in cities. The biggest industries were textiles and clothing manufacture, shoes, and transportation.

Serious political issues have arisen out of Quebec's place in Canada, before and after Confederation. In 1837 there were uprisings here as well as Upper Canada. Confederation was a contentious issue, and in the twentieth century the issues have been conscription during the two world wars and a rising sense of national identity, which has created a series of crises over the separation of the province from Canada.

FINDING LOCALITIES

The principal units for organization of records are counties, districts, parishes, and townships. The bigger units have changed, which means a township may have been in different districts and counties. The counties of Quebec were changed in 1855 and reorganized into municipal districts in 1980.

To find locations, a modern place-name database is available at the website of the Commission de toponymie du Québec. The resource is known as Topos sur le Web, and it gives access to all official place-names, their locations, origin, and meaning. There is also an Atlas of Quebec online.

John Lovell's *Canadian Dominion Directory* for 1871 gives place locations. You can find out the township and county of each community and read short descriptions of towns and villages. It is online in the directories collection at Library and Archives Canada (LAC).

Our Roots has at least two old books on place-names: *A Topographical Dictionary of the Province of Lower Canada* (Bouchette, 1832) and *Les Noms Géographiques de la province de Québec* (Roy, 1906).

CENSUS RETURNS

The province of Quebec is within all available enumerations of Canada 1871 to 1911. Using Ancestry and Automated Genealogy you can find indexes for the returns of 1901 and 1911 on the Web. At both sites, search results are linked to the record images at LAC. A detailed index for the 1881 census for Canada is at FamilySearch, but images need to be viewed on microfilm.

The 1851 and 1861 censuses for Quebec name everyone. Only part of the 1851 census survives, but it is accessible using the online index at Ancestry, which is linked to the images at LAC. The 1861 census gives each person's occupation, birthplace, religion, and age (next birthday). Both censuses are widely available on microfilm.

Many census enumerations have been made from the time of the French regime; the first one was in 1666. Some of those before 1850 cover a wide area, but others are for small areas, just one parish or seigneury. Begin a search for transcriptions and indexes online by checking the district and county sections within Quebec GenWeb. You should also search the Family History Library Catalog (FHLC) at FamilySearch because Family History Library (FHL) holdings are extensive.

The materials held by LAC can be checked by place-name using the online version of the *Catalogue of Census Returns on Microfilm, 1666–1901*. A summary of census records appears in *French-Canadian Sources: A Guide for Genealogists* (Geyh et al., 2002), which describes survival and access for all censuses of Quebec from earliest times.

You can zero in on ancestors and possible connections better if you know the census districts. A table within *Traité de Généalogie* (Jetté, 1991) sets out the correlations between counties and census districts from 1792 to 1981.

CIVIL REGISTRATION

Through most of Quebec's history, civil records were the copies made by parish priests and subsequently submitted to local notaries. In 1926 it became possible to report a record of birth, marriage, or death directly to a civil office in Quebec, but four decades passed before a significant number of vital events were recorded only by this office. In 1994 the provincial government established a vital statistics department.

The colonial authorities kept records of marriage bonds for those intending to marry by license. There is a collection of Lower Canada Marriage Bonds at LAC and an online index to names for the years 1779 to 1858. The records have been filmed and are in the FHL.

From 1840 to 1968 one could not obtain a divorce in Quebec except by act of Parliament. There is a database of federal divorces at the Canadian Genealogy Centre website.

CHURCH REGISTERS

Church registers are the most important class of records for Quebec research. Duplicates were made because copies had to go to the government, which is why so many records have survived. Their value is enhanced because maiden names are always recorded, and many excellent indexes are available.

Large amounts of information are already online, and more is coming. Ancestry has uploaded images of the Drouin Collection, which is largely made up of French-Canadian parish records from the 1600s to 1940. At present the images can be searched by place-name and browsed. The great majority of the records are from Catholic churches, but because the requirement for duplicate copies applied to all churches, records of many other denominations, such as Anglican, Baptist, Methodist, and Presbyterian, can be found.

Ancestry will be adding indexes to the Drouin images. When complete, these indexes will provide access to nearly 12 million records and more than 35 million names. The Drouin Collection includes baptisms, marriages, burials, and miscellaneous other events such as confirmations; most other indexes available up to now have been to marriages only.

At the University of Montreal, the Research Program in Historical Demography (Programme de recherche en démographie historique, or PRDH) is another online database. PRDH has collected all parish register data for inhabitants of the St. Lawrence Valley before 1800 and created three online databases: vital events in Quebec, 1621–1799; a genealogical dictionary of families, 1621–1765; and couples and filial relations, 1621–1799. Searching requires a full name.

Original civil copies from earliest entries to the end of 1800s are at Bibliothèque et Archives nationales du Québec (BAnQ) and are widely available in other places on microfilm. The FHL has filmed the records up to 1877.

Many parish indexes, mainly for marriage entries, were made by individuals and genealogical societies. They are called *répertoires* and are available for most Catholic parishes of Quebec. Some répertoires cover large areas. Collections of répertoires can be found at LAC, the FHL, and in repositories in regions of the U.S. where French-Canadians settled. Check catalogs for details of parishes available.

The Loiselle Marriage Index, on microfiche or microfilm, is the biggest and best known. It indexes Catholic marriages in Quebec and some parts of Ontario, New Brunswick, and New England from 1750 to the early 1900s. Loiselle, and its supplementary additions, are at BAnQ, LAC, and the FHL, and can circulate to Family History Centers.

The *Fichier Histor*, available at BAnQ and LAC, is an index to Catholic and Protestant marriages in Quebec from 1730 to 1825 and includes some records from forts in the West, such as Detroit, and from Acadia. It is available at BAnQ and LAC, but is unlikely to be found in U.S. repositories.

Even with all these finding aids you will need to check parish locations and the survival of records. There are several useful resources, including

- Inventaire des registres paroissiaux catholiques du Québec, 1621–1876 (Bélanger and Landry, 1990);
- Guide des registres d'état civil et recensements du Québec: catholiques, protestants et autres dénominations, 1621–2000 (Fortin, 2001);
- A *Checklist of Registers of Protestant & Jewish Congregations in Quebec* (Broadhurst, 1994).

Events for other denominations appear in some of the larger indexes, but the répertoires are mostly for Catholic parishes. There are links to non-Catholic finding aids within Quebec GenWeb, notably in the sections for Montreal and Huntingdon. The BAnQ website has finding aids: an Index of Non-Catholic Marriages in the Montreal Area, 1766–1899, and another to Non-Catholic Burials in the Montréal Area, 1768–1875.

Records of Anglican parishes more than one hundred years old are likely to be in diocesan archives; recent ones are retained by the church. The United Church regional archives for the Montreal and Ottawa Conference holds church records in four locations; contact information is at their website. Many registers will be with local churches. Most Methodist and Presbyterian congregations joined the United Church in 1925.

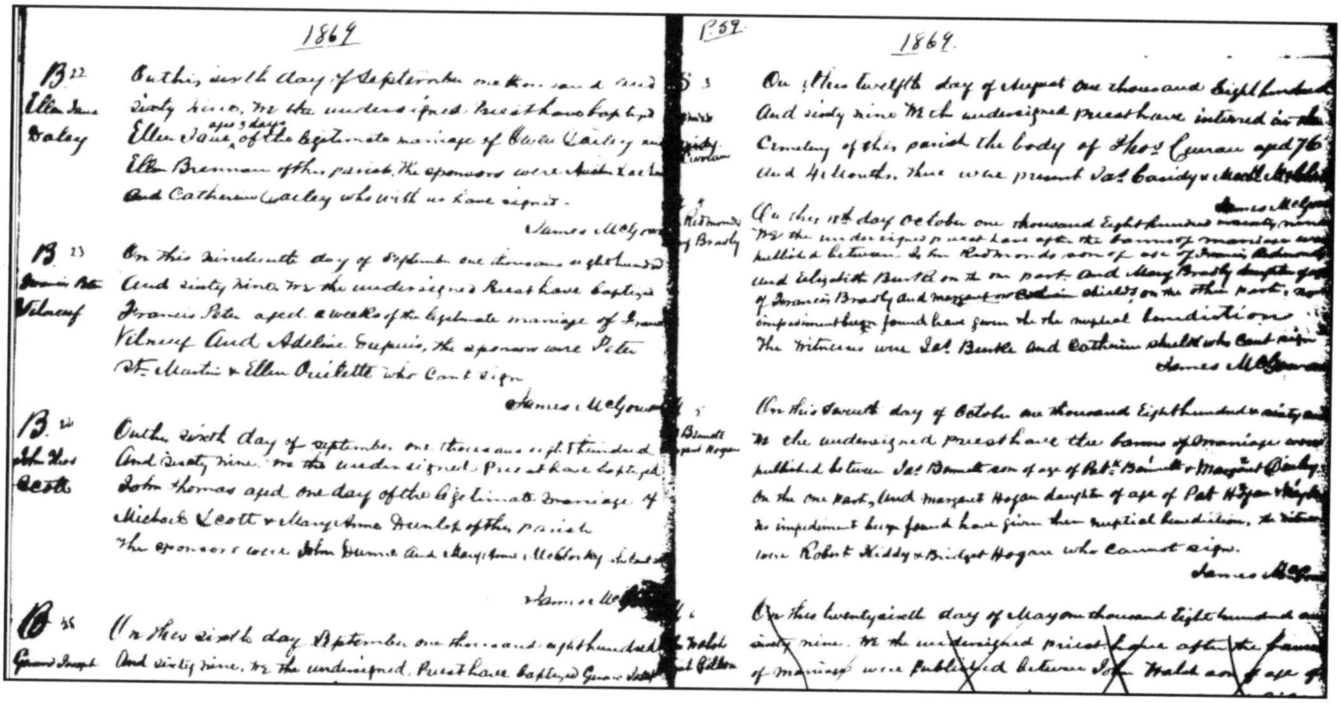

Figure 24-2. Drouin Collection, Page of a Register of Baptisms

This page, from the register of an Anglican Church, shows that the baptism record includes the maiden name of the mother and full names of the sponsors. The first entry on the left reads: "On this sixth day of September one thousand and sixty nine we the undersigned priest have baptized Ellen Jane aged 3 days of the legitimate marriage of Owen Dailey and Ellen Brennan of this parish. The sponsors were Austin Lach---and Catherine Dailey who with we have signed. James McGowan.

(Quebec, Old Chelsea, 1863–1884, church register. Quebec Vital Records Drouin Collection 1621–1967, online at Ancestry.ca)

CEMETERY RECORDS

Online gravestone transcriptions and cemetery information can be found at Canada GenWeb both within the Quebec pages and through the site of the main Canada transcription project. Look at both sites because the information is not identical. Also worth checking is the list of Quebec cemeteries at Interment.net; it has links to transcriptions for cemeteries in sixteen counties. These transcriptions are mostly for Protestant cemeteries.

There are extensive holdings of cemetery records in BAnQ. You can use both the catalog search tool (IRIS) and the archives search tool (PISTARD) to locate descriptions. When you search, use both the English and French terms, *cemetery* and *cemetière*.

Many transcriptions and indexes are in other locations, and three Web search tools will help you find them. The Canadian Genealogy Centre has an article about LAC holdings, and the AVITUS genealogy search tool turns up links to several Quebec cemeteries. The FHLC has more than two hundred entries for cemeteries and family plot transcriptions in the Family History Library.

LAND RECORDS

The seigneurial system was well established in Quebec by 1650 and lasted until 1854. Lands were granted to seigneurs—the upper middle class, officers, gentry, and nobility—and they in turn granted lands to tenants. A system of rules governed the relationships, spelling out rights and obligations.

When a seigneur granted land to a tenant, this was recorded in a notarial contract. People did not own the land they occupied, but they could sell the right to occupy it. These transactions also are found in notarial records.

Alongside this system, and after 1763, the British authorities introduced their own, basing the division of land on townships. They made free land grants to Loyalist settlers and other immigrants. To receive a grant it was necessary to present a petition. Land grants continued after Confederation.

Lower Canada Land Petitions, 1764 to 1841, contains petitions, reports from the surveyor general, and administrative documents. Library and Archives Canada has a nominal database covering all records. In addition, at its website you can view 20,000 digitized images, roughly 25 percent of the collection. The remaining land petitions must be consulted on microfilm at LAC, at the FHL, or through a Family History Center.

The Quebec Family History Society has prepared a finding aid to land grants, *Alphabetical Index to the Land Grants by the Crown in the Province of Quebec from 1763 to 31st December 1890*. The volumes are sold by the society. Records of land grants are at BAnQ and in the FHL.

Special land grants to families with twelve children or more were available for several years after legislation was passed in 1890. The records are mainly for the counties of Beauce, Ottawa, Rimouski, and Temiscouata; about five thousand families applied. The records include details and documentation for marriages and children. The records are at BAnQ, and there is an index at the website.

Today Quebec has a modern land registration system that includes online access to a digital land registry database. The land registry system had its beginnings in 1830 when, to protect property rights and prevent fraud, it became necessary to register all land transactions and for this information to be public. This is called "publication of rights" (*publicité des droits*). Formerly the records had to be consulted in one of the many land registry offices throughout Quebec, but now, following registration, remote access is possible, and documents can be accessed online for a fee. There are quite extensive explanations of the system in English on the website.

NOTARIAL RECORDS

The local notary played an important role, acting as a registrar for legal affairs including marriage contracts, land transfers, inventories of estates, donations (division of assets among children), and business contracts. You may find apprenticeships, settling of neighborhood disputes, and the working agreements of men going west with fur-trading companies among notarial records.

All surviving notarial records to 1937 are at BAnQ, and roughly 85 percent still exist. Abstracts to a large portion, into the twentieth century, are in the FHL (entitled *Instruments de recherches des registres notariaux*).

Every notarial act states name, title, and jurisdiction of the notary; date and place of writing; names and places of residence of the parties; name and place of residence of the witnesses. Frequently you will find age, marital status, and occupation of the parties; age, marital status, and occupation of witnesses; and names of parents.

To access notarial records you must, for anything after 1785, identify the notary or notaries used by your ancestors. There are books that list notaries, and their names and places of business appear in library or archives catalogs. People did not always choose the one close by, but they did tend to return to the same notary again and again. The term *greffe de notaires* refers to the original record held by the notary. He also made copies for other parties involved.

Name searches for the period 1647–1942 will become available at the Ancestry website. Within the Drouin Collection there are record répetoires and indexes prepared by the notaries. Notaries were required to make two finding aids, a chronological catalog and an alphabetical surname index (arranged within each year by first letter of the last name). Images are online now, mostly of répetoires, and can be browsed according to the name of the notary. There are no actual records available. Searching for all individual names will eventually be possible; check the Ancestry website regularly. The screen grabs on the next page show répetoires in French and English. You can see the groupings by month and that each entry provides a reference number, the type of notarial instrument, and names of people involved.

It is possible to search notarial records by name for records from 1626 to 1785 using Parchemin, a database on CD-ROM prepared by Archiv-Histro; there is a charge for the record. Some libraries in Canada and the United States have acquired the database. A few small databases are online at BAnQ: indexes to some coroners' inquests, inventories after death, and marriage contracts.

There are many books about notaries and their records and many finding aids, particularly lists of notaries and their locations. Search the FHLC for more resources, and look for lists of notaries within Quebec GenWeb.

NEWSPAPERS

Several old newspapers can be searched at the BAnQ website. The titles available include the *Quebec Chronicle*, 1847 to 1924, and *La Patrie*, 1879 to 1978.

Some Quebec newspapers, such as the *Quebec Gazette*, have been indexed. They can be identified by consulting the Checklist of Indexes to Canadian Newspapers held by Library and Archives Canada at the LAC website. The checklist also mentions online indexes to Canadian newspapers. Many of the newspapers, indexed and unindexed, can be borrowed on microfilm through interlibrary loan.

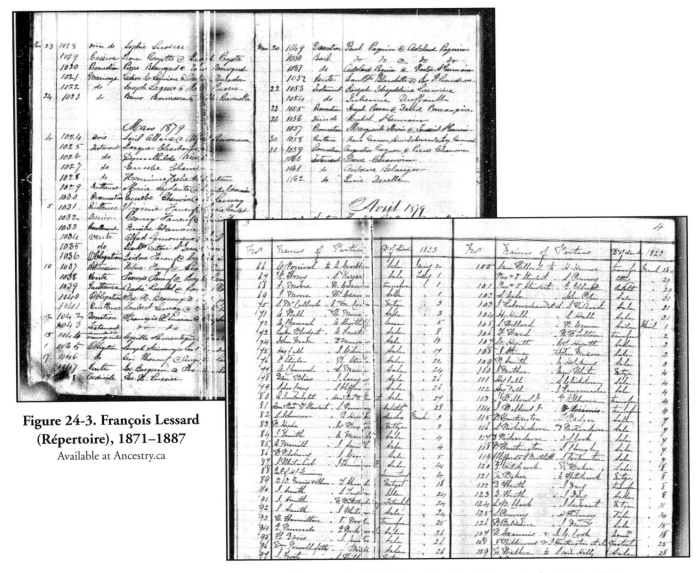

Figure 24-3. François Lessard (Répertoire), 1871–1887
Available at Ancestry.ca

Figure 24-4. William Ritchie (Répertoire), 1822–1871
Available at Ancestry.ca

The Family History Library has both microfiche and microfilm versions of *Two Partial Indexes to Newspapers in the Province of Quebec from 1666–1993* (Bangsberg et al., 1993). They are listed according to town and newspaper name.

OTHER WAYS TO FIND PEOPLE

Quebec has many dictionary-style resources about French-Canadian families and individuals. The best known is Cyprien Tanguay's monumental work, *Dictionnaire Généalogique des familles canadiennes depuis la fondation de la colonie jusqu'à nos jours*, published from 1871 to 1890. Others have come along since then to correct and expand on Tanguay's work.

The complete work is available in a digitized and searchable form online at BAnQ. Subjects of the study are French-Canadians who lived and died up until 1764, though some later entries are included.

The first to improve on Tanquay was J. Arthur Leboeuf, who compiled *Complément au Dictionaire Généalogique Tanguay* (1957–64). His publication makes thousands of additions and corrections.

More recently, René Jetté completed *Dictionnaire Généalogique des Familles du Québec* in 1990. This work covers the time from the start of French settlement to 1730. All three works use coding and abbreviations, so it is helpful to consult *French-Canadian Sources: A Guide for Genealogists* (Geyh et al., 2002).

Names of many residents of Quebec, with document sources, are contained in *The French Canadians, 1600–1900: An Alphabetized Directory of the People, Places and Vital Dates* (Elliot, 1992). This is online at Ancestry, part of the Canadian Genealogy Index, 1600s to 1900s.

From the middle of the 1800s, many provincial and city directories were published. The largest collection on the Web is at BAnQ, a sequence of Montreal directories from 1842 to 1999. They are in PDF format and use bookmarks to help you get around within each volume. Other directories are online at LAC in the Who Was Where database and at the Our Roots website. Collections of original copies can be found at BAnQ, in public libraries in Quebec, and at LAC.

RESEARCH CONSIDERATIONS

Care must be taken with names because of the prevalence of *dit* names, or alternate names. You may not know your ancestors used *dit* names, but you should watch for evidence of them. Many people went by another name, sometimes a translation and sometimes a name that appears to have no connection. If a man who was not French married a French girl, he might adopt the French form of his name. The use of two names was common among French-Canadians who moved to the United States. They used their French name for church records and gave an English name for civil records. You can find guidance in *French-Canadian Surnames: Aliases, Adulterations and Anglicizations* (R. J. Quintin, 1993).

The residents of Quebec who were neither Catholic nor French can sometimes be harder to trace because less attention has been given to creating finding aids to parish records. However, they appear in many records, including censuses, notarial records, non-Catholic church registers, land records, and cemetery transcriptions.

WEBSITES

American-Canadian Genealogical Society: <www.acgs.org>
Ancestry: <www.ancestry.ca>
Atlas of Quebec online:
Bibliothèque et Archives nationales du Québec: <www.banq.qc.ca>

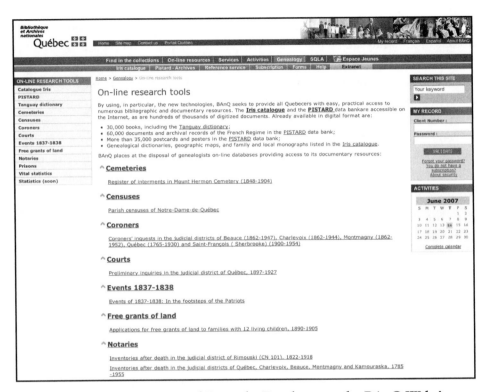

Figure 24-5. Using Notarial Records: Databases at the BAnQ Website
<http://www.banq.qc.ca/portal/dt/genealogie/inst_recherche_ligne/inst_recherche_ligne.jsp?bnq_
langue=en>

Commission de toponymie du Québec (TOPOS sur le Web): <www.toponymie.
gouv.qc.ca>

Directeur de l'état civil (vital statistics): <www.etatcivil.gouv.qc.ca/English/index.
htm>

Fédération québécoise des sociétés de généalogie:
Interment.net, Quebec: <www.interment.net/can/qc/index.htm>

La Société généalogique canadienne-française:

Lovell Directories of Montreal 1842–1999: <http://bibnum2.bnquebec.ca/bna/
lovell/index.html>

New France New Horizons: On French Soil in America: <www.archivescanadafrance.
org/english/accueil_en.html>

Programme de recherche en démographie historique:
Quebec and Eastern Townships Genealogy Research Page: <http://simmons.
b2b2c.ca/>

Quebec Family History Society: <www.qfhs.ca>

Quebec GenWeb: <www.rootsweb.com/~canqc/>

Quebec Land Survey and access to the land register: <www.mrn.gouv.qc.ca/
english/land/ <http://www.mrn.gouv.qc.ca/english/land/>

South West Quebec Old Placenames:
  <www.rootsweb.com/~qcchatea/placenames/names.htm>
United Church Archives Network: <www.united-church.ca/archives/home.shtm>
United Church Montreal and Ottawa Conference Archives:
  <www.montrealandottawaconference.ca/Archives/index2.htm>
University of Montreal (parish locator and record details): <www.genealogie.
  umontreal.ca/en/Carte.asp>

BIBLIOGRAPHY

Bangsberg, Tara L., Sandra Burrows, and Jon W. Bangsberg. *Two Partial Indexes to Newspapers in the Province of Quebec from 1666–1993.* Salt Lake City, UT: Genealogical Society of Utah, 1993.

Bélanger, Pauline, and Yves Landry. *Inventaire des registres paroissiaux catholiques du Québec, 1621–1876.* Montréal: Presses de l'Université de Montréal, 1990.

Bernard, Pierre. *Répertoire des naissances des Métis et Amérindiens(nes), extrait du P.R.D.H. du début de la colonie à 1765.* Kanesatake, QC: P. Bernard, 1996.

Bouchette, Joseph. *A Topographical Dictionary of the Province of Lower Canada.* London: Longman, Rees, Orme, Brown, Green and Longman, 1832. (online at Our Roots)

Broadhurst, R. Neil. *A Checklist of Registers of Protestant & Jewish Congregations in Quebec.* Calgary, AL: Kintracers, 1994.

Elliot, Noel M. *The French Canadians, 1600–1900: An Alphabetized Directory of the People, Places and Vital Dates.* 3 vols. Toronto: Genealogical Research Library, 1992. (online at Ancestry)

Fortin, Francine. *Guide des registres d'état civil et recensements du Québec: catholiques, protestants et autres dénominations, 1621–2000.* Montréal: Société généalogique canadienne-française, 2001.

Geyh, Patricia Keeney, et al. *French-Canadian Sources: A Guide for Genealogists.* Orem, UT: Ancestry, 2002.

Jetté, René. *Dictionnaire généalogique des familles du Québec.* Montréal: Presses de l'Université de Montréal, 1983.

Jetté, René. *Traité de généalogie.* Montréal: Les Presses de L'Université Montréal, 1991.

Leboeuf, J.-Arthur. *Complément au dictionnaire généalogique Tanguay.* Montréal: Société généalogique canadienne-française, 1957–1964.

LaFontaine, André. *Recensements annotés de la Nouvelle-France, 1666 & 1667.* Sherbrooke, QC: A. Fontaine, 1985.

———. *Recensement annoté de la Nouvelle-France, 1681.* Sherbrooke, QC: A. Fontaine, 1981, rev. 1995.

———. *Recensements annotés de la ville de Québec, 1716 & 1744.* Sherbrooke, QC: A. Fontaine, 1983.

Laliberté, Jean-Marie. *Index des lieux de résidence et de pratique des commis, des garde-notes, des greffiers, des tabellions, autres, et des notaires, 1621-1991 : ainsi que les lieu de dépôt de leurs minutiers avec leurs cotes aux A.N.Q.* Montréal: Jean-Marie Laliberté, 1991.

Lovell, John, ed. *Canadian Dominion Directory for 1871.* Montreal: John Lovell, 1871.

Quebec Family History Society. *Alphabetical Index to the Land Grants by the Crown in the Province of Quebec from 1763 to 31st December 1890.* 22 vols. Pointe Claire, QC: Quebec Family History Society, n.d. (available from the society)

Quebec Family History Society. *A Directory of Monumental Inscription Lists: Cemeteries in and Near the Province of Quebec.* Rev. ed. Pointe Claire, QC: Quebec Family History Society, 1997.

Quintin, Robert J. *French-Canadian Surnames: Aliases, Adulterations and Anglicizations.* Pawtucket, RI: Quintin Publications, 1993.

Quintin, Robert J. *The Notaries of French Canada 1626 to 1900.* Pawtucket, RI: Quintin Publications, 1994.

Roy, Pierre-Georges. *Les Noms géographiques de la province de Québec.* Quebec, QC: 1906. (online at Our Roots)

Tanguay, Cyprien. *Dictionnaire généalogique des familles canadiennes depuis la fondation de la colonie jusqu'à nos jours.* Baltimore: Genealogical Publishing Company, 1967. (originally pub. 1871–1890)

White, Jeanne Suave. *Guide to Quebec Catholic Parishes and Published Parish Marriage Records.* Baltimore: Genealogical Publishing Co., 2003. (online at Ancestry)

ADDRESSES

American-Canadian Genealogical Society
PO Box 6478
Manchester, NH   03108-6478

Bibliothèque et Archives nationales du Québec
Pavillon Louis-Jacques-Casault
1055, avenue du Séminaire
Case postale 10450 Succersale Sainte-Foy, QC G1V 4N1

Centre d'archives de l'Abitibi-Témiscamingue et du Nord-du-Québec
27, rue du Terminus Ouest
Rouyn-Noranda, QC J9X 2P3

Centre d'archives de la Côte-Nord
700, boulevard Laure
Bureau 190-2
Sept-Îles, QC G4R 1Y1

Centre d'archives de l'Estrie
225, rue Frontenac, bureau 401
Sherbrooke, QC J1H 1K1

Centre d'archives de la Mauricie et du Centre-du-Québec
225, rue des Forges, bureau 208
Trois-Rivières, QC G9A 2G7

Centre d'archives de Montréal
Édifice Gilles-Hocquart
535, avenue Viger Est
Montréal, QC H2L 2P3

Centre d'archives de l'Outaouais
855, boulevard de la Gappe
Gatineau, QC J8T 8H9

Centre d'archives de Québec
Pavillon Louis-Jacques-Casault
Cité universitaire, C.P. 10450
Sainte-Foy, QC G1V 4N1

Centre d'archives du Saguenay–Lac-Saint-Jean
930, rue Jacques-Cartier Est
Bureau C-103, 1 er étage
Chicoutimi, QC G7H 7K9

Commission de toponymie
750, boulevard Charest Est, rez-de-chaussée
Québec, QC G1K 9M1

Grande Bibliothèque
475, boulevard De Maisonneuve Est
Montréal, QC H2L 5C4

Library and Archives Canada
395 Wellington Street
Ottawa, ON K1A 0N4

Ministère de la Justice
Directeur de l'état civil
2535, boulevard Laurier
Sainte-Foy, QC G1V 5C5

Programme de recherche en démographie historique (PRDH)
Département de démographie
Université de Montréal
C.P. 6128, succ. Centre-ville
Montréal, QC H3C 3J7

Regional Centers of Bibliothèque et Archives nationales du Québec
Centre d'archives du Bas-Saint-Laurent et
de la Gaspésie-Îles-de-la-Madeleine
Édifice Louis-Joseph-Moreault
337, rue Moreault
Rimouski, QC G5L 1P4

Société généalogique canadienne-française
3440 Davidson
Montréal, QC H1W 2Z5

Société de recherche historique Archiv-Histo
2320, rue des Carrières
Montréal, QC H2G 3G9

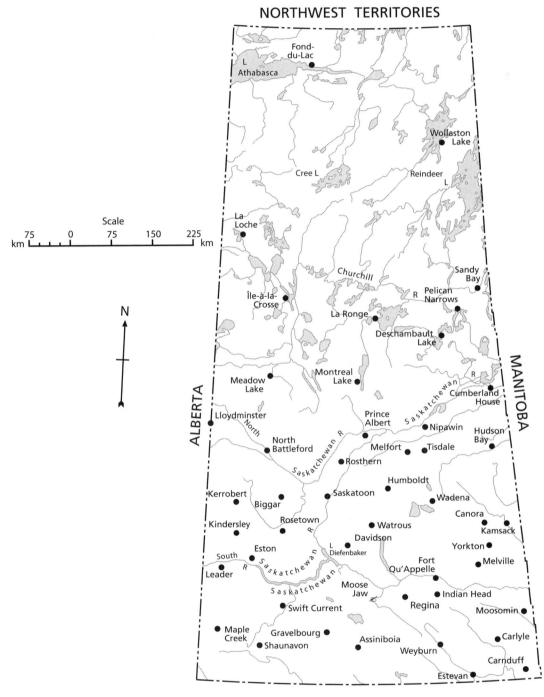

Figure 25-1. Saskatchewan

25

SASKATCHEWAN

Saskatchewan became a province on 1 September 1905, created from territory in four administrative districts: Assiniboia East, Assiniboia West, Athabasca, and Saskatchewan. The districts had been created by the Canadian government in 1882. The flood of immigration that followed the completion of the Canadian Pacific Railway in 1885 generated the pressure for change.

Until Saskatchewan experienced a dramatic population boom in the early years of the twentieth century, it was home to fur traders, First Nations, and a few daring homesteaders, primarily in the southeastern corner. The 1901 census recorded 91,279 people there, and in ten years the population increased fivefold. The number of people continued to increase until the late 1930s, when most of the good agricultural land had been taken. The Great Depression and a lengthy drought started to take its toll.

The 1936 census shows that of those people living in Saskatchewan who had not been born in the province, Ontario was the most common birthplace, followed by the United States and England. Most people identified themselves as being of British stock, with German second, and Ukrainian third.

Saskatchewan settlement included a patchwork of ethnic blocks, with Hungarians in the Esterhazy area in 1886, six Jewish farm colonies between 1886 and 1906, Doukhobors from the Crimea region of the Russian Empire in three districts in 1899, and the Barr Colonists from England in the Lloydminster area in 1903.

The number of farms in Saskatchewan peaked with the 1936 census, but the province remained the most populous in western Canada until the 1940s. Today, Saskatchewan has about 1 million people, and mining, forestry, and oil and gas production have joined agriculture as key industries.

FINDING LOCALITIES

The creation of Saskatchewan introduced the potential for confusion. There was an old district of the same name comprising the central part of the province as well as pieces of Alberta and Manitoba. In addition, the two Assiniboia districts, which included most of the population of Saskatchewan, disappeared. When researching before 1905 you will find that records may refer to any of the former administrative districts or simply to the Northwest Territories (N.W.T.).

After 1905, regional boundaries are less important. Saskatchewan has a network of rural municipalities as well as town and city governments, but most records are at the federal or provincial levels.

The Canadian Geographical Names website and contemporary directories can help you find most communities. Another readily available online reference is the provincial government's Saskatchewan Highway Grid Map; it includes township boundaries. Small rural settlements, perhaps with only a store and a community hall, can be found on modern maps. Consult the detailed landowner maps published by the rural municipalities.

Saskatchewan Wheat Pool maps from 1924 through 1984 are reproduced on the Saskatchewan GenWeb site. These include lists of communities with their locations.

CENSUS

Censuses have been taken in Saskatchewan since 1881. The first three were completed in 1881, 1891, and 1901, when Saskatchewan was still part of the Northwest Territories, and split into four administrative districts.

All censuses covering Saskatchewan have been indexed. An index to the 1881 census is on the FamilySearch website. It has some errors, and you should consult the more accurate *Index to 1881 Canadian Census of Northwest Territories and Algoma, Ontario* (Main, 1984). Indexes to the 1901, 1906, and 1911 censuses are online at Ancestry and Automated Genealogy; index results are linked to images at the Library and Archives Canada (LAC) website. You can browse by census district or search by place-name at the LAC site.

A published index to the 1891 census, done on a district-by-district basis, is available for sale by the Regina branch of the Saskatchewan Genealogical Society. It is also available on microfiche through the Family History Library (FHL). The Edmonton branch of the Alberta Genealogical Society prepared an index to the 1901 census, giving you a third search option for this particular year. It can be consulted at the society website or purchased as a series of published volumes.

All of the federal census returns are available on microfilm from LAC, and those from 1881 to 1906 are available through Family History Centers.

There are some additional enumerations. The Hudson's Bay Company took a census of the Prince Albert District in 1871, which is at its archives in Winnipeg and at the Glenbow Museum and Archives in Calgary. The Doukhobor population was enumerated in 1905, and there are some local government lists. Check with the Saskatchewan Archives.

CIVIL REGISTRATION

Registration of marriages began in the Northwest Territories in 1878, and registration of births and deaths started ten years later. The new provincial government continued with registrations when Saskatchewan was created in 1905.

Indexes to early vital registrations, including the territorial ones, are available on a Saskatchewan government website. Births from one hundred or more years ago and deaths from before 1917 are already on the site. It will eventually have all deaths from more than seventy years ago and marriages from more than seventy-five years ago.

Copies of the birth, marriage, and death registration documents included in the site's database are available from Saskatchewan Vital Statistics. More recent documents are available only to the people named on them or close relatives.

Saskatchewan created local divorce courts in 1920. Before that, couples seeking a divorce had to apply to the Canadian Parliament. Records up to 1950 have been microfilmed by the Genealogical Society of Utah and are available at the FHL.

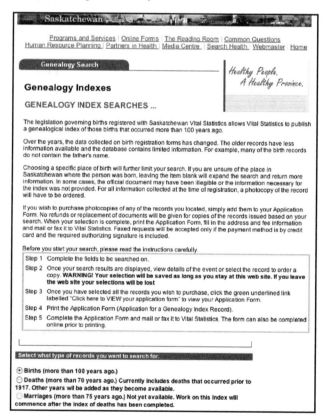

Figure 25-2. Saskatchewan Vital Statistics Online Search Page
<http://vsgs.health.gov.sk.ca/vsgs_srch.aspx>

CHURCH RECORDS

The Saskatchewan Archives Board has many original and microfilm copies of parish registers, primarily from the United, Anglican, and Presbyterian churches. In most cases, access is subject to the permission of the conference or diocese. Those offices can help you determine which church your ancestor attended if you do not know that already.

The Saskatchewan Archives Board serves as the archives for the United Church Conference of Saskatchewan and for the Anglican Diocese of Qu'Appelle and the Ecclesiastical Province of Rupert's Land.

The Roman Catholic Archdiocese of Regina has archives that are open only by appointment for historical research. For baptismal records, check with individual churches.

The Lutheran Church keeps its archives for the central district, which includes Saskatchewan, in Regina. Only a few Saskatchewan church registers are available through LAC or the FHL.

CEMETERY RECORDS

The Saskatchewan Genealogical Society has a comprehensive list of cemeteries and plans to add references to burials for people mentioned in its Saskatchewan Residents Index. Indexes of burials from several dozen Saskatchewan communities are on the Internet. The largest cemeteries available on the Web include ones in Saskatoon, Moose Jaw, and Lloydminster.

Some cemetery records are also held at the Saskatchewan Genealogical Society and the Saskatchewan Archives Board. The Saskatchewan GenWeb includes a listing of online cemetery transcriptions throughout the province.

Cemeteries might have been owned by local churches or municipalities, so there is no set rule as to where you will find the records.

WILLS AND PROBATE RECORDS

Probate records, which started in 1882, are kept by Saskatchewan's Surrogate Courts. Check for them at the courthouse closest to where the deceased person lived: Estevan, La Ronge, Lloydminster, Meadow Lake, Melfort, Moose Jaw, North Battleford, Prince Albert, Regina, Saskatoon, Swift Current, Wynyard, or Yorkton.

Copies of probated wills are also filed with the Surrogate Registrar at the Regina Court House, but to gain access requires the full name of the deceased, the date of death, and the place of last residence.

Surrogate court records have been microfilmed by the Genealogical Society of Utah. They include Arcola, 1907–1933; Assiniboia, 1922–1935; Battleford, 1897–1935; Estevan, 1913–1936; Gravelbourg, 1918–1932; Humboldt, 1913–1932; Kerrobert, 1913–1930; Kindersley, 1913–1938; Leader, 1923–1950; Maple Creek, 1923–1932; Melfort, 1920–1930; Moosomin, 1887–1932; Prince Albert, 1884–1934; Regina, 1882–1930; Saskatoon, 1908–1932; Scott and Wilkie, 1913–1931; Swift Current, 1913–1933; Weyburn, 1913–1940; Wynyard, 1913–1932; and Yorkton, 1897–1936. Most of the records have indexes or docket books, which can be used to determine the number of the will.

LAND RECORDS

Homestead records include biographical information. They are available at the provincial archives, and the Saskatchewan Homestead Index has references to 360,000 records from 1872 through 1930. It provides enough information to allow a file to be ordered from the Saskatchewan Archives Board.

The amount of information in a file varies, depending on whether or not the homesteader made a serious effort to establish the land as a working farm. Not all files are for those who received a patent to the land. Some include little more than an application or a request to abandon the land.

The Saskatchewan Genealogical Society has produced a CD-ROM titled *HOME*, for Home Ownership Mapping Endeavour. The CD provides the names, dates, and locations of about 400,000 original Dominion land grantees in the province. It also has an explanation of the Dominion land survey system, a digital copy of the 2005 Saskatchewan Highway Grid Map, and historical background.

An index of western land grants is on the LAC website. It includes only those people who successfully met the requirement and obtained ownership of their land. Images of the patents are being added to the website. The Glenbow Archives has an online database of land sold by the Canadian Pacific Railway.

Another database of land grants, along with a database of modern landowners, is on the website of the Information Services Corporation of Saskatchewan, a provincial government service. It includes records of people who bought land directly from the Crown.

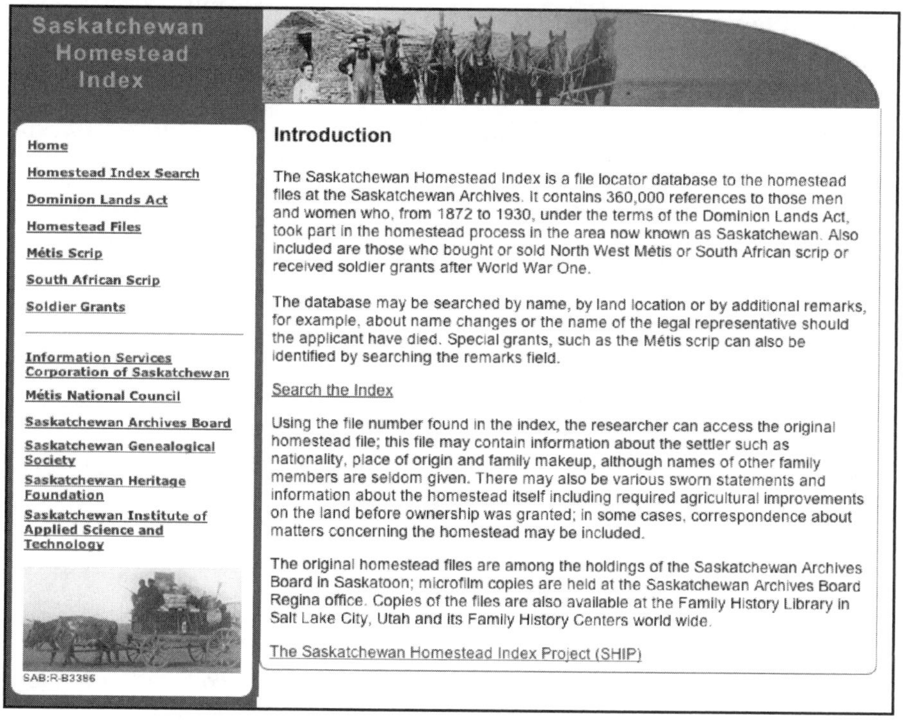

Saskatchewan Homestead Index

Home

Homestead Index Search

Dominion Lands Act

Homestead Files

Métis Scrip

South African Scrip

Soldier Grants

Information Services Corporation of Saskatchewan

Métis National Council

Saskatchewan Archives Board

Saskatchewan Genealogical Society

Saskatchewan Heritage Foundation

Saskatchewan Institute of Applied Science and Technology

SAB:R-B3386

Introduction

The Saskatchewan Homestead Index is a file locator database to the homestead files at the Saskatchewan Archives. It contains 360,000 references to those men and women who, from 1872 to 1930, under the terms of the Dominion Lands Act, took part in the homestead process in the area now known as Saskatchewan. Also included are those who bought or sold North West Métis or South African scrip or received soldier grants after World War One.

The database may be searched by name, by land location or by additional remarks, for example, about name changes or the name of the legal representative should the applicant have died. Special grants, such as the Métis scrip can also be identified by searching the remarks field.

Search the Index

Using the file number found in the index, the researcher can access the original homestead file; this file may contain information about the settler such as nationality, place of origin and family makeup, although names of other family members are seldom given. There may also be various sworn statements and information about the homestead itself including required agricultural improvements on the land before ownership was granted; in some cases, correspondence about matters concerning the homestead may be included.

The original homestead files are among the holdings of the Saskatchewan Archives Board in Saskatoon; microfilm copies are held at the Saskatchewan Archives Board Regina office. Copies of the files are also available at the Family History Library in Salt Lake City, Utah and its Family History Centers world wide.

The Saskatchewan Homestead Index Project (SHIP)

Figure 25-3. Website for the Saskatchewan Homestead Index
<http://www.saskhomesteads.com/>

If a land description shows the meridian was W2 or W3, that land is in Saskatchewan. W2 is in the eastern half, and W3 is in the western half. And if the meridian is W1, with a range number of 30, 31, 32, 33, or 34, the land is in the southeast corner of Saskatchewan, next to the Manitoba border.

The Saskatchewan GenWeb has a page on how to read homestead records.

NEWSPAPERS

The first newspaper published in Saskatchewan was the *Saskatchewan Herald*, published in Battleford from 1878. The *Regina Leader-Post* traces its roots to 1883, and the Saskatoon *Star-Phoenix* began publication in 1902.

The province's newspapers are available at the offices of the Saskatchewan Archives Board. The Saskatoon office has the newspapers from the northern half of the province, and the Regina office holds those from the southern half.

An index of major news stories from 1884 through 2000 is on the University of Saskatchewan website. Indexes to births, marriages, and deaths in Regina newspapers to 1910 are available at the Saskatchewan Genealogical Society.

OTHER WAYS TO FIND PEOPLE

The first directories for Saskatchewan were published in Winnipeg in the 1880s, part of volumes covering all three Prairie Provinces. As a result, only the most prominent people were included. These Prairie-wide directories continued until 1908. A directory covering all of Saskatchewan was published in 1921, but like the others, it included only the most prominent people.

City directories, designed to include every household, were published in several cities until the late 1990s. They started in Moose Jaw in 1890, Saskatoon in 1908, Regina in 1911, and North Battleford and Battleford, Swift Current, Weyburn, Yorkton, and Prince Albert in 1913.

In rural areas, check brand books, which listed the owners of cattle brands. Maps showing the names of landowners were published by the Cummins Map Company of Winnipeg for certain years between 1917 and 1930. Maps showing the names of farmers are available from rural municipalities.

The Peel's Prairie Provinces website includes directories, such as the 1919 Henderson's edition for Regina. This website is searchable by name and gives you access to local histories and government reports.

Federal voters lists are available from 1935 through 1979. Municipal voters lists may also be available; many have been deposited with the Saskatchewan Archives Board.

SPECIAL SOURCES

The Saskatchewan Genealogical Society has an exceptional collection of resources in its Regina library. The Saskatchewan Residents Index is a continuing program of indexing names, with more than 2 million so far from a wide variety of sources.

Another particularly helpful resource is its Saskatchewan Obituary File containing more than 750,000 death notices. In addition, the society runs the largest genealogical lending library in Canada; members can borrow books from anywhere in Canada.

The biggest battle on Canadian soil since Confederation took place in Saskatchewan. The Northwest Resistance of 1885 followed an attempt by the Métis people to establish their own sovereign nation in what is today north-central Saskatchewan. The rebellion was suppressed by 3,000 troops, 2,000 volunteers (mostly from the Prairies), and members of the North-West Mounted Police.

The names of the volunteers may be found, on a district-by-district basis, in contemporary government reports and newspapers. The University of Saskatchewan website has a database of materials about the 1885 resistance.

As mentioned previously, before the province was opened to homesteaders, most of the residents of Saskatchewan were members of First Nations, Hudson's Bay Company fur traders, or Métis—people of mixed ancestry. Aboriginal research is important in Saskatchewan. LAC has superb collections, and other valuable resources are with the Hudson's Bay Company Archives, the Saskatchewan Archives Board, and the University of Saskatchewan. Refer to chapter 14 for more detailed information.

WEBSITES

Ancestry: <www.ancestry.ca>

Anglican Diocese of Saskatchewan: < http://www.skdiocese.com/archives/>

Atlas of Saskatchewan: <www.rootsweb.com/~cansk/maps/saskatchewanatlas. html>

Information Services Corporation of Saskatchewan: <www.isc.ca>

Lutheran Central District Archives: <www.lcccentral.ca>

Northwest Resistance: <library2.usask.ca/northwest>

Roman Catholic Archdiocese of Regina: <www.archregina.sk.ca/Archives.htm>

Saskatchewan Archival Information Network: <scaa.usask.ca/sain>

Saskatchewan Archives Board: <www.saskarchives.com>

Saskatchewan cemetery transcripts: <www.rootsweb.com/~cansk/Saskatchewan/ cemetery.html>

Saskatchewan Genealogical Society: <www.saskgenealogy.com>

Saskatchewan GenWeb: <www.rootsweb.com/~cansk>

Saskatchewan Homestead Index: <www.saskhomesteads.com>

Saskatchewan News Index, 1884–2000: <library.usask.ca/sni>

Saskatchewan Vital Statistics: <vsgs.health.gov.sk.ca/vsgs_srch.aspx>

Saskatchewan Wheat Pool Maps, 1924–1984: <www.rootsweb.com/~skwheat/>

Saskatoon Obituary Index:
<http://spldatabase.saskatoonlibrary.ca/OBIQuery.htm >

Saskobits: <www.saskobits.com>

Virtual Museum of Métis History and Culture: <www.metismuseum.ca>

BIBLIOGRAPHY

Barry, Bill. *Geographic Names of Saskatchewan.* Regina: People Places Publishing, 2005.

Condon, Eileen P. *Index to the 1891 Census of Canada: Assiniboia East, Assiniboia West and Saskatchewan.* Regina: Regina Branch, Saskatchewan Genealogical Society, 1988–1992.

Gazetteer of Canada: Saskatchewan. Ottawa: Canadian Permanent Committee on Geographical Names, 1969.

Hanowski, Laura M., ed. *Tracing Your Aboriginal Ancestors in the Prairie Provinces: A Guide to the Records and How to Use Them.* Regina: Saskatchewan Genealogical Society, 2006.

———. *Tracing Your Saskatchewan Ancestors.* 3rd ed. Regina: Saskatchewan Genealogical Society, 2006.

Main, Lorne W. *Index to 1881 Canadian Census of North West Territories and Algoma, Ontario.* Vancouver: L.W. Main, 1984.

ADDRESSES

Anglican Church Diocese of Qu'Appelle
and the Ecclesiastical Province of Rupert's Land
c/o Saskatchewan Archives Board
University of Regina
3737 Wascana Parkway
Regina, SK S4S 0A2

Anglican Church Diocese of Saskatchewan
1308 Fifth Avenue East
Prince Albert, SK S6V 2H7

Anglican Church Diocese of Saskatoon
PO Box 1965
Saskatoon, SK S7K 3S5
(Housed in the Saskatchewan Archives Board—Saskatoon Office)

Glenbow Museum and Archives
130 9th Avenue S.E.
Calgary, AB T2G 0P3

Hudson's Bay Company Archives
130-200 Vaughan Street
Winnipeg, MB R3C 1T5

Library and Archives Canada
395 Wellington Street
Ottawa, ON K1A 0N4

Lutheran Church of Canada Central District
1927 Grant Drive
Regina, SK S4S 4V6

Roman Catholic Archdiocese of Regina
445 Broad Street N.
Regina, SK S4R 2X8

Roman Catholic Diocese of Prince Albert Archives
1415 4th Avenue West
Prince Albert, SK S6V 5H1

Roman Catholic Diocese of Saskatoon
Catholic Pastoral Centre
100 5th Ave. North
Saskatoon, SK S7K 2N7

Saskatchewan Genealogical Society
Second Floor, 1870 Lorne Street
PO Box 1894
Regina, SK S4P 3E1

Saskatchewan Archives Board Regina
3303 Hillsdale Street, Regina
mailing address:
Saskatchewan Archives Board,
University of Regina
Regina, SK S4S 0A2

Saskatchewan Archives Board Saskatoon
Murray Building, University of Saskatchewan
3 Campus Drive
Saskatoon, SK S7N 5A4

Saskatchewan Vital Statistics
100-1942 Hamilton Street
Regina, SK S4P 4W2

United Church Saskatchewan Conference Archives
418A McDonald Street
Regina, SK S4N 6E1

Figure 26-1. The Territories

THE TERRITORIES

The Northwest Territories are not what they used to be—a fact that family history researchers working in Western Canada need to remember.

The Northwest Territories came into being on 22 June 1869, when the lands of the Hudson's Bay Company were transferred to the government of Canada. The area was immense: everything between British Columbia and Ontario north of the United States border, plus all of Quebec and Ontario that drained into Hudson Bay.

The Northwest Territories became the largest single geographic jurisdiction in Canada, a title it held for more than a century, even as more and more land was taken from it. In 1870, the settlements in the Red River area were removed from the Territories, forming the core of the new province of Manitoba. Six years later, the District of Keewatin, north of Manitoba and west of Ontario, was also removed. In 1880, Manitoba was expanded, again cutting into the territorial land.

Within the Territories, provisional districts—named Assiniboia, Alberta, Saskatchewan, and Athabaska—were set up in 1882 for postal and administrative purposes. Farther north, unorganized districts were created and named Yukon, Mackenzie, Franklin, and Ungava.

A sharp increase in immigration at the end of the nineteenth century prompted the removal of more land. Yukon, the scene of a gold rush, became a territory of its own in 1897. The four provisional districts in the south were replaced in 1905 with two new provinces, Alberta and Saskatchewan.

The population of the Territories rose dramatically in those years, from 98,967 in 1891 to 158,940 in 1901. Population boomed in the areas that became Alberta and Saskatchewan, with a total population of 443,175 by 1906, the first census taken after the provinces were created. In 1911, the population of the Territories was just 26,993.

The Territories lost land again when Quebec, Ontario, and Manitoba were extended north in 1912. The boundaries didn't change again until 1999, when more than half the land area was split off to create the new territory of Nunavut. From 1869 through 1999, the Northwest Territories was Canada's largest jurisdiction by area. Today, it is in third place, behind Nunavut and Quebec.

A tremendous flow of people entered the Yukon during the gold rush from 1897 to 1900. Their stories and their names can be found on the Internet. To this day, the Yukon's population has not recovered to its level at the peak of the rush.

The total population of the three territories (Yukon, Nunavut, and Northwest) is about 100,000. In Nunavut and the Northwest Territories, aboriginal residents, mostly Inuit, make up more than half the total population.

The former territorial areas in the three Prairie Provinces are covered in the sections in this book on Manitoba, Saskatchewan, and Alberta. This chapter deals only with today's Northwest Territories as well as the Yukon and Nunavut.

FINDING LOCALITIES

The Canadian Geographic Names database is the best source for locating places in the three territories. Be sure to search for a formerly official name as well as a current name because there have been many changes in Canada's north.

If you find a reference that includes the geographical abbreviation N.W.T., look for the date. If it is from before 1905, check to find out whether it is in today's Alberta or Saskatchewan. If it is from after 1905 but before 1999, there is a chance it refers to land in Nunavut. And remember that other Northwest Territories land has gone to the Yukon, Manitoba, Ontario, and Quebec.

You won't need to worry about counties or other local jurisdictions in the territories because most records are handled on a territory-wide basis or by the federal government.

Many communities were given English names over the years, but these are being changed in favor of native ones. Frobisher Bay, for example, was renamed Iqaluit in 1987. In everyday usage there are still references to the English or native names. Most people in the area are familiar with both names, and if your roots are there, it would make sense for you to learn them as well. The dual names include Fort Norman (also Tulit'a); Fort Good Hope (Radlei Ko); Coppermine (Kugluktuk); the Mackenzie River, also known as Deh Cho; and Arctic Red River (Tsiigehtchic).

CENSUS

The North-West Territories (the hyphen was dropped in 1912) appeared in the census starting in 1881, but most of the people were living in the districts that later became parts of Alberta or Saskatchewan. The 1911 census was the first in which territory boundaries referred to the northern territory rather than the provinces. Subsequent censuses were taken every ten years until 1956, when enumerations switched to every five years, in line with the rest of Canada.

Indexes to the 1901 and 1911 censuses for the territories are on the Ancestry website, and they are also complete at Automated Genealogy. At both sites, search results are linked to online images of the returns at Library and Archives Canada

(LAC). In 1901 the area is called Unorganized Territories and in 1911, Yukon and Northwest Territories. The small population of the north is included in the 1881 index at FamilySearch.

The censuses from 1881, 1891, 1901, and 1911 can be viewed on microfilm using Family History Centers.

CIVIL REGISTRATION

Birth, death, and marriage certificates since 1925 are available from the Northwest Territories government's Vital Statistics Registrar General in Inuvik. The early records are not complete because of the remoteness of many of the communities. There are restrictions on access. A death certificate, for example, is available only to immediate family or for legal or official reasons.

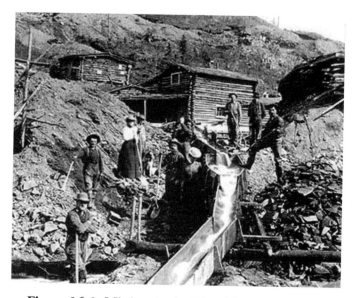

Figure 26-2. Mining in the Klondike, 1898–1900
Photo courtesy of Library and Archives Canada / C-005394

Birth, death, and marriage certificates for events in the Yukon since 1896 are available from the Department of Health and Social Services in Whitehorse. Civil registration documents for Nunavut can be obtained from Nunavut Health and Social Services in Rankin Inlet.

The Native and Inuit people were under the jurisdiction of the federal government. Descriptions of records containing personal information appear in chapter 13. Records for Inuit people begin in 1939.

CHURCH RECORDS

A few early records were made in the 1880s. If the records are not held locally, you may have to look outside the territories and thousands of miles to the south. In addition to the websites and addresses for this chapter, check into location and contents of church archives for provinces from Ontario west.

The main Christian churches in the north were the Church of England (Anglican), Roman Catholic, and United, which was created in 1925 by an amalgamation of Methodists, Congregationalists, and Presbyterians.

A printed source that may be helpful is *Lost and Found in Alaska and the Klondike* (Beeman, 1997). It is an index based on a variety of sources, including some church records.

WILLS AND PROBATE RECORDS

Probate records for the Northwest Territories are handled by the Supreme Court in Yellowknife. In Yukon they are the responsibility of the Department of Justice in Whitehorse. In Nunavut, contact the public trustee in Iqaluit.

Figure 26-3. Yukon Genealogy Website
<www.yukongenealogy.com>

LAND RECORDS

All registered documents, plans, and titles maintained in the land titles office in Yellowknife are available for inspection by the public. Information on land grants in the Territories can be found through the Registrar of Titles in Yellowknife.

In Nunavut the land titles office is in Iqaluit. Historic records are in Yellowknife. In the Yukon the land titles office in Whitehorse holds all original land titles and related documents.

NEWSPAPERS

The only daily newspaper north of the sixtieth parallel, the southern boundary of all three territories, is the *Whitehorse Daily Star* in the Yukon. The University of Washington Special Collections Library holds an index to the *Yukon Nugget* newspaper.

In Yellowknife the major newspaper for decades has been *News of the North*, or *News/North*. It is published weekly and distributed throughout the territories. There is also a biweekly, the *Yellowknifer*. In Nunavut the most important newspaper is the *Nunatsiaq News*, published in Iqaluit.

OTHER WAYS TO FIND PEOPLE

The Yukon Genealogy website has two databases, Yukon Archives Genealogy Database and Dawson City Museum Pan for Gold Database. The first is derived from many lists: civil servants, teachers, voters, Anglican Church records, are a few. Pan for Gold includes names from the Dawson City 1901 census, police records, death records, list of travelers, and placer mining applications.

You can search by surname only or full name. Each result tells you the original source by reference code or list title.

Parts of the Yukon have been included in some directories of the province of British Columbia and the state of Alaska. There are many Yukon directories in the Pacific Northwest Collection of the University of Washington Special Collections Library.

SPECIAL RESOURCES

The territory of the Hudson's Bay Company surrounded the bay and included part of the Northwest Territories. However, the company concentrated its activities in the southern part of its lands. If an ancestor served with the company in the far north, you need to consult records at the Archives of Manitoba. The website has a section for the Hudson's Bay Company with descriptions of various classes of records and guides to contents.

Post histories and biographies are the most helpful. The post histories contain records of the operation of the post, location, and history. Biographies record the service of individuals and usually state birthplace, places of service, and positions held. There may be details about the employee's family. There were at one time seven posts in the Yukon and more than fifty in the Northwest Territories.

The Inuit are the Aboriginal people of the Arctic, formerly referred to as Eskimos. In 1939 the courts determined that "Eskimos" did come under the definition of Indian and that the federal government should have administrative responsibilities for the native population of the north. Before that time it is not easy to find information. To see the sorts of records held by government, use the Government of Canada Files database on the LAC website, searching for place or personal names or using "Eskimo$" or "Inuit$." Also refer to the chapter in this book on Aboriginal records.

WEBSITES

Ancestry: <www.ancestry.ca>
Anglican Diocese of the Arctic: <www.arcticnet.org>
Dawson City Museum and Historical Society: <users.yknet.yk.ca/dcpages/Museum.html>
Government of Canada Files Database:
    <www.collectionscanada.ca/archivianet/020105_e.html>
Library and Archives Canada, Canadian Genealogy Centre:
    <www.collectionscanada.ca/genealogy>
Northwest Territories Archives: <pwnhc.learnnet.nt.ca/programs/archive.htm>
Northwest Territories GenWeb: <www.rootsweb.com/~cannt/nwt.htm>
Nunavut GenWeb: <www.rootsweb.com/~cannt/nunavut.htm>
United Church Alberta and Northwest Conference Archives: <http://www.archivesalberta.org/walls/united.htm>
University of Washington Library: <www.lib.washington.edu/specialcoll/>
Yukon Archives: <www.btc.gov.yk.ca/archives/>
Yukon Genealogy (two databases):
Yukon GenWeb: <www.rootsweb.com/~canyk/>

BIBLIOGRAPHY

Beeman, Marydith. *Lost and Found in Alaska and the Klondike.* Volumes 1 and 2. Chugiak, AK: M.W. Beeman, 1997.

Coutts, R. C. *Yukon Places and Names.* Sidney, BC: Gray's Publishing, 1980.

Fletcher, Roy Jackson. *Settlements of Northern Canada: A Gazetteer and Index.* Edmonton: Boreal Institute for Northern Studies, 1975.

Genealogical Research at the Yukon Archives. Whitehorse: Yukon Archives, 2003. (free download on the Yukon Genealogy website)

ADDRESSES

Anglican Diocese of Yukon
Box 31136
Whitehorse, YT Y1A 5P7
(Records are at the Yukon Territorial Archives.)

Anglican Archives, Diocese of the Arctic
General Synod Archives
80 Hayden Street
Toronto, ON M4Y 3G2

Dawson City Museum and Historical Society
PO Box 303
Dawson City, YT Y0B 1G0

Library and Archives Canada
395 Wellington Street
Ottawa, ON K1A 0N4

Northwest Territories Archives
Prince of Wales Northern Heritage Centre
PO Box 1320
Yellowknife, NT X1A 2L9

Nunavut Archives
PO Box 310
Igloolik, NU X0A 0L0

United Church of Canada Alberta and Northwest Conference Archives
c/o Provincial Archives of Alberta
8555 Roper Road
Edmonton, AB T6E 5W1

University of Washington Libraries
Special Collections and Preservation Division
University of Washington Libraries
Box 352900
Seattle, WA 98195-2900

Yukon Archives
400 College Drive
Yukon Place
PO Box 2703
Whitehorse, YT Y1A 2C6

RESEARCH FUNDAMENTALS

Lucky genealogists hear firsthand personal accounts about their family's past from grandparents and other relations. Stories stir the imagination and are a reminder to start work at home with the remembered past. Photographs, letters, diaries, heirlooms, and the stories that surround them are often the sources of facts vital to research.

An early focus on home helps create the habit of gathering information even if you cannot see the immediate value. Besides the fun of collecting, there is the interesting exercise of organizing and reviewing what you have collected before you get down to serious research. Review is a valuable search tool, one you will turn to again and again.

Your ancestors' homes were happy and sad places, comfortable and harsh, safe and dangerous. They were integral parts of their lives. That is another value of a home focus from the start—you will better understand the fabric of the past in your family.

METHOD

Have you ever been to an auction? Sometimes what is going on the block is an Aladdin's Cave of delights; if you simply go, you may be caught up in the excitement and spend too much on things you don't want. If you go in advance, preview items, and select those of interest, you can plan ahead to get the best value.

Method in genealogy is like that. Without any, the excitement of the pursuit can carry you off on tangents, ultimately wasting time and perhaps money, too. With advance planning and review, your results are better and usually come faster.

Organization is part of method. You need to be able to find things and to make comparisons. Modern genealogy software performs many of these tasks easily. There is also plenty of choice, and you should think carefully about the features you need before choosing a program. If the basics are all you require, there are free programs and shareware. Greater complexity comes at a price. Talk to others, and look for software reviews in computer and genealogy magazines.

Genealogy software is helpful but not essential. There are options online, places to input data that keep it for you. Some genealogists use word processing and spreadsheet software. The only drawback is the necessity of planning the layout yourself. Others continue to sort information into shoeboxes or three-ring binders. The need for organization is absolute, but how you do it is entirely up to you.

FLOW

Using method in research creates flow. You can see where your conclusions came from and predict to some extent where they are leading. It really helps to keep track of flow, and that is best done with charts. Make lots of them often so you always have up-to-date charts handy.

Pedigree charts present the skeletal drawing of the route back through the bloodlines. The principle is simple: everyone has a mother and father. Working left to right, several generations of parents and just the one child in the family line appear on the same page. The chart design never changes, and a numbering system keeps generations, and pages, in order. It matches the flow of research progress.

Drop-line charts or family trees plot all the descendents of one ancestor. You see direct ancestors, brothers, sisters, uncles, aunts, and cousins. When bloodline ancestors are poorly represented in records, your attention may have to shift to someone else in the family, and this style of chart helps you "see" where.

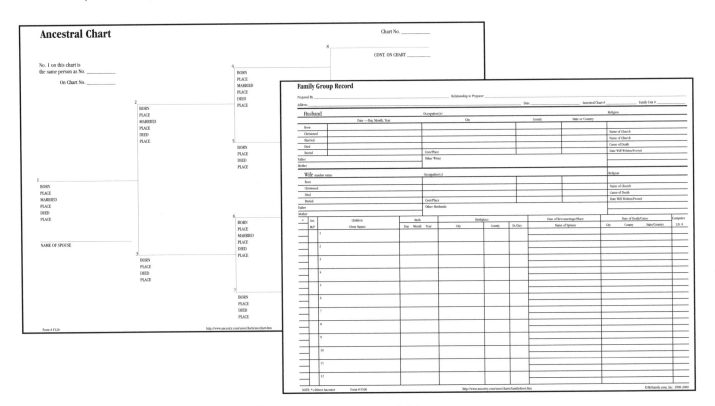

Figure A-1. Charts Available at Ancestry.ca

Family group sheets present a factual summary of the individuals making up a single family. They round out the information on the two styles of relationship charts because they have room for extra details, and they help you keep track of an entire family.

SOURCE CITATIONS

Source information is essential because unsupported facts are nothing more than possibilities. Without citations, facts cannot be accepted as true.

When citations are provided, facts can be checked against the source. Citations are evidence of the care that went into the research, and they provide valid evidence for you, or others, to use in building a family history.

Sources come in many formats today, reflecting the many ways you view records and documents. Among them are original records in archives, microform copies, digitized images on CD-ROM or online, personal papers in private hands, transcripts, extracts, and abstracts.

The person reading your citations has to understand exactly what was consulted in any format. Citations do the job if they answer four questions.

Is it clear what sort of a resource was consulted?

Will I find this again easily?

Can others find this fact from my citation?

Will this citation be as good in ten years as it is today?

The generally accepted guide on citation style for genealogists is Elizabeth Mills. Consult either of her books, *Evidence!* (Mills, 2006) or *Evidence Explained* (2007). There is also a quick reference sheet for Internet data, *Citing Online Historical Resources* (Mills, 2005). There are other acceptable forms, such as the *Chicago Manual of Style*. Online, many university libraries offer guides to citations, and you may want to look at the Citation Machine, a site that can do some of the work for you.

PRIMARY SOURCES, SECONDARY SOURCES, AND PROOF

Genealogists are always weighing evidence and assessing the reliability of sources. These three terms—*primary sources, secondary sources*, and *proof*—are terms you are familiar with, but there are other, related factors to consider that reveal more about the strength of genealogical evidence. Some sources are direct, and others indirect; some sources are original, and others are derived from something else, which may or may not be original.

More than the words *primary* and *secondary, direct* and *indirect, original* and *derived* are descriptive terms that guide your assessment of any source. The following three questions apply to basic vital records, but questions like these should be asked whenever you record facts and their citations.

Were the facts recorded at the time and place of the event?

Were the facts recorded by someone who was at the event?

If you are using facts collected by someone else, what do you know about when, where, and who recorded the original information?

Fortunately, when you pay attention to methodology, carry out thorough searches, weigh your evidence, and plan your research steps, proof becomes less of a worry. Thorough work provides checks and cross-checks, and guides such as this book help you plan your research. With good methodology, you are more likely to build a good case for the facts in your family history. If you want to learn more about the this topic read *Genealogical Proof Standard: Building a Solid Case* (Rose, 2005).

ANALYSIS

It is hard to put a stop to family history research. You keep going because there is always another generation to be found. There is constant challenge. It is also the source of speculation. Your conversation with other genealogists is often made up of ideas about what happened and why.

So analysis is something you are doing already. Like your research, it will be better with some method applied. Bouncing ideas around is important, but make sure that happens within a framework of knowledge and leads to methodical planning.

You are probably doing homework already, too. Most genealogists read magazines, watch mailing lists, or attend society meetings and lectures. Structure these activities around your research interests, checking into geography, history, and records.

A mix of results, review, theories, and new knowledge is going to give you the strategy for the next stage of your research.

EXPERIENCE

Talk to others either in person at society meetings or online. Read constantly in all formats: e-mail, websites, magazines, and books. For a Canadian focus, look to GenWeb, and the resources provided by the Canadian Genealogy Centre.

Use the Internet effectively and gain experience there; appendix C has some advice on that. Then stop and visit your library and the nearest Family History Center. If you have not visited an archive, do so.

There is no substitute for experience, but to be valuable it must be varied. Help this building process along by seeking out what is new and different. You will be a better genealogist.

EXPECTATIONS

Some of you may have no expectations at all; family history is totally absorbing, it is what you want to do, and that's that. Others have definite expectations and goals in sight. If you are still thinking about whether or not researching your roots will be fun, consider these reasons:

- You want to hold the best family reunion ever.
- You want to discover and visit all the places associated with your parents, grandparents, and great-grandparents.
- Your interests have few limitations; it is the broad sweep that you want, as many ancestors and as far back as possible—the thrill is in the hunt.
- You are intrigued by one line, perhaps that of your father, perhaps the line associated with a family treasure.
- You are fascinated by history but not as you learned it years ago; instead, it is history at a more personal level, through the lives of your ancestors.

Then work hard and have a good time.

WEBSITES

Ancestry Family Trees Center: <www.ancestry.com/learn/contentcenters/contentCenter.aspx?page=trees>
Canadian Genealogy Centre: <www.collectionscanada.ca/genealogy/index-e.html>
Canada GenWeb: <www.rootsweb.com/~canwgw/>
Citation Machine: <www.citationmachine.net>

BIBLIOGRAPHY

Mahan, M. D. F., and Chicago University Press. *Chicago Manual of Style: The Essential Guide for Writers, Editors and Publishers.* 15th ed. Chicago: University of Chicago Press, 2005.

Merriman, Brenda. *About Genealogical Standards of Evidence.* 2nd ed. Toronto: Ontario Genealogical Society, 2004.

Mills, Elizabeth. *Citing Online Historical Resources.* Baltimore: Genealogical Publishing Company, 2005.

———. *Evidence!* 1997. Reprint, Baltimore: Genealogical Publishing Company, 2006.

———. *Evidence Explained* Baltimore: Genealogical Publishing Company, 2007.

Rose, Christine. *Genealogical Proof Standard: Building a Solid Case.* San Jose, CA: CR Publications, 2005.

APPENDIX B

PAY ATTENTION TO THE HAZARDS

An old cliché applies to genealogical research: forewarned is forearmed. There are pitfalls in family history, and if not spotted in advance, they can lead to hours of wasted effort. The digital world of today has not made the problems disappear; it just changes some and introduces a few more.

PITFALLS WITH PERSONAL NAMES

Rarely was a name written one way all the time until relatively recently. Variant spellings occurred because clergymen could not spell or people could not read and paid no attention to what a registrar wrote. Universal education and an official interest in accuracy did not come along until late in the nineteenth century. A man might spell his name several ways in his lifetime because there was no official necessity for an exact name. Accents, difficulties with language, poor handwriting, and inattention led to many errors in recording and copying.

Eight Name Problems

1. What you do and don't hear: information about any different languages, dialects, or accents may help you figure out the evolution of a surname.
2. Spelling differences can totally transform a name; one cause is translation of the meaning (*Schwarz* becomes *Black*).
3. Middle names easily confuse, and sometimes name order is switched by indexers; watch out for names that sound good in any order, like James Gordon Russell.
4. Is there just one name? This happened with some Aboriginal people and immigrants, and the name could be indexed as a surname or as a given name.
5. You cannot rely on the first letter of the name. Some capitals are easily confused, and a misspelled name can sound plausible; this uncertainty makes searching more tedious.
6. You don't know the way the name was recorded; you may be looking for Bill White and not realize your search term should be Wm. White or Wilhelm Weiss.
7. The first name used all the time could be different from what was entered into records; nicknames can be very different from baptismal names.
8. The person had an alias or alternate surname. You may come across other terms for alternate names: *dit names* is a French term, and *to-names* is a Scottish one. Some records show the alternative, entering both surnames (e.g., Mary Smith, alias Cooper). In many records there is no clue that the surname is an alternate. Use of aliases might occur because a child was born illegitimate under one surname, which changed when the mother married. Sometimes there were so few surnames in a community, new ones were created to avoid confusion; also, immigrants might use one name among their own people and one for official records.

Solutions

Three steps can help with personal name problems: put the problem in context, read about name problems in Canadian records and indexes, and find out about names for the language and nationality of origin.

Context refers to where the name appears. For handwriting problems, look through several pages if you can, checking the style, noting other names and words where you see a similarly shaped letter and can figure out what it is. Historical context may help as well because in some time periods and places, people wanted to hide their origins and changed or translated their names.

Refer to the FamilySearch website for two helpful guides to names and spelling. Books or websites about genealogy in the country of origin can guide you to books about name difficulties.

PITFALLS WITH PLACES AND BOUNDARIES

Place-names suffer from language and transcription problems, too. Some are translated all the time, having both English and French forms. Other places changed their names for good. Île Saint-Jean became Island of St. John and then Prince Edward Island to honor a son of George III. No doubt some variations of long, hard-to-spell

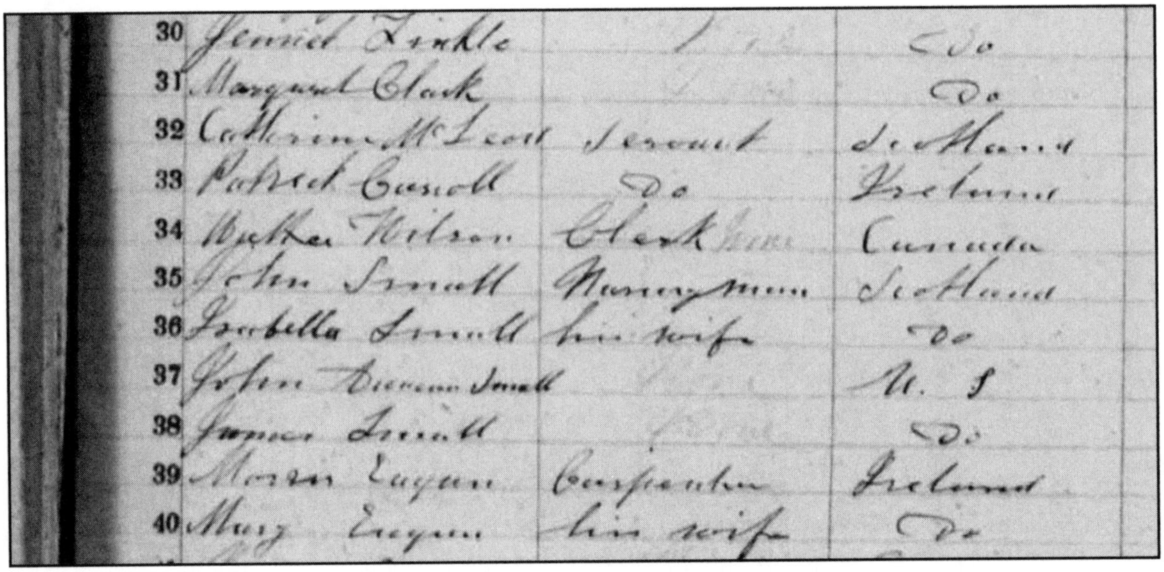

30	Jennet Tinkle		Do
31	Margaret Clark		Do
32	Catherine McLeod	Servant	Scotland
33	Patrick Carroll	Do	Ireland
34	Walter Wilson	Clerk	Canada
35	John Small	Merchant	Scotland
36	Isabella Small	his wife	Do
37	John Duncan Small		U. S
38	James Small		Do
39	Moses Eagan	Carpenter	Ireland
40	Mary Eagan	his wife	Do

Figure B-1. Deciphering Names Is a Challenge for Genealogists and Indexers

1851 Census, Canada West, Oxford County, District 27, Subdistrict 266, page 69, Library and Archives Canada film #C11745

Available at Ancestry.ca

names have never been figured out by puzzled descendents. Words like *Musquodoboit* can be difficult to say and harder to write.

Location is such an important factor in searching records that chapter 2 is devoted to it. Canadian boundaries have been anything but static, and the division of responsibility between levels of government in Canada muddies the waters. Most of you will find that boundary changes affect your research.

The solution to this hazard is information. Keep maps and gazetteers handy, whether as bookmarked websites or atlases on your reference shelf, and know your boundaries before you start.

PITFALLS WITH DATES

The most obvious date problems arise because people lie about age. The dead cannot give their age to the registrar or minister, and even family members may not know the exact age of a sibling or parent. Doctors, housekeepers, or neighbors are even less likely to be accurate.

Another source of trouble can be your estimate of the years an ancestor was alive. Don't stop a search too soon—a narrow range of years can mean a record is missed. Be ready to shift a date range, even if it looks like Grandfather lived to be 101. It is better to overestimate, think someone lived longer than average, or assume parents produced children over a long period. Sometimes date problems arise from a late registration or delayed probate.

There is another problem when your research gets back to the middle 1700s. You may come across and perhaps be confused by what is called Old Style dating. In British territories in 1752 the official New Year changed from 25 March to 1 January, and eleven days were "lost" in September of that year as the switch was made from the Julian to the Gregorian calendar. Catholic Europe had made the change in 1582, so French colonies were always on the Gregorian calendar.

COMMON PROBLEMS WITH SOURCES

In any record collection you should know about missing months or years or missing geographical areas before you start searching. It also helps to know in advance about sections of such poor quality that reading is impossible.

You may come across date ranges for sources in catalog descriptions, for example. Limited descriptions frequently omit important facts about gaps in record collections or in their indexes. Also missing may be facts about local lists and any local or regional differences; for example, not all 1851 and 1861 census returns are nominal.

Boundaries changed. Places don't move, but they can switch from one colony to another, one province or territory to another, one county or district to another, one city ward to another. In areas of border disputes, such as New Brunswick and the state of Maine, an area may have changed countries.

Smart genealogists know what they are working with and gather information about records in advance.

THE INFORMATION COULD BE SOMEWHERE ELSE

Movements of people into Canada, within the country, and out of it create the potential hazard of searching in the wrong place. Your information or your family stories may point to one place, and it may not be the right location at all.

The free movement that occurred without any record across the Canada/U.S. border before the 1890s and the fact that Canadian settlement has always been close to the border means that anyone's family can have an American connection.

FIND THESE FACTS BEFORE USING A RESOURCE

- The time period the record covers from start date to end date, with major gaps
- The geographical area the record covers, whether the boundaries change for any period within its full date range, and whether there are subdivisions you need to know about
- The reason the record exists
- The way the record is organized, whether by name, by name with a year or span of years, by name within certain geographic areas, or some other basis
- The facts required to search the record and its indexes or finding aids
- The new information the record can be expected to provide

The special relationship between Canada and the United Kingdom must also be considered. Families of British or Irish origin, or families that came to Canada via a British port, are likely to have some sort of record in the United Kingdom.

Finally, people traveled more than you may realize. New opportunities or family ties generated travel within Canada, and sometimes births, marriages, and deaths happened away from home.

AVOID MADE-AT-HOME PITFALLS

Pitfalls and errors can happen at home, and you may create some of your own problems. If you set high personal standards, you will be more confident about the quality of your work.

1. Read with care. Read or review records, family data, or any sort of family information carefully to avoid making data transcription errors or drawing erroneous conclusions.
2. Be skeptical. Doubting, then checking, details that have little supporting evidence prevents bad family trees. Are you looking in the right place? Have you selected the appropriate date range? Are there other name variants? Are you using the best resources for the problem? Could the family story have changed with repeated telling?
3. Improve your knowledge of Canadian resources, history, and geography. Knowledge really helps and makes your research more successful and more fun.
4. Record your work carefully. Cite every source, even those with no information, and take notes. Be honest with yourself about how you worked—when you were tired or rushed, for example—and if necessary, repeat the work.
5. Go to the original. An index is only an index, and a copy of the original record must be examined.

WEBSITES

Cyndi's List Calendar Page: <www.cyndislist.com/calendar.htm>
Cyndi's List Names Page: <www.cyndislist.com/names.htm>
FamilySearch Research Helps (For advice on Name Variants, select the letter N): <www.familysearch.org/Eng/Search/RG/frameset_rhelps.asp>

BIBLIOGRAPHY

Dilts, David. *Research Guidance: Spelling Substitution Tables for the United States and Canada.* 2001. (PDF version available for download at FamilySearch)

Douglas, Althea. *Here Be Dragons! Navigating the Hazards Found in Canadian Family Research.* Toronto: Ontario Genealogical Society, 1996.

———. *Here Be Dragons, Too! More Navigational Hazards for the Canadian Family Researcher.* 2nd ed. Toronto: Ontario Genealogical Society, 2003.

———. *Tools of the Trade for Canadian Genealogy.* 2nd ed. Toronto: Ontario Genealogical Society, 2003.

FamilySearch. *Research Guidance: Name Variations in Canadian Indexes and Records, 2004.* (PDF version available for download at FamilySearch)

THE INTERNET

Most people begin genealogical searches on the Internet. For Canada, this makes sense. All levels of government, societies, libraries, museums, volunteers, and private companies are contributing online resources. A great deal is free, though some comes with a fee. You can enjoy great benefits from online resources if you master some fundamentals.

YOUR BROWSER

You will visit many websites, and it is going to be impossible to remember what they are and how you found them. Before you get into Canadian research, get ready; make sure you are familiar with the options offered by your browser.

Look at the History feature and how it functions. For some searches you may want this frame open to help you backtrack. New browser versions may offer the advantage of tabs to jump back and forth between websites. This works faster than using separate browser windows.

Tidy up the list of favorite sites saved by your Internet browser. If the list is so long it disappears off the bottom of the monitor screen, shorten it: create file folders for several categories, and put your saved links into them. Make sure you create a folder for Canada.

SEARCH ENGINES

Get acquainted with at least two search engines. You can be sure they will return different results to the same search. Read some neutral assessments of the weaknesses and strengths of several engines, and then take a test drive. The library website at the University of California, Berkeley, offers some helpful assessments.

Part of controlling your search tools is understanding how to construct an effective search request. Most people put in a surname or place-name or a couple of keywords and hit the Search button. All search engines offer advanced options and instructions on how to use them. Read up on them and practice. Also, take a look at the way Free Genealogy Search Help for Google constructs name searches for you; you could be creating your own search expressions with a little practice.

You should also remember that search engines do not reach everything. Names in databases are a good example of what is usually inaccessible to them. Typing a name into a search engine is just one option—and an incomplete one. You have to learn about available databases as well.

GATEWAYS AND PORTALS

Some sites are devoted to pointing Internet users around the online world of a single subject. Cyndi's List does this for genealogy in general. The site is a gateway, a convenient way for you to enter the subject of genealogy and find websites of interest arranged in convenient sections and subsections. A gateway sounds like a big site with a broad sweep across a subject. A portal sounds smaller, perhaps a site pointing to a specific place or topic within the subject of genealogy. You may hear both terms used, but it does not matter what you call these sites;

just remember how they work. Figure out two or three that suit you and your work and save the links in your browser. These websites usually keep their links up to date, and that is going to save you time and frustration.

Cyndi's List has a section for Canada, sections for the provinces, and more sections within each of those. There are two portals (or gateways) devoted only to Canadian genealogy websites: CanGenealogy.com and Canadian Genealogy and History Links. Both select listings according to quality and do not strive to include everything. Their layouts are different, too, which can make a difference. What you miss at one site may be clearly visible at another.

History

Alcan Highway During World War II, 10,607 U.S. soldiers built a road 1,522 miles long in 8 months. This road cut throught the Canadian Wilderness fron Dawson Creek BC to Fairbanks Alaska.

Barkerville Online The Cariboo Sentinel Newspaper provides information about the Gold Rush and the early development of British Columbia.

BC Heritage Your online guide to BC Heritage historic sites and services and an introduction to the programs of the British Columbia Heritage Trust. A BC Government page.

BC Studies - The British Columbian Quarterly Dedicated to the exploration of British Columbia's cultural, economic, and political life, past and present.

Centre for the Study of the Pacific Northwest This site makes accessible some of the University's myriad resources in regional history. Includes the Pacific Northwest Quarterly which is a journal devoted to the history and culture of the northwestern United States, Alaska, and western Canada.

Comox Valley Harbour Authority - Marine History Timeline of events, pictures and stories of Comox Bay events and development.

First Newspapers on Canada's west coast: 1858-1863 Victoria, British Columbia: 1856-1863.

Folklore Heritage In the Pacific Northwest Join us as we journey through modern and historic tales of hardship on the open seas and poke around B.C.'s smaller folk communities.

Fort Steele Heritage Town Come to Fort Steele Heritage Town and be transported back in time to a mining boom town in the 1890s. Information on Archives & Library Holdings.

History of Esquimalt Origin of the Name, Historical Outline, Reeves and Mayors of the Township of Esquimalt.

History of Fort Langley Brief history of Fort Langley and the Hudson's Bay Company.

History of Houston Important people and events in Houston's past. Early pioneers, area place names, past mayors, schools, postal service, etc.

Figure C-1. A Page of Links for History in British Columbia from Canadian Genealogy and History Links

Gateway and portal websites are usually simple in design to pack more detail into less space.

Canada GenWeb is another way into the subject of Canadian genealogy. It is part of the World GenWeb Project. Within the Canadian project is a part for each province and territory, and many of these have internal sections according to counties or districts. All work is done by volunteers, so there is a lot of variety in site structure and content. Some provinces have remarkable sites filled with databases, source lists, advice, and maps.

Finally, another portal exclusively devoted to Canadian genealogy is the Library and Archives Canada (LAC) website. Two parts of the site are genealogical portals: AVITUS and the Sources by Topic section at the Canadian Genealogy Centre. These and other features of the LAC website are described at the beginning of this book.

FAMILYSEARCH

The Church of Jesus Christ of Latter-day Saints presents a storehouse of genealogical data and information at its FamilySearch website. You can find databases such as the International Genealogical Index; census returns for 1880/1881 for the United States, Canada, and England and Wales; and the Family History Library Catalog (FHLC). In addition, there is information about visiting the Family History Library (FHL) and locating Family

History Centers. Hours of service and the size of local collections vary at the Family History Centers, but all of the centers have computer and microform resources to get you started and are where you view any microfilms ordered on loan from the FHL in Salt Lake City.

Additional features include two databases of unverified information derived from charts and individual contributions: Ancestral File and the Pedigree Resource File.

Particularly useful is the great selection of online research outlines. There is one for Canada and for each of the provinces. Read them for research advice, ideas, and information about the collections held by the FHL.

Give yourself a tour of the website and make sure you can find the research outlines. We suggest you start with the home page. There are links to the FHLC, Research Guidance, and a tool for finding the nearest Family History Center. You can start a search on the home page, too, but it is better to click on the Advanced Search link and go directly to the search page. Once there you can select the type of resource to search. It is much better to tackle them one at a time.

You should notice that the items in the blue band near the top change when you are at the Advanced Search screen. Research Helps is another way to get advice (our preferred way). Click on Research Helps and use the options on the left (Place, Title, Subject, and Document Type) to explore the readable and downloadable reference guides.

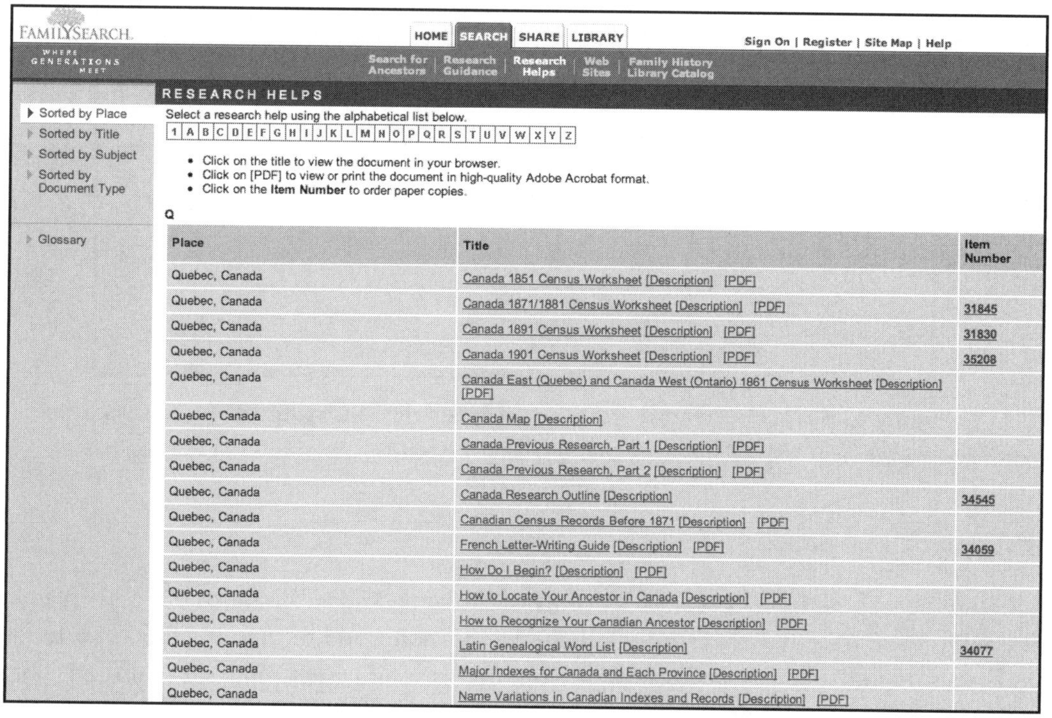

Figure C-2. FamilySearch: Research Helps Page
Use the topics on the left and the letters of the alphabet to navigate.

ANCESTRY

Ancestry is the largest online provider of genealogical data, and this includes Canadian data. There are indexes to census returns, civil vital records, church records, local and regional histories, directories, gazetteers, and much more. Make sure you choose the Search tab near the top of the Ancestry.ca home page and then use the interactive map of Canada to explore the contents of the website listed province by province.

Once you can find your way around the site and get a feel for its different levels, you will be able to construct searches as broad or as narrow as needed. You can also find helpful information here, blank charts, and a place to store your research information.

Ancestry continues to add data on a regular basis, and you should check back regularly for updates. Subscribers can view record details and any available document images. You may be able to access Ancestry at a local public library.

Figure C-3. Quebec Family and Local Histories—Listings at Ancestry.ca
Use the drop-down menu below the map of Canada to change to another province.

FUN TIME

Time on the Internet should feel like work only some of the time. You will want to put aside planned searches occasionally and browse according to whim or follow wherever some odd succession of links leads. Lucky things happen, and you may find a long-lost ancestor. Or you may learn only that some sites don't fit your needs, but either way your experience will grow.

For some of you, fun time online may be sharing using mailing lists or message boards or talking to others. (You can actually speak using some services.) Other ways of interacting include blogs (*blog* is short for Web log) and wikis. *Ancestry Weekly Journal* appears as part of the blog *24/7 Family History Circle,* and the best known wiki is Wikipedia, which happens to have a helpful article on genealogy. Two Canadian genealogical blogs are included in the websites listed at the end of this chapter.

Some people create special websites for particular family lines or for residents of one town or for a special group of immigrants. Genealogical data is often shared or uploaded to a website. If these ideas appeal to you, take a look at recent Internet guides that explain the options in detail.

IT DEPENDS ON YOU

The Web can produce startling progress, helping you add many names or several generations to a family tree. What took months or years a few years ago can be accomplished in days or weeks. The advantages come with a warning, though, and you will learn the dangers from experience: the faster you travel, the greater the potential for errors.

The pitfalls have not changed with the Internet, but an entirely new set of problems has been added. Digitizing records means that yet another level of human interpretation can compound errors. There is also the danger that you will search hastily and draw conclusions based on imperfect understanding of what has been searched. You need to stop and record what you are searching and what you do or do not find. Take time to investigate the website and its data. Can you find answers to questions like these?

- What is in the database—records, dates, and geographic areas?
- Are there citation details for the results?
- Do I trust the provider of the database?
- Can I find instructions for the search tool?
- Is it possible to browse through the records forward and backward?
- Does the site offer background information to the records?
- Are document images available, and what is their quality?

There is plenty to learn, plenty to practice, fun time, serious work, and great satisfaction in pursuing family history online.

WEBSITES

Ancestry: <www.ancestry.ca>
Ancestry Weekly Journal: <http://blogs.ancestry.com/circle/>
Anglo-Celtic Connections (a Canadian blog): <http://anglo-celtic-connections.blogspot.com/>
AVITUS, Directory of Canadian Genealogical Resources:
    <www.collectionscanada.ca/genealogy/022-501-e.html>
Canadian Genealogy Centre, Index of Topics: <www.collectionscanada.ca/genealogy/022-904-e.html>
Canadian Genealogy and History Links: <www.islandnet.com/~jveinot/cghl/cghl.html>
CanGenealogy:
Cyndi's List: <www.cyndislist.com>
FamilySearch: <www.familysearch.org>
Free Genealogy Search Help for Google: <www.genealogy-search-help.com/index.html>
GenWeb Canada: <www.rootsweb.com/~canwgw/>
Library and Archives Canada, Canadian Genealogy Centre: <www.collectionscanada.ca/genealogy/>
Library, University of California, Berkeley, Guide to Search Engines:
    <www.lib.berkeley.edu/TeachingLib/Guides/Internet/SearchEngines.html>
Olive Tree Genealogy Blog: <www.olivetreegenealogy.blogspot.com>

BIBLIOGRAPHY

Morgan, George G. *The Official Guide to Ancestry.com.* Provo, UT: Ancestry Publishing, 2007.

CANADIAN HISTORY

Succinct and visual, a timeline is an effective way to provide an outline of Canadian history. However, a single line of Canadian events would lack perspective and any meaningful connection to family history. For these reasons, we have chosen to include five parallel timelines, one each for Canada, Canadian records, Britain, France, and the United States. These three countries have had important influences on Canadian history. Dates from the history of records are added because records have a history, too; awareness of that history can be a source of research ideas.

The timelines begin with the early 1600s, the dates of the first permanent settlements of Europeans in Canada, and continue up to the 1960s. Events listed here may or may not have been known to your ancestors and may or may not have had some direct impact on their lives. However, they were historically significant or are in some way related to family history research.

Use the dates for quick reference and to lead you to further research online and in books. Resources are listed at the end.

TIMELINE CANADA

1608 Champlain at site of Quebec City

1615 First French missionaries, *les Récollets*, reach Quebec

1627 Company of New France established

1628 Quebec captured by English; Scots settlers in Nova Scotia

1632 Treaty returns Quebec and all of Acadia to France

1642 First settlement at Montreal

1663 Arrival of *les filles du roi*, daughters of the king (the French king gave each a dowry of money and free transport)

1665 Jean Talon appointed governor; the Cerignan-Salières Regiment arrives in New France

1670 Hudson's Bay Company established by London traders; the company holds trading rights for regions whose rivers drain into Hudson Bay

1672 Frontenac made governor of New France

1690–92 The explorations of Henry Kelsey, first European to see the Prairies

1697 French capture York Factory and hold it for 16 years

1702 War in Europe begins, called Queen Anne's War in America

1713 Treaty of Utrecht; France gives up claims to Hudson Bay and Newfoundland except for fishing rights and surrenders all of Acadia

1713 160 French, displaced from Newfoundland, go to Cape Breton and found Louisbourg

1744 30 years of peace ends; Louisbourg falls to a volunteer force from New England

1748 Treaty returns Louisbourg to France

1749 British establish Halifax

1753 Settlement at Lunenburg, mainly by Germans and Swiss
1755 Governor Lawrence of Nova Scotia orders the expulsion of the Acadians
1756–63 Seven Years' War; Quebec falls in 1759
1763 Treaty of Paris; Britain acquires all French colonies east of the Mississippi
1764 Ban on the Acadians lifted; many return
1774 The Quebec Act recognizes the French language and the Roman Catholic religion, allows seigneurial system to continue
1778 Captain Cook at Vancouver Island
1783 Treaty of Paris ends Revolutionary War; Canadian–U.S. border now drawn at the Great Lakes
1783–90 Loyalist refugees flood into Canada
1791 Constitutional Act; Quebec divided into Lower Canada (present-day Quebec) and Upper Canada (present-day Ontario) along the Ottawa River
1793 Alexander Mackenzie reaches the Pacific

1811 Lord Selkirk establishes the settlement at Red River
1812–14 War of 1812
1818 49th parallel declared the boundary with the U.S. from the Lake of the Woods to Georgia Strait
1821 Hudson's Bay Company and North West Company merge
1829 Completion of Welland Canal; Rideau Canal finished in 1832
1832 Establishment of immigrant quarantine station at Grosse Île; it closed in 1937
1837–38 Armed rebellions in Upper and Lower Canada
1841 United Province of Canada
1842 Large piece of New Brunswick given to U.S. in the Webster-Ashburton Treaty
1849 Vancouver Island becomes a Crown Colony
1867 British North America Act; Canada begins with 4 provinces
1870 Western land opened for settlement; Manitoba becomes fifth province, followed by British Columbia in 1871 and Prince Edward Island in 1873
1871 British regiments cease to be stationed in Canada
1885 Riel Rebellion in Manitoba and completion of the Canadian Pacific Railroad
1897 Klondike gold rush; the Yukon becomes a territory a year later
1899 Canada sends own troops overseas for the first time to the Boer War

1905 Alberta and Saskatchewan become provinces
1911 22-month Springhill, Nova Scotia, coal strike ends
1916 Women in Manitoba are able to vote, first in Canada
1917 Canadians take Vimy Ridge; income tax introduced; Halifax explosion
1918 World War I ends; approximately 50,000 Canadians die in the influenza pandemic
1919 Winnipeg general strike paralyzes city
1921 Canadian women over 21 gain right to vote federally
1935 On-to-Ottawa Trek during the Great Depression
1944 First war brides arrive in Canada
1949 Newfoundland joins Canada
1954 Roger Bannister runs the mile in under 4 minutes at Commonwealth Games in Vancouver
1959 St. Lawrence Seaway opens
1965 The present Canadian flag is adopted
1967 Expo '67 is the main event in Canada's Centennial Celebrations

TIMELINE CANADIAN RECORDS

1621   Date of earliest surviving church records for French Canada
1637   First year of records of inventories of deceased persons in French Canada
1671   Earliest census record of Acadians in New Brunswick

1749   First probate records in British system begin in Nova Scotia
1752   La Rocque's census of Nova Scotia and Île Saint-Jean
1763   Nova Scotia earliest surviving marriage bonds
1766   Earliest Church of England registers in the colony of Quebec
1769   Start of records of land transfer, Island of St. John
1775–85   Earliest Loyalist records and lists date from this period
1784   Start of land records in New Brunswick
1790s   Early newspapers in Upper Canada
1793   Probate records begin in Upper Canada
1798   List of inhabitants of the Island of St. John

1830s   Directories begin in major cities
1832   Start of voters lists in Newfoundland
1842   Census, Upper and Lower Canada
1851   Nominal census in some of the colonies
1854   End of the seigneurial system in Quebec
1858–59   First newspapers in the West, in Victoria and Winnipeg
1869   Civil registration in Ontario
1871   First census of the new Dominion of Canada
1872   Start of some homestead records for Saskatchewan
1865   Passenger arrival records begin
1895   Start of the St. Albans Registers recording those going from Canada to the U.S.

1906   Census of the Northwest Provinces
1908   Start of Canadian border entry records
1911   Most recent census currently available
1914   Start of personnel and attestation papers for World War I service
1935   First year of federal lists of voters
1937   Closure of quarantine station at Grosse Île and end of records after 105 years
1940   National Registration
1945   Most recently available census for Newfoundland and Labrador
1968   Last year for divorce by private act of Parliament

TIMELINE FRANCE

1614   Last meeting of the Estates General until 1789 and start of a period of civil strife
1618–48   Thirty Years' War in Europe
1624   War with England; Cardinal Richelieu becomes principal minister
1629   End of war with England; Hugenots achieve religious freedom

1633   France occupies Lorraine

1639   France begins its occupation of Alsace

1643   Louis XIV becomes king, with Mazarin as principal minister

1656   First manufacture of stockings in Paris

1659   Peace with England, gains for France

1661   Mazarin dies; personal rule of Louis IV begins

1685   Louis revokes the Edict of Nantes

1715   Louis XIV dies; Louis XV accedes

1720   National bankruptcy

1731   France erects a fort at Crown Point on Lake Champlain

1740   Famine in Paris

1744   France declares war on England, lasts until 1748

1778   Offensive-defensive alliance with the American Colonies

1789   French Revolution; storming of La Bastille

1792   Monarchy abolished; war begins

1793   Louis XVI and Queen Marie Antoinette executed in Paris

1794   End of Reign of Terror; first telegraph line, Paris to Lille

1799   General Bonaparte enters Paris

1815   Napoleon defeated at Waterloo

1815   Napoleon deported to St. Helena, an island off the coast of Africa

1824–30   Reign of Charles X

1830–48   Reign of Louis Philippe

1839   Daguerre invents first practical camera

1852   Napoleon I's nephew crowned as Emperor Napoleon III

1853   Haussman redesigns Paris

1870–71   Franco-Prussian War

1871   Third Republic

1889   Eiffel Tower built

1895   Lumière brothers build a portable movie camera.

1914–18   World War I

1919   Peace Conference meets in Paris

1929–39   The Depression

1939   France declares war on Germany

1940   Paris falls; Vichy government formed

1944–45   D-Day and Allied victory; Fourth Republic led by de Gaulle

1946–54   War in Indochina

1954–58   War in Algeria

1958   De Gaulle initiates Fifth Republic

1968   General strikes and students' riots in Paris

TIMELINE UNITED KINGDOM AND IRELAND

1605 Gunpowder Plot

1616 Shakespeare dies

1638 National Covenant; Scots protest ecclesiastical policy of Charles I

1641 Massacre of Protestants in Ulster

1642 First battle of the Civil War

1649 Execution of Charles I

1653 Cromwell transplants people to west of Ireland

1660 Restoration of the monarchy; Charles II returns to London

1665 Great Plague in London

1666 Great Fire of London

1685 Monmouth's rebellion

1690 Battle of the Boyne

1692 11 February, massacre at Glencoe

1702 England joins in the War of the Spanish Succession (Queen Anne's War)

1707 Union of England and Scotland

1713 Treaty of Utrecht

1715 Jacobite uprising in Scotland

1714 Death of Queen Anne, last of the Stuarts; accession of George I of House of Hanover

1733 English becomes the language of legal records

1746 Battle of Culloden; defeat of the Jacobites led by Prince Charles Edward Stuart

1752 Gregorian calendar adopted by England and her possessions

1775 England hires 29,000 German mercenaries for the war in North America

1791 Catholic Relief Act

1793 Start of wars with France

1797–99 Irish Rebellion

1800 Act of Union between Britain and Ireland

1802 First law restricting child labor

1815 Battle of Waterloo

1829 Catholic emancipation

1837 Start of government registration of births, marriages, and deaths

1842 Chartist Riots

1845–47 Famine in Ireland

1854–56 Crimean War

1855 Registration in Scotland

1858 Establishment of the civil principal probate registry in England and Wales

1864 Registration in Ireland

1914 Start of WWI

1921 Irish peace agreement and division of Ireland

1931 Statute of Westminster grants British dominions complete autonomy

1936 Edward VIII abdicates; George VI becomes king

1939–45 Second World War
1947 Canada declared to be of equal status with Great Britain within the Commonwealth; British subjects now required to become naturalized as Canadian citizens
1954 Nine years after end of the Second World War, food rationing ends in the UK
1961 The farthing (quarter penny) ceases to be legal tender
1963 de Gaulle vetoes admission of UK to the European Common Market

TIMELINE USA

1607 Jamestown, Virginia, founded by English settlers
1620 Plymouth Colony, near Cape Cod, founded by the Pilgrim Fathers
1628 Massachusetts Bay Colony
1639 First printing press in U.S.
1664 Surrender of New Amsterdam to the English
1674 Treaty of Westminster ends third Anglo-Dutch war, confirms English possession of New York
1681 Charles II grants a charter to Pennsylvania
1682 Indentured servants allowed to go to America

1706 Unsuccessful attack on Charleston by French and Spanish
1709 First large group of Germans arrive in Pennsylvania
1732 James Ogelthorpe founds Georgia
1763 End of French and Indian War; Britain controls territory east of the Mississippi
1765–66 Stamp Act
1774 First Continental Congress
1775 American Revolution; George Washington leads Continental Army
1776 4 July Declaration of Independence endorsed by Congress
1781 Defeat of the British at the Battle of Yorktown.
1783 Treaty of Paris; Britain concedes loss of colonies
1788 Enough states have ratified the U.S. Constitution to bring into force
1789 George Washington elected first president of U.S.
1791 Bill of Rights guarantees individual freedom

1803 France sells Louisiana territories to U.S.
1808 Atlantic slave trade abolished
1811 American Fur Company establishes post at the mouth of the Columbia River
1812 U.S. declares war on Britain
1842 Webster-Ashburton Treaty; 2,000 French Canadians are in the U.S.
1846–48 U.S. acquires land after Mexican War, including California and New Mexico
1849 Gold rush in California
1860–61 11 pro-slavery Southern states form Confederate States of America
1863 Lincoln issues Emancipation Proclamation
1865 Confederates defeated; slavery abolished; Lincoln assassinated
1866 Irish Fenians in the U.S. attack Canada
1898 U.S. gains Puerto Rico, Guam, the Philippines, and Cuba following the Spanish-American War; U.S. annexes Hawaii

1906 San Francisco earthquake
1917–18 U.S. intervenes in World War I
1920 Women given the right to vote under the Nineteenth Amendment
1924 Congress gives indigenous people right to citizenship
1929–33 13 million are unemployed in the Great Depression
1933 President Franklin D. Roosevelt launches "New Deal" recovery program
1941 World War II; U.S. joins Allied forces
1945 U.S. drops two atomic bombs on Hiroshima and Nagasaki; Japan surrenders
1947 Cold War with Soviet Union begins
1948 The Marshall Plan; aid for Europe begins; some $13 billion is disbursed over 4 years
1950–54 Senator Joseph McCarthy's campaign against communists, real and imagined
1950–53 Korean War
1954 Racial segregation in schools becomes unconstitutional
1963 Assassination of President Kennedy

WEBSITES

Canadian Encyclopedia:
Dictionary of Canadian Biography: <www.biographi.ca/EN/index.html>
Oxford Reference Online (available through some public library websites—check local online services; includes several relevant reference works, such as *Oxford Companion to Canadian History*, the *Oxford Companion to British History*, the *Oxford Companion to Military History*, and the *Oxford Companion to United States History*)
On This Day (find out what happened on any day of the year in history): <www1.sympatico.ca/cgi-bin/on_this_day>

BIBLIOGRAPHY

Bely, Lucien. *The History of France*. Translated by Angela Moyon. Paris: Editions Jean-Paul Gisserot, 2001.

Black, Jeremy. *Eighteenth Century Britain: 1688–1785*. Palgrave History of Britain. London: Palgrave-Macmillan, 2001.

Brinkley, Alan. *Unfinished Nation: A Concise History of the American People*. New York: Knopf, 1997.

Brown, Craig. *The Illustrated History of Canada*. Rev. ed. Toronto: Key Porter Books, 2003.

Colley, Linda. *Britons: Forging the Nation, 1707–1837*. 2nd ed. New Haven, Conn; London: Yale University Press, 2005.

Corey, Melinda, and George Ochoa. *American History: The New York Public Library Book of Answers*. New York: New York Public Library, 1993.

Ferguson, Will. *Canadian History for Dummies*. Toronto: Wiley, 2005.

Hallowell, Gerald A. (ed.). *Oxford Companion to Canadian History*. Don Mills, ON: Oxford University Press, 2004.

Pugh, Martin. *Britain Since 1789: A Concise History*. London: Macmillan, 1999.

Unger, Irwin. *These United States: The Questions of Our Past*. 2nd ed. Upper Saddle River NJ: Prentice-Hall, 2003.

INDEX

ABOUT THE AUTHORS

Sherry Irvine, CG, a native Canadian, has been teaching, speaking, and writing about family history research for twenty-seven years. She has lectured in Australia and New Zealand, England, Canada, and the United States. For ten years she taught courses on English and Scottish research at the Institute of Genealogy and Historical Research at Samford University and led study tours to England and Scotland. She presents online classes through Pharos Teaching and Tutoring Ltd.

Through 2002 and 2003 Sherry was president of the Association of Professional Genealogists and in 2005 was awarded the APG Graham T. Smallwood Award of Merit. She is vice-president of the International Society for British Genealogy and Family History.

Sherry's other books are *Your English Ancestry* and *Scottish Ancestry: Research Methods for Family Historians*. Sherry's articles have appeared in several publications, including *Ancestry Weekly Journal* and the British monthly, *Ancestors*.

Dave Obee has been researching his own family history since 1978 and has authored or compiled six books on genealogical research. On his father's side, he has roots in Canada going back to the early 1800s. His mother arrived in Canada as a child in the 1920s.

Dave runs CanGenealogy, a selective links site that is sorted for ease of use, and served as president of the Federation of East European Family History Societies from 2004 to 2007.